Tne
Equality Act
2010
in Mental Health

The
EQUALITY ACT
2010
IN MENTAL HEALTH

A Guide to Implementation
and Issues for Practice

Edited by Hári Sewell

Foreword by Lord Victor O Adebowale

Jessica Kingsley *Publishers*
London and Philadelphia

Crown copyright material is reproduced with the permission of the Controller of HMSO and the Queen's Printer for Scotland.

First published in 2013
by Jessica Kingsley Publishers
116 Pentonville Road
London N1 9JB, UK
and
400 Market Street, Suite 400
Philadelphia, PA 19106, USA

www.jkp.com

Copyright © Hári Sewell 2013
Foreword copyright © Lord Victor O Adebowale 2013

Library of Congress Cataloging in Publication Data
A CIP catalog record for this book is available from the Library of Congress

British Library Cataloguing in Publication Data
A CIP catalogue record for this book is available from the British Library

ISBN 978 1 84905 284 9
eISBN 978 0 85700 589 2

Printed and bound in Great Britain

This book is dedicated to Aaron and James-Earl. Oh how we laugh...and how I needed to laugh throughout this project. I smile just thinking about our times together (18 cups).

My inspiration remains my amazing parents, Lorenzo and Hazel Sewell.

CONTENTS

PART III: ESSENTIAL CONSIDERATIONS

PART IV: CHANGE AND EQUALITIES

FOREWORD

Hári Sewell's book is very timely. As the recession continues to bite, there is a tendency for organisations in every sector to take the 'short cut' and ignore the importance of knowledge and good practice in the area of equalities. Indeed, my own experience of at least three recessions tells me that this desire for the short cut is often assisted by policy makers and political leaders who will ring their hands at the obvious results of discrimination and prejudice affecting a wide range of groups in society, and will then avoid any legislative or other action that might mitigate and or ameliorate the impacts of discrimination particularly in times of economic stress. So it is with some pride that I write this foreword to an important book in which contributors have considered the issue of equality with rigour and insightful knowledge.

Many people who find themselves in management and leadership positions know that the culture of an organisation revolves around its approach and practice in the area of equalities. This is not just a matter of fairness, it is a matter of efficiency, effective management practice and leadership that is experienced as values driven and authentic.

In my experience organisations can fall into one of three categories. The first type are those that are in denial who often simply don't understand the impact of poor practice on moral, brand and performance. Such organisations are often in the courts or attempt to avoid such risks by not employing anyone from outside 'the circle' at all. The second type of organisation are those that recognise the need but are trapped by their own inability to engage with the issues with clarity and determination. Such organisations often appear to be engaged with the issue through a plethora of internal groups usually defined by race, gender, ethnicity, religion, disability and even class. There is a tendency in such organisations for debates to revolve around hierarchies of oppression or a patronising non-engagement with the issue and the odd pat on the back to members of the various groups. The third type of organisation is rare but will need to be less so if we are to meet the demands of the current economic downturn. Third stage organisations are places where the questions of equality are expressed within their vision for the type of organisations they wish to become. This is underpinned by an intellectual honesty and curiosity which is encouraged through the leadership of the organisation resulting in a workforce that is both diverse and at ease with itself, able to draw upon a wide range of skills and experience and see challenges from many perspectives thus enabling imaginative forward thinking solutions to emerge. It is these organisations that this book speaks to, and to those organisations and individuals who aspire to become like them, that I am happy to commend this book and congratulate Mr Sewell and his contributors on its production.

Lord Victor O Adebowale, MA, CBE

ACKNOWLEDGEMENTS

Thanks to my commissioning editor, Stephen Jones, for his continued support, including online; for his advice, guidance and clever planning. Without your support this would never have happened. Thanks too to the whole JKP team.

Many thanks to all contributors. Your diversity of style and content has made this an engaging book to edit.

Throughout the course of writing this book many people have provided me with advice and moments of joy in both my professional and private lives, enabling me to stay energised: the Sewell family, particularly those nearby (Sharnet and Margaret) and also those far away, including Lady Allen. Also thanks to Emma Squires (Thompson); Sinead Gibson; Simon 'Krugger' Chandler; Pete Precise; Edana Minghella; Josh 'JR' Riley; Trevor Smith; Marcel Vige; Melba Wilson; Sue Waterhouse, Fred Hickling and David Morris.

And thanks too to John Coltrane, Courtney Pinch, Kenny Garrett, Sheldon Lawrence, David Brooks, Adija Palmer and Leroy Russell, Damian Marley and Edana for creating the soundtrack to this book.

INTRODUCTION

Hári Sewell

It is likely that everyone involved in delivering mental health services believes in fairness. The report of the Equality Review Panel set up by the Labour Government that led to the Equality Act 2010 was called *Fairness and Freedom* (The Equalities Review 2007). The new Coalition Government's policy programme was entitled *Freedom, Fairness, Responsibility* (HM Government 2010). The language of fairness dominates the political and public service landscapes. But as the Public services editor of *The Guardian* newspaper noted, 'fairness, of course, lies in some extent in the eye of the beholder' (*The Guardian* 2011). The Equality Act 2010 provides a basis for determining not what is right or fair, but what is legal. The principle of promoting fairness and equality is the bedrock of the legislation. The generalised belief in fairness held by those working in mental health services will be informed by personal values, pre-registration training, continued professional development and requirements of professional codes of practice. Translating the duties of the Equality Act 2010 into front-line and managerial practice in mental health will require more specific understanding. This volume brings together essential information as well as considerations, illustrations, exercises and suggestions about how to infuse the Equality Act 2010 into the workings of mental health organisations.

Chapter 1 provides a thorough briefing on the Act itself. It is an information-rich but concise source of the detail. Readers will be able to learn about the language of protected characteristics, a shift from the previous terminology of equality strands. The similarities and differences between protected characteristics are highlighted, as are the different forms of discrimination set out in law. Relevant for all health and social care sectors, Honigmann's extended chapter is essential reading.

Chapter 2 tackles the merits of a single equalities approach versus a focus on individual protected characteristics, and makes the point that people are complex and not best suited to reductive labels. The concept of intersectionality is presented as a way of understanding the way in which different aspects of identity and different manifestations of discrimination come together in people's lives.

Eleanor Hope's Chapter 3, giving a personal account, exemplifies why equalities needs to be more than a stream of work but an element that runs through the veins of an organisation. If the primary goals of mental health organisations are centred around people benefiting as much as possible from their contact, then these organisations must be equipped to see the complexity of the people with whom they work. Further, they must be designed and function in such a way that human diversity is expected and catered for. To achieve this, organisations should have equalities so embedded in their functioning that wherever attention is focused, there will be evidence that equalities is a core part of business.

Chapters 4 to 12 (Part II: Evidence of Inequality) look at equality in relation to each of the nine protected characteristics. Despite the fact that the protected characteristic of *marriage and civil partnership* applies only to workforce and not service delivery, a brief chapter (Chapter 6) is included for completeness. The contributors present their understanding of the issues specifically relating to mental health and offer suggestions about potential solutions. Of particular note is the detail of the ways in which inequalities emerge. Being able to anticipate and recognise inequality is a key asset in promoting equality and Chapters 4 to 12 present evidence on how ignorance and inactivity can maintain and perpetuate inequality. More positively, these Chapters present examples of what good practice looks like. Without seeking to impose prescriptive guidance on the minutiae of practice, Chapters 4 to 12 provide information to allow ways of thinking that enable readers to apply learning through better informed judgement. *Equalities* is, after all not a science.

Practitioners and front-line managers operate within organisational contexts. Chapters 13 to 16 (Part III: Essential Considerations) cover the prevalence of traditional psychiatric models and the inherent drivers of inequality; conflicts within the equalities agenda; the impact of cost-cutting; and good enough plans and strategies. These subjects are tackled with the purpose of moving tricky issues from the sidelines into the centre of debates about addressing inequalities. For example, the statutory requirements to produce and publish equality schemes on race, gender and disability (and then subsequently single equality schemes) had left some organisations struggling with getting the content right, possibly distracting them from delivering improvement in service user outcomes. The introduction of the non-mandatory Equality Delivery System in the NHS (Crown 2011) added a new possibility for documents to be produced and as the report on *Making Progress on Race Equality in Mental Health* noted (Sewell and Waterhouse 2012), some organisations are flummoxed about incorporating the new approach or replacing existing documents. Chapters 4 to 12 provide perspectives from the point of view of the contributors, and these will either be received with concordance of view or will stimulate oppositional arguments. As such, these chapters celebrate the contribution to improved critical analysis, and ideas for progress to be made, rooted in service user outcomes.

Chapters 17 to 22 (Part IV: Change and Equalities) have a central theme running through them: equalities requires the same attention and professionalism as any other aspect of an organisation's business. The chapters cover management practice; the financial case for tackling inequality; organisational development; skilling the workforce; engaging communities and stakeholders; and knowledge management and new technologies.

Chapter 19, on organisational development, captures the theme of Part IV well, as it considers the need for an organisation to focus change management across all areas of business, drawing on the McKinsey 7S model (Waterman, Peters and Phillips 1980). The authors of Chapter 19 point to the emotive nature of discussions about unfairness and inequalities, and challenge readers to be vigilant that this dimension does not lead to avoidance behaviours that are detrimental to progress on equalities. Financial management, workforce development and community and stakeholder engagement in relation to discrete streams of equality work all need to be rigorously implemented so that initiatives focused on reducing inequalities stand the best chance of success. Opportunities arising from knowledge management and technology need to be capitalised upon. The application of effort and resource needs to be carefully managed, since lack of success could jepardise not only the initiative in question, but future potential investment in equality initiatives as well.

Taken as a whole, this book enables readers to hold technical knowledge about the Equality Act 2010 alongside practice and managerial implications. The centrality of the service user and the focus on improved outcomes is captured well by contributing authors. Achieving equality is just about human beings having their needs met with equal skill, care and effectiveness. The chapters that follow should make a big contribution to achieving these ends.

REFERENCES

Crown (2011) *The Equality Delivery System for the NHS* (Amended January 2012). London: Department of Health. Accessed at www.eastmidlands.nhs.uk/about-us/inclusion/eds/ on 5 March 2012.

Equalities Review, The (2007) *Fairness and Freedom: The Final Report of the Equalities Review.* London: The Equalities Review.

Guardian, The (2011) 'Fair game for fairness failures.' Guardian Society. 16 March, p.4.

HM Government (2010) The Coalition: Our Programme for Government. London: Cabinet Office.

Sewell, H. and Waterhouse, S. (2012) *Making Progress on Race Equality in Mental Health.* London: NHS Confederation. Accessed at www.nhsconfed.org/Publications/ on 3 September 2012.

Waterman, R.H., Peters T.J, and Phillips, J.R. (1980) 'Structure is not organization.' *Business Horizons 23*, 3 June, 14–26.

PART
I

SETTING THE SCENE

Chapter 1

THE EQUALITY ACT 2010
The Letter and the Spirit of the Law

Jo Honigmann

INTRODUCTION

This chapter has been written specifically to set the context for the rest of the book, and as such serves as a useful source for anyone wishing to read an accessible guide on the Equality Act 2010 ('the Act') as it relates to the provision of services and the exercise of public functions (Part 3 of the Act). Subsequent chapters develop the practice, operational and managerial requirements to ensure compliance in relation to each protected characteristic. This chapter is deliberately rich in detail and ensures that readers will have in one place both legal and technical information on the content of the Act (contained in this chapter) and also the issues to consider in implementation (in subsequent chapters).

THE BACKGROUND TO THE ACT

The Equality Act 2010 (which covers England, Wales and, with some exceptions, Scotland) is the latest development in a history of discrimination legislation, starting with the Race Relations Act back in 1965. It brings together all the existing discrimination legislation into one statute; as its explanatory notes explain, it has 'two main purposes – to harmonise discrimination law, and to strengthen the law to support progress on equality' (explanatory note 10 to the Act). Familiar statutes such as the Race Relations Act 1976, the Sex Discrimination Act 1975 and the Disability Discrimination Act 1995 have now been repealed.

The Act received Royal Assent on 8 April 2010 and the majority of its provisions came into force on 1 October 2010, with some key provisions such as the public sector Equality Duty following in 2011. Protection from age discrimination in the provision of goods and services for people aged 18 and came into force on 1 October 2012. At the time of writing, additional key provisions which the Labour Government intended to bring in have been rejected by the Conservative-Liberal Democrat, namely the socio-economic duty and dual discrimination. The Government's Red Tape Challenge[1] is threatening the continued existence of the public sector Equality Duty and the positive action provisions.

The protections the Act contains echo the intent behind the guiding principles of the Code of Practice to the Mental Health Act 1983 and the tenets of the Human Rights Act 1998. They provide a framework in which mental health service providers must operate to avoid unlawful (even if unintentional) discrimination.

OVERVIEW OF THE ACT

The Act offers protection to people if they are discriminated or harassed on the basis of a *protected characteristic*, or if they are victimised as a result of action taken in connection with the Act, in different contexts including employment, access to services, the exercise of public functions (such as the exercise of statutory powers under mental health legislation), education and premises.

There are nine protected characteristics listed in s4 of the Act: age, disability, gender reassignment, marriage and civil partnership, pregnancy and maternity, race, religion or belief, sex and sexual orientation. Not all of these characteristics are protected in every context; for example, a person is protected from discrimination by virtue of being married or in a civil partnership if they are an employee, but not if they are seeking to access services or education, nor in relation to premises. These protected characteristics are explained in more detail below.

There are several different types of discrimination (set out in ss13–22 of the Act): direct (including by association or perception), indirect, pregnancy and maternity discrimination, discrimination arising from disability and a failure to make reasonable adjustments for disabled people. There are additional prohibitions on harassment (s26 of the Act) and victimisation (s27 of the Act). It is also unlawful to instruct, cause or induce discrimination.

In addition to duties towards individuals, public bodies listed in Schedule 19 of the Act (and those exercising a public function) also have a

---

1   The Coalition Government is seeking to reduce regulation across the board and its Red Tape Challenge invites comment as to which regulations they believe should or should not be kept.

duty to improve equality outcomes across all the protected characteristics[2] from within their organisation in the form of the public sector Equality Duty (s149 of the Act). This has two parts: a general duty on all those listed bodies and those exercising a public function referred to above; and specific duties on those bodies listed in Schedules 1 and 2 of the Equality Act 2010 (Specific Duties) Regulations 2011. The NHS and local authorities are covered by both the general and the specific duties.

All types of organisations now have the opportunity to adopt positive action measures to improve equality outcomes, not only for their employees (s159 of the Act in relation to recruitment and promotion) but also for their clients/service users with protected characteristics who experience a disadvantage, have particular needs or a disproportionately low participation rate arising from their protected characteristic (s158 of the Act).

Individuals who think they have been discriminated against can bring a claim under the Act; this may be in a county court (sheriff court in Scotland) or a tribunal, depending on the context. If the claim is in connection with non-compliance with the public sector Equality Duty, any affected person/s (as well as the Equality and Human Rights Commission, EHRC), can bring a High Court (Court of Session in Scotland) action known as a judicial review.

The EHRC also has a variety of other enforcement powers, which are covered in the section on enforcement below.

Key points arising from these different provisions of the Act are considered in more detail in the following sections, but this is by no means an exhaustive explanation of the Act's provisions.

The EHRC has produced statutory[3] and non-statutory[4] guidance for different areas of the Act; some statutory guidance such as that in relation to the public sector Equality Duty has yet to be finalised and other codes have yet to be commenced. The Government's Office for Disability Issues based in the Department for Work and Pensions has produced non-statutory guidance as has the Government's Equalities Office based in the Home Office which leads on the Act.

---

2   With the exception of marriage and civil partnership, to which only the first part of the general public sector duty applies.

3   Statutory guidance is guidance that has been approved by the Secretary of State and laid before Parliament. It is not an authoritative statement of the law. However, it can be used as evidence in court or tribunal proceedings connected with the Equality Act and the court/tribunal must take into account any part of the Code it considers relevant when determining the questions arising.

4   Non-statutory guidance is essentially practical guidance aimed at helping people understand their rights and obligations under the Act, but it has no legal standing.

This chapter focuses on the work of all those involved in mental health services provision, both as service providers (as opposed to employers) and when exercising a public function (such as commissioning decisions about service priorities); in practice, the Act's duties in relation to the provision of services and the exercise of public functions operate in a very similar way. Part 3 of the Act covers services and the exercise of public functions.

PROTECTED CHARACTERISTICS

The protected characteristics covered by Part 3 of the Act at the time of writing are discussed below. The ban on age discrimination in the provision of services and public functions is coming into force on 1 October 2012 but will only apply to people aged 18 and over.

Disability (s6 and Schedule 1 of the Act)

The definition of disability under the Act is essentially the same as under the Disability Discrimination Act 1995 as amended (the DDA); namely, a person is disabled if they have a physical or mental impairment which has a substantial long-term adverse effect on their ability to carry out normal day-to-day activities. As under the DDA (as amended by s18(2) of the Disability Discrimination Act 2005), a mental impairment does not have to be clinically well recognised in order to satisfy the definition. What has changed is that there is no longer a list of capacities (such as speech, hearing or eyesight, memory or ability to concentrate, learn or understand, or perception of the risk of physical danger), at least one of which a person had, under the DDA, to show was affected in order to prove that their ability to carry out normal day-to-day activities was affected by their impairment.

Certain conditions are specifically excluded from the Act, including addiction to, or dependency on, alcohol, nicotine, or any other substance (other than in consequence of the substance being medically prescribed).

Non-statutory guidance on how the definition is applied, including detailed information about how recurring conditions such as depression are treated, has been issued by the Government's Office for Disability Issues (2011).

Gender reassignment (s7 of the Act)

People who are proposing to undergo, or are undergoing a process (or part of a process) to reassign their sex by changing 'physiological or other attributes of sex' (s7(1) of the Act) are covered by the protected characteristic of gender reassignment. The Act does not consider this as a medical process; there is no requirement for someone to have had medical treatment in order to receive the Act's protection. As long as they have proposed to start the process, this does not need to be an irrevocable decision; they will still have this protected characteristic.

If someone has been diagnosed with gender dysphoria or gender identity disorder and satisfies the definition of disability in s1 of the Act, they will have the protected characteristics of both gender reassignment and disability.

Separate legislation (the Gender Recognition Act 2004) covers gender recognition certificates.

There is an exception to the general prohibition on unlawful gender reassignment discrimination in relation to the provision of separate and single-sex only services (Schedule 3 Part 7 Paragraph 28 of the Act): a service provider is permitted to provide a different service, or refuse to let someone with the protected characteristic of gender reassignment access the service, but only if this is a proportionate means of achieving a legitimate aim.

A service provider can refuse communal accommodation (defined in Schedule 23 Paragraph 3(5) of the Act as residential accommodation, including shared sleeping accommodation which should only be used by members of one sex for privacy reasons), to someone with the protected characteristic of gender reassignment – but again, only if this is a proportionate means of achieving a legitimate aim.

However, paragraph 13.60 of the Services, Public Functions and Associations Statutory Code of Practice ('the Services Code') (EHRC 2011) states that 'the denial of a service to a transsexual person should only occur in exceptional circumstances'.

Pregnancy and maternity

Pregnancy and maternity is listed as a protected characteristic in ss4 of the Act, but does not have a separate section devoted to it like the other protected characteristics. It is also listed as a form of discrimination, which is dealt with below.

A service provider can lawfully refuse a service to a pregnant woman, or only offer it on certain conditions if the provider:

1. reasonably believes that if the service were provided, the woman's health and safety would be at risk because of her pregnancy and

2. would not provide the service to people with other physical conditions because of a reasonable belief that the service would put their health or safety at risk.

(Schedule 3 Part 3 Paragraph 14 of the Act)

Race (s9 of the Act)

Race includes colour, nationality and ethnic or national origins.[5]

Where people have or share the same colour, nationality or ethnic or national group, they are considered to be part of a specific racial group. Two or more groups can make up a racial group; for example, British Asians.

Religion or belief (s10 of the Act)

The definition includes any religious or philosophical belief, including lack of such belief. Explanatory note 51 clarifies that in line with Article 9 of the European Convention on Human Rights, a religion 'must have a clear structure and belief system'. A denomination or sect within a religion can be considered to be a religion or belief in its own right.

In terms of philosophical belief, there are strict criteria for defining whether a belief would receive protection under the Equality Act (Explanatory note 52 to the Act). Such a belief must:

- be genuinely held

- be a belief and not an opinion or viewpoint, based on the present state of information available

- be a belief as to a weighty and substantial aspect of human behaviour

- attain a certain level of cogency, seriousness, cohesion and importance

---

5   For more information on these definitions, see paragraphs 2.29 to 2.42 of the Services Code.

- be worthy of respect in a democratic society, compatible with human dignity and not conflicting with the fundamental rights of others.

Paragraph 2.51 of the Services Code highlights that a belief 'must affect how a person lives their life or perceives the world'.

Example: Humanism would be considered a philosophical belief under the Equality Act, for example, but being a devotee of Star Trek or a supporter of a particular sports team would not, as such beliefs would not satisfy the conditions listed above.

Expressions of a religion or belief, such as diets, dress codes or prayer observances, cannot always be separated from the actual religious or philosophical belief.

Sex (s11 of the Act)

This covers a male or female of any age, and in a group context, a group of either men/boys or a group of women/girls.

There are exceptions permitting the provision of separate services for each sex and providing separate services in a different way, if certain conditions are fulfilled (Schedule 3 Part 7 Paragraph 26 of the Act). In relation to the provision of separate services, it would not be unlawful sex discrimination to provide separate services for men and women if:

1. a joint service would be less effective and

2. the separate provision is a proportionate means of achieving a legitimate aim.

The provision of separate services in a different way will not amount to unlawful sex discrimination if:

1. a joint service would be less effective

2. the need for the service by one sex means it is not reasonably practicable to provide the service other than separately and in a different way for each sex and

3. the separate provision is a proportionate means of achieving a legitimate aim.

The provision of single-sex only services will not amount to unlawful sex discrimination, provided it is a proportionate means of achieving a legitimate aim and one of the following six conditions applies (Schedule 3 Part 7 Paragraph 27 of the Act).

1. Only people of that sex need the service.

2. Where a service is provided for both sexes, an additional service exclusively for one sex would be lawful if the joint provision would not be sufficiently effective.

3. If a joint service were provided it would not be as effective, and the need for the service means it is not reasonably practicable to provide separate services for each sex.

4. The service is provided in a hospital or other setting where service users require special care, supervision or attention.

5. The service is either for, or likely to be used by, more than one person at a time, and a woman might reasonably object to a man's presence.

6. It is likely that the service will involve physical contact between the service user and another person, and that other person could reasonably object if the service user is of the opposite sex.

Communal accommodation can be restricted to one sex only so long as it is managed in as fair a way as possible for both sexes.

Sexual orientation (s12 of the Act)

This covers a person's sexual orientation, be it towards persons of the same sex, persons of the opposite sex or persons of either sex. It covers discrimination towards a person because of their sexual orientation and also because of how their sexual orientation is demonstrated.

TYPES OF DISCRIMINATION

For the purposes of this section, the term 'service provider' and 'service user' apply respectively to those providing services and exercising public functions, and to those receiving services or who are in receipt of the exercise of a public function respectively.

Direct discrimination

Direct discrimination arises in services and the exercise of public functions (covered by Part 3 of the Act) when a service provider treats a service user less favourably than it treats (or would treat) another service user, because of a protected characteristic.

> *Example:* A Child and Adolescent Mental Health Service (CAMHS) refuses to treat a boy with mental health difficulties because he is also autistic and the service does not believe it has the necessary expertise to treat him as a result. This is direct disability discrimination.

Generally direct discrimination cannot be justified. Racial segregation is always discriminatory.

When age (for people aged 18 and over) becomes a protected characteristic for the purposes of Part 3 of the Act, age discrimination can be justified if it is a proportionate means of achieving a legitimate aim. However, paragraph 13.2 of the Services Code stresses that 'the basic presumption under the Act is that discrimination because of the protected characteristics is unlawful unless any exception applies and any exception to the prohibition of discrimination should generally be interpreted restrictively'.

> *Example:* An Adult Mental Health Service (AMHS) refuses to allow users who are over 55 to join an exercise class for service users on health and safety grounds. This is likely to amount to direct age discrimination, as there is no reason why it would be unsafe for all service users aged 55 or over to exercise.

It is always lawful to treat a disabled service user more favourably than a non-disabled service user because of their disability. It is also lawful to treat pregnant or breastfeeding women more favourably because of this protected characteristic.

Direct discrimination by association

This arises when a service provider treats a service user less favourably because of their association with another person who has a protected characteristic (other than pregnancy or maternity).

> *Example:* A young man is not allowed to join a group therapy class because his parents are a gay couple, and the therapist considers the fact that he does not come from a heterosexual family background will interfere with the group dynamics. This would be direct discrimination by association because of sexual orientation because of the man's association with his parents.

Direct discrimination by perception

This occurs when a service user is treated less favourably by a service provider because the provider mistakenly thinks the user has a protected characteristic (other than pregnancy and maternity).

> *Example:* A girl who has been on the waiting list for a renowned music therapist is passed over when a slot comes up, as the CAMHS practice manager mistakenly thinks she is Muslim and will not see a male therapist. This would be direct discrimination by perception because of religion and belief.

Indirect discrimination

Indirect discrimination can arise where a service provider applies a provision, practice or criterion in the same way for all service users, and in doing so puts those service users who share a particular protected characteristic (other than pregnancy or maternity) at a particular disadvantage.

However, indirect discrimination can be justified if it is a proportionate means of achieving a legitimate aim. Examples of legitimate aims set out in paragraph 5.30 of the Services Code of Practice include ensuring:

- that services and benefits are targeted at those who most need them

- the health and safety of those using the service provider's service or others, provided risks are clearly specified

- the well-being and dignity of those using the service.

Example: A young man from a Jain family complains that his psychiatrist is indirectly discriminating against him by prescribing tablets which contain animal gelatine, as Jains believe in the sanctity of all life. CAMHS would need to look more closely into the nature of the young man's beliefs to see whether this practice amounts to a particular disadvantage, and if so, whether any other tablets could be used instead, or whether the practice can be justified as a proportionate means of achieving the legitimate aim of helping him to be well.

Pregnancy and maternity discrimination

This form of discrimination will arise if a service provider treats a service user unfavourably because she is or has been pregnant, has given birth within the last 26 weeks, or is breast feeding a baby who is 26 weeks old or under.

Example: A woman is breastfeeding her three-month-old baby in the waiting area and is asked to move outside because other service users have complained about this.

If a service user is treated less favourably because she is breastfeeding a baby who is more than 26 weeks old, this may be direct *sex* discrimination.

Discrimination arising from disability

This form of discrimination and a failure to make reasonable adjustments only applies to disabled people.

Discrimination arising from disability arises when a service provider treats a disabled service user unfavourably for a reason relating to their disability, without justification.

Example: A service user with a severe facial disfigurement is always asked to wait in a room on their own as the service is concerned the user's presence makes other service users uncomfortable. This is unfavourable treatment for a reason relating to the user's disability.

If a service provider has not complied with its duty to make reasonable adjustments (see below) it will be difficult for it to justify the unfavourable treatment.

If a service provider does not know and could not reasonably have known that the service user was disabled, then the unfavourable treatment will not amount to discrimination arising from disability. However, if the service user has told anyone who works or acts for the service about their disability, the whole service is deemed to know (unless the service user has requested strict confidentiality). While the service should be aware of the service user's mental health condition, which may amount to a disability under the Act, there may be other disabilities that the service needs to be aware of.

Failure to make reasonable adjustments

The purpose of the duty is to ensure that the standard of service (or exercise of a public function) received by disabled people is as close as reasonably possible to that offered to service users as a whole.

Service providers and those exercising a public function are required to take reasonable steps to:

- avoid that disadvantage where a practice, provision or criterion puts disabled service users at a substantial disadvantage:

Example: AMHS extends the usual length of their counselling sessions to accommodate the extra time required by a service user who communicates by way of a communication aid and assistance from his personal assistant. This is likely to be a reasonable adjustment to make.

- avoid that disadvantage where a physical feature puts disabled service users at a substantial disadvantage; this covers removing the feature in question, altering it or providing a reasonable means of avoiding it or where the disadvantage cannot be avoided, by providing a reasonable alternative method of providing the service or exercising the function:

Example: An accessible day service is moved to a listed building site which is accessible only by steps. The rooms designated as treatment rooms have very narrow doors. The service enters into discussions with access consultants about how to make the service fully accessible in its new location, for both current and future clients. In the meantime the service ensures that all its users can continue to use the service, by making a temporary ramp available and arranging for appointments for wheelchair users whose wheelchairs will not fit through the narrow doors to take place in the main meeting room, which has double doors.

- provide an auxiliary aid or service where failure to do so would put a disabled service user at a substantial disadvantage:

Example: A service trains a member of staff as a British Sign Language (BSL) signer so as to be able to ensure that deaf service users who use BSL are able to communicate effectively with staff and other users.

'Substantial' is defined in s212(1) of the Equality Act 2010 as 'more than minor or trivial'.

In relation to a disabled person being subjected to a detriment in the exercise of a public function, substantial disadvantage means:

- being placed at a substantial disadvantage where the exercise of the public function confers a benefit or

- suffering an unreasonably adverse experience where the exercise of the function could have an adverse effect on the person on the receiving end (such as being detained in hospital).

If the provision, practice or criterion or the auxiliary aid or service involves the provision of information, the steps it is reasonable to take include steps to ensure the information is provided in an accessible format.

Service providers will be familiar with the concept of the reasonable adjustments duty from the DDA. However, the threshold for the duty to arise in the context of service provision is lower than under the DDA, where failure to comply with the duty would make it 'impossible or unreasonably difficult' for a disabled person to make use of the services.

The duty to make reasonable adjustments is anticipatory and continuing and owed to disabled service users generally. Service providers should therefore think about and plan for the needs of their disabled service users in general and not wait until an individual disabled service user approaches them asking for adjustments to be made.

Failure to make reasonable adjustments cannot be justified; service providers therefore need to consider whether the adjustment being considered is a 'reasonable' one. However, those exercising public functions cannot be required to make any adjustments which are beyond their powers to make.

Service providers cannot charge a disabled service user for the cost of making reasonable adjustments for them.

HARASSMENT AND VICTIMISATION
Harassment (s26 of the Act)

There are three types of unlawful harassment under the Act (covering all the protected characteristics to which Part 3 applies, with the exception of pregnancy and maternity, religion or belief and sexual orientation):

1. Harassment related to a relevant protected characteristic
This is unwanted conduct related to the service user's protected characteristic which has the effect of:

- violating their dignity or

- creating an intimidating, hostile, degrading, humiliating or offensive environment for them.

It also covers situations where there is a connection with a protected characteristic, such as where a service user is associated with someone with a protected characteristic, or wrongly perceived as having a protected characteristic, or where the unwanted conduct is not aimed at the person who is harassed, but at someone else or no one in particular.

Example: A psychologist who runs an inpatient group therapy session frequently makes derogatory comments about the poor quality work of Polish builders who 'come to England to make their fortune'. A Polish inpatient and an English friend in the group find these remarks extremely offensive. This behaviour could amount to racial harassment of both the Polish inpatient and his English friend.

---

2. Sexual harassment

This occurs when a person engages in unwanted conduct as described in section 1 above which is of a sexual nature.

> *Example:* A female nurse is very tactile with a male patient and kisses him. Regardless of whether the patient tries to reject her advances or not, this amounts to sexual harassment.

3. Treating a service user less favourably because they submit to or reject unwanted conduct of a sexual nature or unwanted conduct related to sex or gender reassignment

> *Example:* In the above example, if the nurse then refuses to let the patient have time in the hospital gym for fear that he will have time to speak to other patients and tell them what has happened, this could be less favourable treatment because the patient either had or had not submitted to unwanted conduct of sexual nature.

Victimisation (s27 of the Act)

A service provider victimises someone when they treat them badly because they have carried out (or the provider thinks they have or will carry out) a '*protected act*'.

A '*protected act*' can be any of the following:

- making a claim or complaint of discrimination under the Act
- helping someone else to make a claim by giving evidence or information
- making an allegation that the provider or someone else has breached the Act
- any other action in connection with the Act.

There must be a link between the service provider's action and how it treats the 'victim'.

> *Example:* A service manager does not award a psychologist a pay rise, despite pay rises being handed out across the board, because she has given evidence in support of a client's claim of discrimination against the manager. This is likely to amount to victimisation of the psychologist.

DUTIES TOWARDS INDIVIDUAL CLIENTS

Mental health services (provided by NHS trusts and/or local authorities and the voluntary sector) are services to the public, and have duties towards individual service users in the same way as any other service provider.

Such services also have duties when exercising public functions (defined by the Act as a function of a public nature for the purposes of the Human Rights Act 1998).

DUTIES WHEN PROVIDING SERVICES

A service provider must not discriminate against or victimise a service user (or someone seeking to use a service):

- by not providing that person with a service (s29(1) of the Act)

  ○ including not providing the service user with the service, and also not providing them with the same level of service, or in the same manner or on the same terms as would usually apply to members of the public or to a section of the public to which the service user belongs, such as inpatients

- in relation to the terms on which it provides the service (s29(2)(a) of the Act)

- by terminating the provision of the service (s29(2)(b) of the Act)

- by subjecting the user to any other detriment (s29(2)(c) of the Act).

It is also unlawful to harass someone in connection with the provision of a service to them.

'Detriment' is not defined in the Act, and has a broad meaning. Paragraph 9.7 of the Services Code explains that while it does not need to have any physical or economic consequences, it should amount to something a service user 'might reasonably consider changed their position for the worse or put them at a disadvantage'.

Duties when exercising a public function

In relation to a public authority, the public function provisions only cover those functions which are not services, or do not fall within the premises, work or education provisions of the Act. Private or voluntary organisations may carry out public functions on behalf of the state that are not services that could be performed by private persons.

A service provider must not discriminate, harass or victimise anyone when exercising a public function (s29(6) of the Act). The interpretation of this is broad. Paragraph 11.26 of the Services Code explains that 'refusing to allow someone to benefit from the exercise of a function, or treating someone in a worse manner in the exercise of a function' are examples of the types of discrimination that would be covered by this provision.

PLANNING FROM WITHIN –
THE PUBLIC SECTOR EQUALITY DUTY

National Health Service (NHS) trusts and local authorities are familiar with the concept of public sector equality duties as, prior to the Act, they were subject to the race, gender and disability equality duties under the old discrimination legislation.

However, the Focus Consultancy's 2011 research report commissioned by the EHRC into how strategic health authorities and primary care trusts in England met their race, gender and disability equality duties revealed that, despite some progress being made, there were 'serious concerns regarding performance on the equality duties' (page 7), for a variety of reasons. These included a lack of mainstreaming equality planning and reporting; a weakness in joined-up thinking between regional and local levels and between equality schemes and health and social service user outcomes; failure to translate consultation with equality stakeholders into priorities and outcomes; lack of leadership from the top; and a failure to follow available advice and guidance.

Under the Act, the public sector Equality Duty has been extended to all the protected characteristics that apply to Part 3 of the Act, so there is even more reason for such weaknesses to be addressed, albeit within a changing health service delivery structure. NHS trusts and local authorities are subject to the general and specific public sector equality duties, and voluntary organisations will be subject to the general public sector Equality Duty when exercising a public function, but only in relation to that function.

The purpose of the public sector Equality Duty is to bring about positive change in relation to equality from within an organisation and it applies to all their functions, including procurement.

General duty

The Act states (s149(1) and (2)) that in the exercise of their public functions a public body or anyone exercising public functions must have due regard to the need to:

- eliminate unlawful discrimination, harassment and victimisation and other conduct prohibited by the Act

- advance equality of opportunity between people who share a protected characteristic and those who do not

- foster good relations between people who share a protected characteristic and those who do not.

Section 149(3) of the Act clarifies that the second part of the general duty, *advancing equality of opportunity*, involves having due regard to the need to:

- remove or minimise disadvantages suffered by people due to their protected characteristics

- take steps to meet the needs of people from protected groups where these are different from the needs of other people

- encourage people from protected groups to participate in public life or in other activities where their participation is disproportionately low.

This mirrors the positive action provisions (see section below).

Specific duties

The regulations covering the specific duties for England came into force on 10 September 2011 and apply to all public authorities listed in Schedules 1 (including NHS trusts and local authorities) and 2 of the regulations; those listed in Schedule 2 have more time in which to publish the information set out below (The Equality Act 2010 (Specific Duties) Regulations 2011). The Welsh and Scottish ministers have the power to introduce specific duties on the relevant Welsh and Scottish public authorities; specific duties came into force in Wales on 6 April 2011 and in Scotland on 27 May 2012.

The purpose of the specific duties (as set out in paragraph 2.2 of the explanatory memorandum to the above regulations) is to ensure that the public authorities concerned perform better in their duty to have regard to the three aims of the general duty.

Most public authorities in England, including NHS trusts and local authorities, had to publish sufficient information to demonstrate compliance with the three aims of the general equality duty no later than 31 January 2012, and equality objectives by 6 April 2012 and then at least every four years.

THE EXTRA MILE – THE POSITIVE ACTION PROVISIONS

The positive action provisions in the Act allow service providers to take action (which would otherwise be unlawful) to redress past or present disadvantage or discrimination faced by service users with protected characteristics. The irony of positive action is that it has great capacity to bring about positive change but is voluntary.

Positive action is in the middle of a spectrum of actions to redress the effects of discrimination: at one end there is action which is always lawful, and at the other end there is positive discrimination which is always unlawful. Positive action is lawful under the Act provided it meets the following conditions set out in the Act:

1. The service provider reasonably thinks a group of service users sharing a protected characteristic:

    • experience a disadvantage connected to that characteristic

    • have different needs, or

    • have a disproportionately low participation rate in an activity.

2. The service provider takes action which aims to:

    • enable or encourage that group of service users to remove or reduce the disadvantage

    • meet their different needs, or

    • enable or encourage increased participation.

3. The action is a proportionate means of achieving a legitimate aim.

> *Example:* A CAMHS believes that the local traveller population is under-represented amongst their service users. It reviews its user records and realises that only two traveller families have accessed the service in the last two years, even though there are a significant number of traveller families within its catchment area. It contacts the travellers' Health Visitor to better understand the travellers' needs, and as a result sets up an on-site service which improves take-up of services. Despite complaints from other groups that this special service for travellers is unfair, this on-site service is likely to be a proportionate means of achieving the legitimate aim of encouraging participation of this ethnic group and satisfying the positive action conditions.

It is important for a service implementing positive action measures to review them regularly to ensure that the preconditions for positive action still exist, otherwise the action risks becoming unlawful. It is advisable for a service to keep records detailing the positive action process, including the nature of any positive action measures taken, why they were taken, why the service considered the steps to be proportionate and the monitoring undertaken.

WHEN THINGS GO WRONG – THE ENFORCEMENT PROVISIONS

Individual claims about unlawful discrimination, harassment or victimisation in connection with Part 3 of the Act are made to the county court (England and Wales) or the sheriff court (Scotland).

Such claims normally have to be brought within six months of the alleged discriminatory act, but the courts have a discretion to allow cases to be brought out of time. This time limit can also be extended to nine months if the case has been referred to conciliation by the EHRC.

Service users can use the procedure for obtaining information before bringing proceedings to find out more information from the service provider to establish whether or not they have a claim. The service provider is not obliged to answer the users' questions, but if they fail to do so within the eight-week allotted time, a court may draw an adverse inference. The Government issued a consultation about whether to remove this provision, which closed on 7 August 2012.

There is a range of remedies a court can award if the case is successful, from declarations of the rights and responsibilities of the parties, to injunctions (interdicts in Scotland) preventing the repeat of an unlawful act in the future, and damages.

Claims in relation to the public sector Equality Duty are by means of judicial review in the High Court (Court of Session in Scotland).

The EHRC has a range of enforcement powers at its disposal, including intervention in court cases, bringing judicial review proceedings inquiries, investigations, assessments and compliance notices. For example, in December 2009, prior to the Equality Act 2010, the Commission issued compliance notices to Frimley Park Hospital NHS Foundation Trust, Kent and Medway NHS and Social Care Partnership Trust and NHS Surrey in relation to their need to take action to address race equality or face legal action for failing to comply with the Race Relations Act 1976 (EHRC Legal Enforcement Update April 2010).

A BRIEF WORD ON EMPLOYMENT

While this book is primarily about the provision of services and the exercise of public functions covered by Part 3 of the Act, given that service providers will be helping some users back into employment, it is worth pointing out a few key issues about employment and the Act. The main employment provisions are contained in Part 5 of the Act.

Protected characteristics

In addition to the protected characteristics that apply to both Part 3 and Part 5 of the Act and which have been discussed above, Part 5 has the additional protected characteristic of marriage and civil partnership. It is important to stress that people who are unmarried or single are not protected under this ground; only those who are married or in a civil partnership are. The protected characteristic of age is already in force in an employment context and applies to all ages, not just people who are 18 or over.

The reasonable adjustments duty

Unlike the reasonable adjustment duty for service providers, which is owed to disabled people at large, the reasonable adjustments duty on employers is only owed to those disabled employees/applicants that the employer knows, or could reasonably be expected to know, are disabled.

Pre-employment enquiries about disability and health

In relation to recruitment, the Act has introduced a new provision, namely, a prohibition on employers asking about a job applicant's health until after they have either been offered a position (on either a conditional or unconditional basis) or have been included in a pool of successful applicants who will be offered a job when one is available. There are six specified exceptions to this prohibition:

- to ask whether reasonable adjustments are required during the recruitment process

- for diversity monitoring

- to implement positive action measures

- to find out whether the applicant satisfies a genuine occupational requirement

- for national security vetting

- to establish whether the applicant can perform functions which are intrinsic to the job.

Disability-related absences from work

It may well be a reasonable adjustment to discount some or all of a worker's disability-related sickness absences. This will depend on the circumstances of each case. It is advisable to record disability-related absences separately from other sickness-related absences so as to avoid unlawful discrimination in relation to allocation of bonuses or other employment decisions.

Liability of employers for harassment by third parties

Employers can be liable for harassment of their employees or of job applicants by third parties such as customers or clients. The duty arises where an employee or applicant has been harassed by a third party on at least two previous occasions (it can be different third parties on each occasion), and the employer, although aware of the harassment, does not take 'reasonably practical steps' to prevent harassment by a third party happening again. However, the Coalition Government wishes to remove this provision and its response to the public consultation concerning its removal is expected within three months of the consultation's closing date of 7 August 2012.

Exceptions

There are a number of exceptions relating to the employment provisions, including:

Occupational requirements – where an employer can lawfully require a job applicant or worker to have a particular protected characteristic, if the relevant statutory conditions are met.

> *Example:* An organisation for deaf people might legitimately employ a deaf person who uses BSL to work as a counsellor to other deaf people whose first or preferred language is BSL (Explanatory note 798 to the Act).

Armed forces exceptions – the armed forces are permitted under the Act to refuse a woman or a transsexual employment or access to opportunities for promotion, transfer or training if such action amounts to a proportionate method of ensuring the combat effectiveness of the forces. Age and disability are not protected characteristics for the purposes of service in the armed forces, and in addition, disability is not a protected characteristic for work experience in the armed forces.

Enforcement

Claims about discrimination in relation to employment are made to the Employment Tribunal.

CONCLUSION

These are challenging times for those working to combat inequality, as the Government is seeking to limit the scope of the Equality Act 2010 and the power of the equalities and human rights regulator, the EHRC, in the name of reducing what it regards as unnecessary duties and powers. However, thanks to previous legislation and greater awareness, a momentum has been built up to combat discrimination, which it is hoped will develop further by taking advantage of the potential offered by provisions such as positive action to continue to bring about positive and lasting change.

USEFUL GUIDANCE
Statutory guidance

- EHRC (2011) *Services, Public Functions and Associations Statutory Code of Practice.*

- EHRC (2011) *Employment Statutory Code of Practice.*

- EHRC (expected 2012) *Public Sector Equality Duty Technical Guidance.*

Non-statutory guidance

- Non-statutory guidance for the public sector Equality Duty: www.equalityhumanrights.com/uploaded_files/EqualityAct/PSED/essential_guide_guidance.pdf

- Office for Disability Issues (2011) *Equality Act 2010: Guidance on Matters to be Taken into Account in Determining Questions Relating to the Definition of Disability.*

- Various guidance produced by the Government's Equalities Office at www.homeoffice.gov.uk/publications/equalities/equality-act-publications/equality-act-guidance

REFERENCES

EHRC (Equality and Human Rights Commission) (2010) *Legal Enforcement Update.* Accessed at www.equalityhumanrights.com/legal-and-policy/enforcement on 15 January 2012.

EHRC (2011) *Services, Public Functions and Associations Statutory Code of Practice.* London: The Stationery Office. Accessed at www.equalityhumanrights.com/uploaded_files/EqualityAct/servicescode.pdf.

Equality Act (2010) (Specific Duties) Regulations 2011; SI 2011 No 2260. London: The Stationery Office.

Focus Consultancy (2011) *The Performance of the Health Sector in Meeting the Public Sector Equality Duties: Moving toward Effective Equality Outcomes.* London: Focus Consultancy and the Equality and Human Rights Commission.

Office for Disability Issues (2011) *Equality Act 2010: Guidance on Matters to be Taken into Account in Determining Questions Relating to the Definition of Disability.* May. London: Office for Disability Issues.

Chapter 2

THE CASE FOR A SINGLE EQUALITIES APPROACH

Melba Wilson

INTRODUCTION

Policy implementation in health and social care and mental health is currently governed by a single equalities approach. This is welcome. To understand fully the impact and implications in a health and social care context, however, it is useful to:

- examine the components contained within a single equalities approach – its individual elements as well as areas of overlap

- understand equality within the context of inequality, i.e. promoting equality is also, inevitably, about recognising the need to reduce inequality

- contextualise the single equalities approach in order to promote greater meaning, emphasis and practicality in commissioning and delivery.

This chapter looks at the existing legislative and policy context; discusses the issues which can arise when services attempt to meet the needs of a range of diverse constituents; considers the potential for change in learning from existing evidence; and identifies some options for embedding change.

UNDERSTANDING EQUALITY

Recent legislation, guidance and policy has been aimed at promoting equality and reducing inequality. Two key areas of focus here are:

- the Equality Act 2010 (particularly the public sector Equality Duty) – set out extensively in the preceding chapter

- the Equality Delivery System, whose intent is to foster greater accountability for promoting equality within the NHS.

Equality Act 2010 – public sector Equality Duty (PSED)

The Home Office has identified that:

> the Equality Duty supports good decision making [through] encouraging public bodies to understand how different people will be affected by their activities, so that their policies and services are appropriate and accessible to all and meet different people's needs. By understanding the effect of their activities on different people, and how inclusive public services can support and open up people's opportunities, public bodies can be more efficient and effective. The Equality Duty therefore aims to help public bodies to deliver the government's overall objectives for public services. (Home Office 2012)

The Equality Act also calls for public sector bodies to demonstrate how they comply with the duties under the Act. For most public sector bodies this requirement had to be demonstrated by 31 January 2012 (Equality and Human Rights Commission (EHRC) 2012).

The PSED thus provides a framework and structure to enable public sector bodies to comply with the letter and intent of the legislation. As such, it is an important opportunity and mandate to enable agencies to plan and deliver services based on the real and assessed needs of their populations. Understanding how various groups and constituencies experience services is central to understanding how services can be made better and more relevant in meeting people's needs.

The Equality Delivery System (EDS)

The Equality and Human Rights Commission (EHRC) and National Health Service (NHS) employers have published guidance on the PSED, and a toolkit – the EDS – is now available to help NHS organisations comply with the PSED.

The EDS was initiated by the NHS Equality and Diversity Council (EDC), chaired by Sir David Nicholson, chief executive of the NHS, and developed in association with the NHS (Crown 2011).

The NHS has been sponsored and supported by the EDC to develop the EDS for the NHS. Work on the EDS was initiated by the EDC in early 2010. The EDC is a sub-committee of the NHS Management Board. Sir David Nicholson chairs both groups. It aims to provide 'visible leadership on equality issues across the NHS, through influencing, encouraging and empowering people throughout the NHS, government and communities to drive real improvements in health and care outcomes' (NHS EDC 2010).

The EDS is one of the first products initiated by the NHS EDC. Its purpose is to drive up equality performance and embed equality into mainstream NHS business. It has been designed to help NHS organisations, in the current and new NHS structures, to meet:

- the requirements of the PSED

- equality aspects of the NHS Constitution

- equality aspects of the NHS Outcomes Framework

- equality aspects of the Care Quality Commission's Essential Standards

- equality aspects of the Human Resources Transition Framework.

(Crown 2011)

The PSED and EDS are important markers for health and social care and provide clear parameters for public sector bodies to develop services which meet diverse needs.

UNDERSTANDING INEQUALITY – 'LIBERTY, EQUALITY AND FRATERNITY'

The mantra of the French Revolution focused attention on the dimensions of social relations that matter most if we are to create a better society and make a difference to the real quality of our lives. (Wilkinson and Pickett 2010, p.45)

Poor mental health is…both a cause and a consequence of the experience of social, economic and environmental inequalities (p.35); [and] mental health is also a key pathway through which inequality impacts on health (p.38). (Friedli 2009)

The Marmot Review (2010) into evidence-based strategies for reducing inequalities concluded that:

health inequalities result from social inequalities; that action on health inequalities requires action across all the social determinants of health;

and that reducing health inequalities is a matter of fairness and social justice. (Marmot 2010, p.7)

Inequality is associated with lower life expectancy, higher rates of infant mortality, shorter height, poor self-reported health, low birthweight, AIDS and depression (Wilkinson and Pickett 2010, p.81).

The link between promoting equality and reducing inequality is also acknowledged in the Coalition Government's mental health (*No Health without Mental Health* (HM Government 2011) and public health strategies (*Healthy Lives, Healthy People* (Department of Health (DoH) 2010). The mental health strategy states that 'tackling health inequalities and promoting equality, as enshrined in the Equality Act 2010, is vital if the Government is to deliver health outcomes that are among the best in the world' (HM Government 2011).

The strategy emphasises that:

> A fundamental principle in tackling inequality is that all protected characteristics should be considered so as to avoid unjustifiable discrimination…[and that] At local level, needs assessment will determine the areas of greatest inequality that local strategies will need to address. (HM Government 2011, p.57)

Given the acknowledged correlation in macro terms, the practical next step is for commissioners and providers to better understand how to accomplish this at a micro level. However, getting the balance right within a context of competing priorities, economic constraints, fast-paced political and organisational change, and increasing demands on health and social care services is no easy task for those with responsibility for commissioning and delivery on the ground.

Attempts to 'get it right' may seem overwhelming and may lead to service responses that do not adequately address need. Sentiments such as 'everyone is treated equally' or 'we treat everyone the same' fail to acknowledge or take account of the realities and the complexities of meeting diversely presenting needs. Tackling the effects of health inequality, for instance, will require services to think differently about what is needed. This, in turn, will mean looking at the disparities within and between communities and groups.

Targeted approaches are required. Providing services for an older black woman with depression and on a low income will necessitate a different approach from that for meeting the needs of a young, mixed-race woman from a middle-class background with a similar diagnosis. Issues of class, race, social perspectives and expectations must be taken into account in framing service responses that address the needs of both.

When considering the dichotomies within and between different groups of protected characteristics, as outlined in the Equality Act 2010, it becomes apparent that underpinning narratives which capture history, culture and identity, as well as social and economic disparities, must be taken on board.

Taking a single equalities approach, as set out in the PSED, is not only about demonstrating compliance with the statute, it is also good practice for helping to ensure that no one protected characteristic area can effectively 'trump' another. Promoting equality and reducing inequality in a mental health context, therefore, is not about treating everyone the same – for example, by contending that a focus on 'dignity and respect' will result in all groups receiving fair treatment; experience has shown that this is simply not sufficient to ensure that people's needs are met. It *is* about understanding need and taking steps in a context of proportionality to address mental ill-health.

USING THE EVIDENCE BASE

The social anthropological approach set out by Kleinman and others (see Kleinman, Eisenberg and Good 1978; Kleinman 2008) is one example of how practitioners and policymakers can more easily incorporate a diversity of perspectives. This promotes evidence-based learning, beginning with practitioners' self-awareness and reflection, to encourage a non-silo approach in working with varied cultures and frames of reference. This explanatory model of care (Bhui and Bhugra 2003; Kleinman 1978) states the need to negotiate care and treatment in a context that acknowledges and takes account of the differing perspectives and world views of caregivers and patients. It advances the view that both perspectives are valid and therefore deserving of integration within the care and treatment interface. However, this involves understanding by each. This model subscribes to the need for mutually beneficial discussion and reflection in order to arrive at more productive clinical relationships.

The work of the mental health equalities programme (National Mental Health Development Unit 2009–2011; www.nmhdu.org.uk) also provides a useful evidence base. The programme broadened its initial focus on race, gender and age equality to embrace an equality-wide remit. This was more in line with the ideals and the intent of the Equality Act, but also was reflective of evidence-based learning.

Another significant area of learning is found in the Canadian experience relating to intersectionality. Although focusing within a gender and economic justice context, the work contains key learning for going forward in a single equalities context.

'Intersectionality' is a term coined in black feminist thought (Crenshaw 1989, 1991; Hill Collins 2012). It refers to the multiple ways in which a person can be marginalised or discriminated against, and is most often discussed in relation to black women with regard to the political, social and economic impact upon them as a consequence of the intersection of race, gender and class.

The Canadian work (Association for Women's Rights in Development (AWID) 2004) notes that *intersectionality* starts from the premise that *people live multiple, layered identities* derived from social relations, history and the operation of structures of power, and is a 'tool for analysis, advocacy and policy development that addresses multiple discriminations and helps us understand how different sets of identities impact on access to rights and opportunities.'

BOX 2.1 INTERSECTIONAL DISCRIMINATION: THE CANADIAN EXPERIENCE

The Canadian experience shows that in the market for rental housing, single, black women may have a particularly difficult time in finding apartments, especially if they are recipients of social assistance and/ or single parents. Many landlords buy into various stereotypes and believe them to be less dependable tenants.

On the basis of sex alone, this discrimination would not be apparent. Similarly, if considering race alone, this discrimination would not be evident. Using standard discrimination analysis, courts would fail to see that there is discrimination against those who are single, black and female. It is the singular identity of *single–black–woman* that is the subject of discrimination in the housing market. This is intersectional discrimination (AWID 2004).

The Canadian tool calls for:

- better use of data

- allocation of resources based on 'intersecting discriminations'

- advocacy to increase awareness of multiple discrimination

- respecting diverse identities.

CONCLUSION

The mental health strategy *No Health without Mental Health* reinforces the Coalition Government's commitment to 'delivering equity of access to treatment, prevention and promotion interventions, as well as equality of experience and outcomes across all protected groups' (Crown 2011, p.17).

Taking a single equalities approach can and should enable commissioners and providers to better understand, and, as a result, develop better services that are appropriate to the needs of their client populations.

REFERENCES

AWID (Association for *Women's Rights in Development) (2004) 'Intersectionality: a tool for gender and economic justice.' Women's Rights and Economic Change, Facts and Issues, No. 9,* August. Accessed at www.awid.org.

Bhui, K. and Bhugra, D. (2003) 'Explanatory models in psychiatry.' *British Journal of Psychiatry 183,* 170.

Crenshaw, K. (1989) 'Demarginalizing the intersection of race and sex: a black feminist critique of antidiscrimination doctrine, feminist theory, and antiracist politics.' University of Chicago *Legal Forum 139.*

Crenshaw, K. (1991) 'Mapping the margins: intersectionality, identity politics, and violence against women of colour.' *Stanford Law Review 43,* 1241.

Crown (2011) *The Equality Delivery System for the NHS* (Amended January 2012). London: Department of Health. Accessed at www.eastmidlands.nhs.uk/about-us/inclusion/eds/ on 5 March 2012.

DoH (Department of Health) (2010) *Healthy Lives, Healthy People: Our Strategy for Public Health in England.* London: DoH.

EHRC (Equality and Human Rights Commission) (2012) *The Essential Guide to the Public Sector Equality Duty.* Revised (second) edition. January. Accessed at www.equalityhumanrights.com/advice-and-guidance/public-sector-equality-duty/guidance-on-the-equality-duty on 6 March 2012.

Friedli, L. (2009) *Mental Health, Resilience and Inequalities.* Geneva: World Health Organization. Accessed at www.euro.who.int on 6 March 2012.

Hill Collins, P. (2012) 'Intersecting Oppressions.' Accessed at www.uk.sagepub.com/upm-data/13299_Chapter_16_Web_Byte_Patricia_Hill_Collins.pdf on 6 March 2012.

HM Government (2011) *No Health without Mental Health: A Cross-government Mental Health Outcomes Strategy for People of All Ages.* London: Department of Health.

Home Office (2012) *Public sector Equality Duty.* London: Home Office. Accessed at www.homeoffice.gov.uk/equalities/equality-act/equality-duty/home on 6 March 2012.

Kleinman. A. (1978) 'Concepts and a model for the comparison of medical systems as cultural systems.' *Social Science & Medicine 12,* 85-91.

Kleinman, A. (2008) 'The art of medicine, catastrophe and caregiving: the failure of medicine as an art.' *The Lancet 371,* 5 January, p.22.

Kleinman, A., Eisenberg, L. and Good, B. (1978) 'Culture, illness and care: clinical lessons from anthropologic and cross-cultural research.' *Annals of Internal Medicine 88,* 2, 1 February, 251–258.

Marmot, M. (2010) *Fair Society, Healthy Lives: Strategic Review of Health Inequalities in England Post 2010 (Executive Summary)*. London: The Marmot Review. Accessed at www.instituteofhealthequity.org/projects/fair-society-healthy-lives-the-marmot-review on 5 March 2012.

NHS EDC (Equality and Diversity Council) (2010) *Terms of Reference*. November. Accessed at www.dh.gov.uk/prod_consum_dh/groups/dh_digitalassets/documents/digitalasset/dh_127136.pdf on 6 February 2012.

Wilkinson, R. and Pickett, K. (2010) *The Spirit Level: Why Equality is Better for Everyone*. London: Penguin Books.

Chapter 3

BEYOND CATEGORIES
Service Users as Complex Beings

Eleanor Hope

Keep the Faith

INTRODUCTION

This chapter highlights the complexity of the human experience from a service user perspective. It explores the interaction between race and other social categories such as gender and class, and considers how they affect the development and delivery of appropriate mental health provisions. The chapter examines how complex identities shape who we are, and how self-discovery is a pathway to recovery, well-being and equality.

I use the Equality Act 2010 throughout this chapter to demonstrate how some of the nine 'protected characteristics' intersect.

CLASS

One characteristic not 'protected' is that of social class. Yet studies show that people perceived to be at the lower end of the social hierarchy are more likely to be discriminated against. One study (Narayan, Pritchett and Kapoor 1990) suggests that one of the root causes of poverty is in the underlying assumptions of policymakers:

> As we trace backward to root causes, we see that the underlying assumptions and residues of ideologies about poverty have left deep imprints on policy choices. Confronting these assumptions leads us to a series of questions. Are poor people dysfunctional or are the contexts in which they live dysfunctional? Is poverty the result of lack of initiative

among the poor, or is the problem lack of opportunity? (Narayan *et al.* 1990, p.7)

Our beliefs, values, underlying assumptions and stereotypes shape the culture we live in and advantage some over others.

RACE

Similarly, in the case of race, the Stephen Lawrence Inquiry defined 'institutional racism' as:

> The collective failure of an organisation to provide an appropriate and professional service to people because of their colour, culture, or ethnic origin. It can be seen or detected in processes, attitudes and behaviour which amount to discrimination through unwitting prejudice, ignorance, thoughtlessness and racist stereotyping which disadvantage minority ethnic people. (Macpherson 1999, p.28)

Similarly, African–American journalist and editor Cose also suggests 'that people do not have to be racist or have any malicious intent in order to make decisions that unfairly harm members of another race. They simply have to do what comes naturally' (Cose 1993, p.4).

How do we change what comes naturally, when we perceive other people as different from us? A white American professor of sociology suggests that 'The trouble around difference is really about privilege and power – the existence of privilege and the lop-sided distribution of power that keeps it going. The trouble is rooted in a legacy we all inherited and while we are here, it belongs to us' (Johnson 2001, p.15).

The first step, then, in changing is to be able to acknowledge and accept that racial discrimination does exist. Having anti-discrimination law under one roof within the Equality Act 2010 is an opportunity to acknowledge and examine the multiple ways in which social and cultural categories permeate the elements of power and privilege that contribute to structural and social inequalities.

INTERSECTIONALITY

Black feminism in the 1970s coined the term 'intersectionality' to define the 'various ways in which race and gender intersect in shaping structural, political and representational aspects of violence against women of color'. Crenshaw (1991) challenges notions that characterise race and gender as essentially separate categories.

Over a century ago, at a convention in 1852, Sojourner Truth, a freed slave and campaigner, combined her passion for both the abolition of slavery and equal rights for women in a famous speech. In her book of the same title, bell hooks[1] (1981) reports the story, including the passage below:

> That man over there says that women need to be helped into carriages, and lifted over ditches, and to have the best place everywhere. Nobody ever helps me into carriages, or over mud-puddles, or gives me any best place! And ain't I a woman? Look at me! Look at my arm! I have ploughed and planted, and gathered into barns, and no man could head me! And ain't I a woman? (hooks 1981, p.160)

We have explored the interaction of race, gender, and class, and now turn to my personal story to consider whether 'intersectionality' is considered in the development and delivery of appropriate provision of service.

MY STORY: INTERSECTION OF TWO WORLDS – SERVICE USER /COMMUNITY DEVELOPMENT/TRAINER

As Sojourner Truth, in my own story, when dealing with traumas of institutional racism, sexism, classism, homophobia and disability still, ain't I a woman?

I grew up in New York, after migrating with my family from Jamaica. After high school I continued to study, but, uncertain of which direction to take, I did not complete my degree, leaving instead to join a grassroots community group to organise and get involved in local politics in the early 1980s. I campaigned and engaged people in discussions and encouraged people to vote, and many did for the first time. Organising also allowed me an opportunity to travel from New York to several cities in the South and back, talking with and listening to people's stories, sharing their concerns, frustrations and dreams.

I was to migrate once again in 1989, when I met and fell in love with my partner, a Turkish Cypriot of African descent, living in London. I had to adjust and almost learn a new language of race, class and culture. This was very prominent on the housing estate we lived in – a culture shock to someone coming from NY where all my neighbours were black and so I had to adjust to a diverse community in South London.

---

1   bell hooks chooses deliberately not to capitalise her name, believing that her writings are more important than the writer.

I attended university and worked throughout my studies, and continued to work in the community, coordinating and managing various local community organisations. I became actively involved with the work of my union, both locally and nationally.

We moved to the southeast coast, seeking a better quality of life. I was employed as a community development worker for a local authority in 2002, and made redundant in 2004. Both experiences were to affect my mental well-being. Below I give a brief background to explain what happened, and what led up to it.

Background

As a community development worker, I was employed to work in a predominantly white, working-class community with high unemployment and poor housing. The area was known for problems of antisocial behaviour – bullying and harassment, domestic violence, homophobic and racial abuse. (New to the area, I was to learn the extent of the 'problem' only six months later, at a forum where the local police identified the area as a 'racial hotspot'.)

The first year – a learning experience

The first year was a learning experience; I would travel from the office to the community, meeting and networking. I met two youth workers who were starting at the same time as me, and one or two community leaders who were already involved with the local authority. I was welcomed by some and visited them in their homes. I was disturbed by some living conditions and was an advocate to arrange more appropriate housing. I would meet parents of children attending the local primary school and hear concerns about bullying and harassment of their children, and racial harassment by their neighbours. Others I met were concerned about the 'significant' number of black and minority ethnic (BME) families moving into their area, while some were concerned about young people hanging about with nothing to do; I also met and worked with some local service providers.

Year 2 – community research / teamwork

After almost a year I was successful in getting additional funding from a variety of sources to develop a six-month project for local residents to be trained and accredited as community researchers. They were paid to work in their community to find out what the local issues were and to make recommendations in a final report.

During the research we were writing up the findings under the two themes of 'Community Safety' and 'Children and Young People'. The local community was asked how they would describe their community and what would help them to feel safe. They talked to us about well-being, safety, inclusion, and feelings of trust. Problems of antisocial behaviour, such as racism, drugs, alcohol, violence, and lack of appropriate housing were also identified. Issues for young people and children were the lack of activities and physical environment. Overall the community responses showed they cared about their community and did not see themselves as 'deprived'; they were a community consisting of families and friends who looked out for each other. There was no denying that there were serious problems – but local residents as community researchers, consulted, engaged and involved their community in addressing issues from a solution-focused and problem solving process.

Incidental consultation

Midway through the research project we were notified that our department would be disbanded, and consultation involved senior managers. Community development workers would be transferred to the community and voluntary sector.

Meanwhile the community research had ended. We submitted a draft report, and I took annual leave. While on leave, I was informed by letter of my end date. I was given a month to wind down my work and was told I could take the rest of the time off as 'garden' leave.

I requested an extension and explained where we were on the project, that we had a draft report and were waiting for feedback from the funders to complete report. I also wanted to ensure that residents completed their assignments to receive their Open College Network (OCN) accreditation. This request was not initially accepted; instead a series of incidents followed. Two are outlined below.

The first incident occurred while I was on annual leave. I decided to attend a community steering group and was forcibly blocked at the door by my line manager preventing me access. I was told that, as I was on annual leave, I could not attend the local community meeting. Months later, I saw on the news an elderly white male being forcibly ejected from a party convention. Reliving the incident, I became distressed again by the way those in power treat people to whom they are supposed to provide a service.

The second incident, just as shocking and distressing, occurred when council staff were sent to pack up and remove my computer and filing cabinets (without any warning or notification). Local residents working on the research discovered what had happened, and called the council, threatening to go to the local press. Everything was immediately returned, with no explanation for why it had been taken.

These incidents also impacted on some of the local residents, and quite a few later resigned from the local steering group in protest at the lack of meaningful consultation with local residents.

The council finally agreed to an extension to complete the report, and I was asked to sign a confidentiality agreement, which I refused. It was all a bit confusing; perhaps it had been too successful? I had developed a project that was building social capital in the area, successful in reaching so-called 'hard to reach' communities, and which engaged residents to work together to create a safe community. There were also long-term benefits, with much potential to continue the project. For example, Sure Start discussed the commissioning of the community researchers to do further research for their organisation. The disbanding of the department without meaningful consultation with the community ended the process and disrupted the trust that had been developed.

Fight or flight

In complying with my job role, I had established trust and engaged residents' enthusiastic participation in change, and this was perceived as radical. It did not occur to me that in arguing with conviction on behalf of true community involvement I would be perceived as radical. I mistakenly took full personal responsibility for badly handled policy changes, resulting in huge disappointment for those involved. I felt guilty that I had misled and let down local residents with promises of being involved in the decision making about issues that affected them. Their contribution had clearly not been considered in this restructuring.

I was unable to get any support from Human Resources (to whom I had sent a long list of incidents including the two described above), and received a letter back to say that they could find no fault. Seeking any small measure of support and feeling the need to engage in an objective appraisal of what was going on, I went to my union and the local union representative within the council to express how I felt the local community had been disregarded in an important policy decision that affected them badly. I also wished to report how I had been treated in the process. There was no mention as to the loss of a department and of possible jobs. Instead the union representative's response was to ask me whether I wanted to start a revolution. No, I had only been talking about community empowerment, engagement and social justice – core principles of community development.

I went to the union solicitors, who told me that I did not have a case for race discrimination, although I had experienced a whole range of discriminatory practices on several grounds – so much so that it was very hard to distinguish what was what.

Kimberle Crenshaw (who coined the term 'intersectionality' introduced above) was asked in an interview how the idea came about. She said:

> It grew out of trying to conceptualize the way the law responded to issues where both race and gender discrimination were involved. What happened was like an accident, a collision. Intersectionality simply came from the idea that if you're standing in the path of multiple forms of exclusion, you are likely to get hit by both. These women are injured, but when the race ambulance and the gender ambulance arrive at the scene, they see these women of color lying in the intersection and they say, 'Well, we can't figure out if this was just race or just sex discrimination. And unless they can show us which one it was, we can't help them.' (Women's Perspectives 2004, p.2)

My union did not know how to respond to these injuries and I was told that it would be hard to prove race discrimination. The only avenue open for me was to pay for my own defense and I was not able to afford it. Also, at this stage I was not physically or mentally well enough to defend myself and sustain the process. I had suffered months of work-related stress caused by an accumulation of incidents as I had stood as a buffer in the middle, unsupported by the council management, while striving ethically to meet openly negotiated agreements with the community. I perceived and experienced both subtle and overt forms of what I recognised as abuse and bullying, with avenues for meaningful or productive communication with management blocked to me. At the end I was exhausted, censored and silenced.

Redundancy

Redundancy was very hard, for it seems we are only valued when we are employed. As a result, I became withdrawn and depressed (I just knew I would not get another job at 48). I blamed myself, and went over and over in my mind trying to figure out how I could have done things differently. I became more and more withdrawn, unable to leave home; I put on weight and began to have severe back pains; I was soon unable to be active as I had always been before. I was unable to walk longer than 10–15 minutes, ride my bike or find anything positive about myself and my life. It would take me almost two years to learn to let go.

Journey – a question of faith and deep self-belief

Finally I began looking for ways to relieve the pain and suffering, and discovered yoga. I was encouraged to visit my GP and request counselling and agreed to this one day while walking along the seaside taking time to pick up and examine stones with a friend who had previous experience of mental health difficulties. I stood looking out to sea, and was reminded of the ebb and flow of life, and I knew I needed to get back into the flow, and to do that I would search for new meaning and purpose. I believed we each have a role to play and that no one is better than another, regardless of where we fit into society's hierarchal structures.

I was introduced to others who shared their mental health challenges with me, and through conversations and laughter I started to have positive feelings about the future; it seemed that I could begin to see opportunities and possibilities to get back to life, back to reality.

Mental health stigma – another barrier to overcome

I grappled with discrimination associated with mental health and the stigma of being defined as a service user; and became aware of the negative stereotyping of people with lived experiences of mental health problems. I was increasingly becoming aware of my own issues. Finally, I was referred to a counsellor, and on my first visit I saw on her desk a tray of stones, which I took as a good omen. Eventually I shared my recent experiences, and things shifted for me when, for the first time, someone acknowledged that what I had experienced constituted abuse on many levels. I attended weekly sessions for several weeks and was told that this was short-term, but could continue, though I would need to be referred again. The counsellor had helped, but I remained undecided whether this person understood some of the deeper and more complex issues of racial discrimination that I had experienced.

Summoning up resilience developed over years of overcoming challenges in many areas, including the above categories, I managed my mental health challenges. The ongoing and unconditional support of my partner was a crucial factor during my journey to recovery.

Recovery

A group of us started meeting in each other's homes and slowly we formed a support group that developed into a well-being creative group. We met monthly to have jamming sessions with percussion instruments and drums. The sessions were beneficial for us and for others, and we grew in number. The act of making music together stimulated a positive learning environment, with those with experience teaching others. The sharing of skills and experiences created a safe space for people to develop friendships that had a positive affect on our well-being.

In 2008, while still involved with this group and coordinating the work, I saw the advert for the NHS post of Mental Health Community Development Worker (CDW) for BME communities. I thought about applying but was uncertain; members of the group encouraged me to apply. I read the CDW handbook and identified with the role of 'change agent' (Department of Health (DoH) 2006, p.12). I applied for the position and was shortlisted.

Peer support training – a new beginning

While waiting for the interview date, I was accepted on an intensive two-week peer support training delivered by an American company, for users of mental health services to be trained to use our lived experience of mental health challenges and to work as peer support specialists. The journey of recovery that I had started now began in earnest. The training helped us to identify our strengths and build confidence in our own knowledge and skills; to role-model recovery.

Moving on – one day at a time

In time I moved on from feeling guilt and blaming myself, and learned to accept that I had done the best I could. I needed to listen and to trust the warning signs I was feeling and develop strategies to protect myself.

Through this experience, I discovered mental health and well-being. Before that, mental health was about other people. As in *No Health without Mental Health* (HM Government 2011), I recognised that mental well-being is for everyone and we are all in it together.

NHS community development work

I am now in my third year as a CDW, working to improve mental health services for BME communities. I work with local community groups, facilitating discussions on well-being, race equality and recovery. I deliver training to staff within my organisation and to BME groups in the community, and support groups to set up as independent, self-help, peer support groups – and for me this was the clearest way to challenge the stigma of mental health. It was a way to break down barriers between 'us and them'.

Developing processes where peer-led groups work together with services in new and innovative ways enables us, as users of mental health services, to be involved in all stages, from planning to delivery of services. Brown and Floyd (2011) suggest this as the way forward for mental health services, and it has been a remarkable opportunity to see people grow and develop, setting and achieving goals they had only dreamed of before.

WHAT NEXT?

I work with uncertainty about the future, as cuts are inevitable and redundancy is again imminent. Many of the CDW posts have been decommissioned, and many innovative projects developed as part of the Delivering Race Equality (DoH 2005) programme have ended. I know and work with people who use mental health services, particularly women, who volunteer their time and effort to provide a service for their community without funding, recognition, and support. I continue to focus on sustainable projects that are beneficial and empower communities. How important is our work and how committed are policymakers to improving the lives of BME communities?

I participated in recent research that consulted with service users from BME communities on their views of local mental health services. One of the main themes was the repeated call for intervention and preventive care; the need for alternative therapies, peer support and complementary services. This has been raised before by people who use our service and also reported by the Sainsbury Centre for Mental Health (2002) report, which also found that BME 'access to psychology, psychotherapy and counseling was extremely rare' (p.52).

It is my experience that it is difficult for BME user-led groups to be valued, funded and supported for the important work they do, due to the stigma and discrimination of mental health and racial discrimination.

This again has been noted previously (Sainsbury Centre for Mental Health 2002, p.9).

I am interested in best practices for creating safe spaces for dialogue on a range of issues that we find difficult to talk about, but need to. Finding ways to speak truthfully and honestly with each other helps to create a healthy economic and well-being society. Amartya Sen, in his book *Development as Freedom* (2001), argues for an integrated approach of economic opportunities and political freedoms and advocates for 'the role of public discussions as a vehicle of social change and economic progress...' (p.xiii).

PERSONAL DEVELOPMENT

I still have daily challenges and difficult days, I have much personal work to do and am learning creative strategies for my well-being. I am focused on my strengths and areas I want to improve. I work to empower myself and others through creativity, recovery and peer support training rooted in equalities and anti-discrimination. I am one of three directors of Recovery Partners, a not-for-profit social enterprise that offers peer support services in Sussex.

CONCLUSION

This chapter has revealed the complexities of race, gender and class from both a personal and a community level, understanding the way in which these simultaneously intersect in understanding people, institutional systems, social issues, and the potential for change in the development of a mental health strategy. In examining black feminist theory of the 'intersectionality' of race, class and gender (as well as other protected characteristics) it is important to understand how they interlock and affect those who stand at the intersection of multiple discriminations. Understanding these experiences is important when assessing, developing and delivering mental health services. Legislation, education and the willingness to change make every day an opportunity to learn that we are interconnected and we will either fall or grow together.

If we are to improve the quality of life for people, and work to eliminate all inequalities, we will need to begin to improve the mental health and well-being of our communities.

REFERENCES

Brown, M. and Floyd, D. (2011) *Better Mental Health in a Bigger Society?* London: Mental Health Providers Forum.

Cose, E. (1993) *The Rage of a Privileged Class. Why Are Middle-class Blacks Angry? Why Should America Care?* New York: HarperCollins.

Crenshaw, K. (1991) 'Mapping the margins: intersectionality, identity politics, and violence against women of color.' *Stanford Law Review 43*, 6, 1241–1299.

DoH (Department of Health) (2005) *Delivering Race Equality in Mental Health Care: An Action Plan for Reform Inside and Outside Services and the Government's Response to the Independent Inquiry into the Death of David Bennett.* London: DoH.

DoH (2006) *Mental Health Policy Implementation Guide: Community Development Workers for Black and Minority Ethnic Communities. Final Handbook.* London: DoH

HM Government (2011) *No Health without Mental Health: A Cross-government Mental Health Outcomes Strategy for People of All Ages.* London: Department of Health.

hooks, b. (1981) *Ain't I a Woman? Black Women and Feminism.* Boston, MA: South End Press.

Johnson, A. (2001) *Privilege, Power and Difference.* New York: McGraw-Hill.

McPherson, W. (1999) *The Stephen Lawrence Inquiry.* London: The Stationery Office.

Narayan, D., Pritchett L. and Kapoor, S. (1990) *The Moving Out of Poverty Study: Volume 2, Success from the Bottom Up.* New York: Palgrave Macmillan and The World Bank.

Sen, A. (2001) *Development as Freedom.* Oxford: Oxford University Press.

Sainsbury Centre for Mental Health (2002) *Breaking the Circles of Fear: A Review of the Relationship between Mental Health Services and African and Caribbean Communities.* London: Sainsbury Centre for Mental Health.

Women's Perspectives (2004) *Intersectionality: The Double Bind of Race and Gender: Interview with Crenshaw.* New York: Publishing Perspectives.

PART
II

EVIDENCE OF INEQUALITY

Chapter 4

GENDERED PRACTICE

Sue Waterhouse

INTRODUCTION

Gender inequalities in mental health arise for both men and women, and occur in different ways. This chapter sets out the nature of gender differences and implications for mental health service provision. It identifies the origins of gender inequality, however simplistically, in the hope that this will be helpful for understanding why it continues. The chapter also proposes some potential solutions for reducing or eliminating gender inequalities and outlines the main policy drivers that can help. First, to set the scene, a brief review of the legislative history is provided.

LEGISLATION

The move towards gender equality commenced with the suffragette movement in the nineteenth century. This brought about some crucial legislative changes regarding the right of women to vote. This was graduated, with women receiving equal rights with men in 1928. Legislative changes primarily focused on women were related to equal pay in 1970 and employment in 1975. The Equality Act 2006 (which came into force during 2007) Equal Opportunities Commission (EOC) 2006a) known as Gender Public Sector Duty, introduced a positive duty on public bodies to promote equality between men and women. The Gender Public Sector Duty included transgender for the purposes of gender equality; however, the Equality Act 2010 now considers 'transgender' separately as 'gender reassignment'.

The Equality Act 2010 consolidated the numerous array of previous Acts and Regulations. Gender in this Act is now referred to as 'sex' – a term that many argue is inappropriate, as it often refers to biological attributes rather than wider social influences.

Moves to eliminate gender inequality have been an international focus for several decades. A clear set of international standards in this area is set out in the 1979 Convention on the Elimination of all Forms of Discrimination Against Women (CEDAW) (United Nations 1979). A hundred and eighty-six countries worldwide have committed to this convention, which requires ratifying states to abolish sex discrimination and to promote the equality of women with men in all aspects of political, social, economic and cultural life. The UK Government committed to this in 1986.

MASCULINITY AND FEMININITY

Popular commentaries acknowledge the differences between men and women in terms of how they think, feel, communicate and behave. This is sometimes used to justify the existence of inequalities, and even to support the view that they are natural (COMAB 2009). There is, however, a weight of evidence from the social sciences arena suggesting the cognitive and linguistic capacities of men and women are very similar (Cameron 2007). Kimmel (2008) explains that, rather than inequalities and differences being biologically determined, they are actively produced by a range of social and economic processes: men and women are different because they are taught to be different and gradually acquire the traits, behaviours and attitudes that our culture defines as 'masculine' or 'feminine'. This means that we are not born different but become different through the process of socialisation (Kimmel 2008; Schaller and Crandall 2004). It is widely recognised that in most cultures and societies men are the dominant group, and are more influential than women (Carli 2001). Services can create an environment where these inequalities continue, because they are often staffed with individuals who have been socialised with these beliefs and lack awareness of the impact.

In recognising that men are the dominant group we also need to recognise that men do not benefit equally from their supposed dominance in our society. Connell's (1995) theory of 'hegemonic masculinity' relates to the belief in the existence of a culturally normative ideal of male behaviour. It describes the dynamic processes through which some groups of men establish and wield enormous economic, social and political power over other men, women and children. In Western countries these men are often white, university-educated and on high incomes. This view is arguably supported by some feminists who believe that men's liberation is a necessary part of feminism, and that men are also harmed by sexism and gender roles.

SOCIAL INEQUALITY PERSPECTIVE

'Social inequality' denotes the way in which socially defined categories of people, as described above, affect access to a variety of social 'goods' (Walker 2009), such as the labour market and other sources of income, education and healthcare, and forms of political representation and participation. Simply put, it affects an individual's access to money, status and power, determining a person's chances of enjoying relative privilege or suffering disadvantage (Williams and Keating 2005). Social inequality is a way of explaining and understanding imbalances in our society, and how power and advantage are held by one group within society at the expense of other groups (Williams 2005). Inequalities are often difficult to detect and challenge because they are concealed by beliefs that call the processes associated with their perpetuation normal and just (Williams and Keating 2005). It is easier to blame the disadvantaged, rather than recognise the origins of their disadvantage. Addressing these inequalities requires reducing the power of the dominant group.

GENDER INEQUALITY IN OUTCOME

The differences observed in general terms are highlighted below. It is an area where a lot of data has been gathered, but little progress has been made.

Work

Work, both formal and informal, paid and unpaid, plays an important part in determining women's and men's relative wealth, power and prestige (World Health Organization (WHO) 2006). Evidence indicates that women's work is devalued precisely because it is women's work, and that women's jobs pay less than men's jobs because they are 'women's jobs' (Magnusson 2009; Stone and Kuperberg 2005; Wolford 2005). An example is women and men working for local councils. Women working as care workers are paid less than men who generally work in refuse collection. Figures from the Office for National Statistics (ONS 2011) showed that the gender pay gap had narrowed by one per cent for the first time in many years. There is evidence that when women and men work in the same jobs, women often earn less than men, and men are more likely to hold leadership positions than women in the same occupations.

Education

Gender differences in educational performance and participation has changed since 1990. Girls now out-perform boys at school at all levels (EOC 2006b). There remain differences in patterns of subject choice. Women make up the majority of undergraduates in higher education, and at postgraduate level there are broadly equal numbers of men and women. Women are under-represented in most science subjects, and over-represented in social science and arts subjects. Gender differences in first degree subject choice appear to be declining over time, but there remains significantly high gender segregation in vocational training (Equality and Human Rights Commission (EHRC) 2010). Gender differences in subject choices have an impact on employment choices and earnings.

Health

There is a need to recognise gender differences in relation to health risks, the responses men and women experience from health systems, their respective health-seeking behaviours, and differing health outcomes (WHO 2009). Both men and women report high levels of stress at work (COMAB 2009). For men, this is often related to long hours and poor management; for women factors include doing low-status jobs, combining work and caring, and experiencing discrimination and sexual harassment. Men have a higher mortality rate than women. Whereas men are a higher proportion than women of 16–24 year olds, at 51 per cent of that demographic, men represent only 48 per cent of the 65–74 age group, and only a third of people over 85 are men (EHRC 2010).

Violence

Men, in general, are more likely to experience physical assault than women (EHRC 2010). Whilst some women engage in acts of violence, men commit more serious and violent crimes than women (COMAB 2009). Women are more likely to be victims of rape, and to experience domestic violence or partner abuse. In some cultural minorities women are also more likely to experience forced marriage and violence at the hands of relatives in so-called 'honour' attacks, and in some groups they are also uniquely likely to experience female genital mutilation.

IMPLICATIONS FOR MENTAL HEALTH

There are psychological consequences of inequality. Some aspects are likely to have greater significance than others. Williams and Keating (2005) suggest that gender inequality has particular significance for mental health, as a result of the way gender identities are constructed in early life – through experience of a structural relationship of inequality between male and female within the family. It is commonly in the family that gender identities are first constructed. Gender inequalities therefore have particular importance for individuals' private lives and psychological functioning (Williams 2005).

Mental health implications arise from gender inequalities in the following domains.

Socio-economic factors

Low social status is associated with health-damaging emotional and physiological consequences (Belle and Doucet 2003). Deprivation and poverty are strongly linked to mental ill-health in communities (Department of Health (DoH) 2002). Earlier discussion regarding pay differentials between men and women have particular relevance to this. Women have a long history of being treated less favourably than men. Within the household women may have less access to resources, and often spend their income on dependants. The discussion above regarding some men's status in society is also relevant. Arguably unemployment, during an 'economic downturn', is likely to have a greater impact on men, as they are still predominantly assumed to be the main breadwinner in the family unit (Men's Health Forum 2010). Discussion of the drawbacks associated with conventional perception of masculinity helps to shed light on this issue. Marmot (2010) highlights the link between socio-economic inequalities and health inequalities generally.

Physiological factors

Physical ill-health is known to be associated with mental ill-health. In women and men, emotional well-being is a strong predictor of physical health (DoH 2002). Having a mental health problem increases the risk of physical ill-health (HM Government 2011a). One of the symptoms of mental illness can be 'somatisation' (DoH 2002). Somatic complaints are two to three times more common in women. Men are reluctant to seek help for both physical and psychological ailments. This means that men are more vulnerable to untreated physical illnesses.

Psychological factors

Men are reported to have fewer social outlets in comparison to women. The social dominance of men is at the cost of emotional entitlement (Williams and Keating 2005). Successful male socialisation requires men to be silent and strong, leaving individuals little scope to acknowledge and deal constructively with feelings of vulnerability and powerlessness, and leading to a relative lack of emotional expressiveness and a tendency to 'act out' emotional distress.

Women are particularly vulnerable to social isolation as they have higher rates of poverty; and are more likely to be lone parents and/or dependent on men, live longer, and fear going out at night alone (DoH 2002).

Williams and Keating (2005) highlighted evidence that crimes motivated by hatred are particularly damaging to psychological well-being (for example, domestic violence, rape and racial oppression).

EXPERIENCES OF VIOLENCE AND ABUSE

Gender inequality is regarded as both a cause and a consequence of violence against women and girls (Women's National Commission 2009). The existence of social inequality can lead to abuses of power. These can take many forms, but the most widely recognised are domestic violence and sexual abuse. These have particularly damaging effects on the individuals concerned. Williams (2005) suggests that the belief commonly held by men, that they should have their needs, including sexual needs, met by women, should not be questioned. There is substantial evidence (DoH 2002) that links women's experience of child sexual abuse and domestic violence with long-term mental illness, as well as with physical and sexual health problems. It is widely believed that all types of sexual violence are under-reported. Prevalence rates for child sexual abuse vary across studies, depending on the definitions used. Estimates from international literature (DoH 2002) suggest that as many as 30 per cent of girls and 13 per cent of boys may be affected. Studies show (HM Government 2011a) that around half of the women in psychiatric wards have experienced sexual abuse, and this proportion increases in correlation with increasing levels of security within mental health services.

The fact that men and boys are more likely to be involved in violent acts has been highlighted above. The mental health consequences of this are rarely commented on, but it is reasonable to assume that these will be similar to the effects normally assoicated with psychological trauma.

PRACTICES IMPACTING ON INEQUALITY

Further to the factors discussed above, Williams (2005) highlights that there are '*processes and practices*' that contribute to the continuance of gender inequality. These includes the perpetuation of stereotypes that maintain the status quo, e.g. women being seen as submissive, nurturing and warm. Processes and practices that maintain inequality are evident in judgements of women as 'bad' or 'mad' (amongst other terms) in circumstances where they do not conform to these female stereotypes, and in 'victim-blaming', as when, for example, a woman is seen as in some way responsible for her own experience of violence or abuse, because of the way she dressed or behaved. A practice often seen in mental health services is the use or overuse of medication to 'quieten' both men and women in their presentation of distress. This practice is linked with failure to identify the causes of the problem.

BOX 4.1: THE IMPACT OF CULTURE AND PRACTICE

One NHS Foundation Trust recognised that many women who were self-harming and perceived to be making inappropriate demands on trust resources through high levels of help-seeking behaviour were labelled as suffering from borderline personality disorders. The focus was on what was wrong clinically with the women, and failed to take fully into account the fact that a high proportion of the women had experienced childhood sexual abuse or other trauma. A shift in culture and practice was facilitated by consistently asking not 'What is wrong with this person?' but 'What has happened to this person?' as outlined in *Informed Gender Practice* (National Institute for Mental Health in England (NIMHE) 2008). This approach generated deeper exploration of cause and effect and how experience impacts on the development of mental health issues. There was acknowledgement of life experiences, and higher priority was given to improving relationships and trust. In turn, this improved patients' engagement and recovery.

CONSEQUENCES FOR SERVICES

There are many examples of gender differences in the way men and women use and experience services. It is important to understand these differences for the purpose of planning and provision of services.

There are differences in the prevalence of mental health presentations. For example, rates of psychosis in the UK general population (DoH 2002) are estimated at 0.5 per cent for women and 0.6 per cent for men; there are indications that schizophrenia has an earlier onset and a more disabling course in men than in women.

Studies suggest that depression and anxiety are at least one-and-a-half to two times more common in women (DoH 2002). However, later authors suggest that depression in men is under-diagnosed (Men's Health Forum 2011) because the conventional method of diagnosis is more likely to detect depression in women. It may be that in men depression, as symptom of psychological distress, manifests differently – as they are three times more likely to commit suicide than women. Male mental distress is more likely to result in violent behaviours towards self and others, to the extent that men are three times more likely to die by suicide than women. Suicide rates are particularly high among younger black men and unemployed men. Men are also more likely to receive treatment for mental health problems under the Mental Health Act (HM Government 2011a). African Caribbean people are particularly likely to be subject to compulsory treatment under the Mental Health Act, and are disproportionately highly represented in secure units.

More women than men present in secondary care. However, more men present than women access tertiary services. Men tend to present in services later, and therefore their conditions are reported as more severe. This may be a result of men's reluctance to seek help.

The shift in focus to community services, with the development of crisis resolution and home treatment teams, has resulted in inpatient environments being more volatile and containing individuals who present higher risk. Mixed-sex acute inpatient wards are 'particularly unsafe' (Phillips and Jackson 2012). As already mentioned, many women admitted to acute services have a history of abuse. Inpatient staff need to recognise how violence and abuse contribute to the development of mental health issues. In addition, they need to recognise that mental health services users are at increased risk of experiencing violence and abuse (Taskforce 2010) as a result of suffering from a mental illness.

Due to a greater focus on the development of services in relation to women, men-only services have emerged by default, sometimes without the necessary service planning.

It is necessary to pay particular attention to this issue, given the number of service users, particularly women, who have a history of experiencing sexual abuse. Many clinicians continue to debate whether they should routinely enquire whether an individual has experienced violence and/or abuse. One research study found that one of the main reasons for clinicians not enquiring was because they did not see it as part of their role (Rose *et al.* 2011).

Many women who use services report being treated with a dismissive attitude to their disclosure of abuse, and interpret this as not being believed or acknowledged. This in itself has a damaging effect on these women's mental well-being. As already noted, there are significant links between physical violence and abuse and the abuse of power. This can be replicated within services, where clinicians show little awareness of the power with which their roles invest them.

There is a particular need to ensure that mental health services are safe places where service users can recover. It has long been argued that this is not the case. The National Patient Safety Agency (2006) reported that 19 alleged rapes occurred in services between November 2003 and September 2005; eight cases were reported to have been perpetrated by other service users, and 11 by members of staff. These figures have since been disputed because they did not end in criminal convictions (which is an unreliable argument, given the low success rate of rape convictions in general). The issue highlights that sexual safety is not just a mixed-sex ward issue.

In responding to the varying needs of individuals it is important to recognise that more than one protected characteristic may be relevant to an individual case, as this will have implications for mental health service provision. For example, services will need to consider the impact of loss of role in older age men or cultural issues influencing high rates of self-harm in South Asian women.

POTENTIAL SOLUTIONS AND RESOURCES

The ultimate aim of modernising mental health care is to ensure that the needs of the individual are addressed with respect and an understanding of diversity, and that inequalities are tackled (DoH 2002).

Mental health providers need to be alert to the major determinants of inequality in our society. These include gender, race, class, age, disability and sexual orientation (Williams and Keating 2005). Particular attention needs to be paid to the power relationship between those who provide and those who use mental health services, and to the disempowering consequences of being labelled as a user of psychiatric services.

Well-informed 'analysis of impact on equality' processes will be key in the task of improving services. Below are some suggestions of what it may be helpful to consider when providing services.

Personalisation

As with all of the equality agenda, personalisation is a key government policy that will assist with tackling inequality. The personalisation agenda challenges the traditional psychiatry and illness model. The personalised approach (National Mental Health Development Unit (NMHDU) 2011) means that service users have:

- more say and control in all aspects of public life, and participate as active and equal citizens

- maximum control of their lives, including control of their own health and healthcare

- support to live independently, stay healthy and recover quickly

- choice and control so that any support they may need fits the way they wish to live their lives.

The benefits of this approach should be evident, in that individualised care that is self-directed offers the most potential to meet individual need. Individual budgets provide people with the means and opportunity to buy the care that they want from the provider that best responds to their gender needs.

Service evaluation and monitoring

Service planners and providers need to ensure that service evaluation and monitoring include a gender (and other protected characteristics) dimension so that they can accurately measure whether the needs of both men and women are addressed on an equal basis (DoH 2003). There is no shortcut for listening to what service users have to say about their lives (Kalikhat 2004) and we need to be cautious in making assumptions about what we believe are individuals' views and needs. Service users must be supported to influence any service evaluation and monitoring regime, if it is to be robust and able to ensure that gender-specific and gender-sensitive services are sustainable and continue to meet service users' needs (NMHDU 2010).

Safe and effective inpatient services

The gender equality programme that formed part of the National Institute for Mental Health in England commissioned a piece of work that saw the development of a resource to help mental health inpatient units improve their response to women (NIMHE 2008). The need for this work was identified through the Healthcare Commission's review of acute inpatient care (Healthcare Commission 2008). *Informed Gender Practice* (NIMHE 2008) identifies that inpatient treatment will only bring maximum benefit if it is felt to be safe, respectful and accepting. This can be achieved when:

- there is a commitment to equality and a just and transparent use of power

- staff are supported to gain the skills and knowledge to practise in gender-informed ways, able to respond to disclosures of abuse and to understand the relationship of these experiences to observed behaviour

- consistent and non-judgemental relationships between staff and patients and within the staff group are the central element of engagement and recovery.

Informed Gender Practice focused on women, but can equally apply to improving services for men.

There is a need to readdress some of the imbalances that have occurred as a result of progress that has been made in services for women. In the instance of single-sex wards, in many cases, women-only wards have developed after a considerable amount of planning, resulting in men-only wards materialising by default, without any consideration to tailoring these wards to meet the specific needs of men.

Violence and abuse

Interventions that prevent violence and abuse reduce subsequent risk of mental ill-health and promote resilience (Royal College of Psychiatrists 2010). *Together We Can End Violence against Women and Girls* (Home Office 2009) was a cross-government strategy, published by the then Labour Government, which set out a coordinated approach to ending violence again women and girls. It includes a range of actions for the police, councils, the NHS and government departments across three areas: prevention, provision and protection. The Department of Health set up an independent taskforce to set out the response the NHS should make to victims of violence and abuse. The taskforce report (Taskforce 2010) makes recommendations around improving early identification of victims; enhancing the quality of and access to services; raising awareness of violence against women and children; training and development; and partnership working.

Delivering Male

The Men's Health Forum was commissioned, by the equality programme within the NMHDU, in order to expand understanding of the specific mental health needs of men in order to carry out a review of the essential issues in the mental health of men and boys (Men's Health Forum 2010). A second publication followed: *Delivering Male* (Men's Health Forum 2011, in collaboration with Mind), which sets out guidelines for effective practice in male mental health. These are two very useful documents that can be used to expand our understanding of the direction mental healthcare needs to take to meet the needs of men.

Working Towards Women's Well-being

Into the Mainstream (DoH 2002) and *Mainstreaming Gender and Women's Mental Health* (DoH 2003) set out the policy direction for women's mental healthcare. *Working Towards Women's Well-being* (NMHDU 2011) was a report that examined the evidence for progress on the recommendations set out in the two earlier documents. The report provides an overview of the next steps to build on and sustain achievements to date. The essential elements in the process are:

- strong leadership
- building coherent multi-agency workforce development
- ensuring the development of integrated care pathways
- improved response to diverse needs
- maintaining and extending action to tackle violence and abuse as a priority.

CONCLUSION

There are clear gender differences, and, contrary to popular belief, these differences are not inherent but formed through socialisation. Society values one set of gender attributes more highly than others, and this creates the environment for the formation of gender inequality. Whilst men possess the attributes that are most valued in society, men who do not fit the masculine stereotype face disadvantages similar to those that women face. Gender inequalities manifest in differing outcomes for men and women in all areas of life, such as work, education, health and use of power. Such inequalities influence the development of mental health issues in men and women, and also the different ways they use services. These differences have implications for service delivery, and the need for individualised care should be emphasised. There are a number of policy developments and resources available to help clinicians and providers make improvements to services.

REFERENCES

Belle, D. and Doucet J. (2003) 'Poverty, inequality, and discrimination as sources of depression among US women.' *Psychology of Women Quarterly 27*, 2, June, 101–113.

Cameron, D. (2007) 'What language barrier?' *The Guardian,* 1 October.

Carli, L. (2001) 'Gender and social influence.' *Journal of Social Issues 57*, 725–741.

COMAB (Coalition on Men and Boys) (2009) *Man Made: Men, Masculinities and Equality in Public Policy.* London: COMAB. Accessed at www.comab.org.uk.

Connell, R. (1995) *Masculinities. Second edition.* Cambridge: Polity Press.

DoH (Department of Health) (2002) *Women's Mental Health: Into the Mainstream.* London: DoH.

Department of Health (2003) *Mainstreaming Gender and Women's Mental Health: Implementation Guidance.* London: DoH.

EHRC (Equality and Human Rights Commission) (2010) *How Fair is Britain? Equality, Human Rights and Good Relations in 2010: The First Triennial Review.* Accessed at www. equalityhumanrights.com/key-projects/how-fair-is-britain/.

EOC (Equal Opportunities Commission) (2006a) *Gender Equality Duty Code of Practice, England and Wales.* Manchester: EOC. Accessed at www.equalityhumanrights.com/ uploaded_files/PSD/gender_equality_duty_cop_england_wales.doc.

EOC (2006b) *Gender Statistics: An Evaluation. Working Paper Series 51.* Manchester: EOC.

Healthcare Commission (2008) *The Pathway to Recovery: A Review of NHS Acute Inpatient Mental Health Services.* London: Commission for Healthcare Audit and Inspection.

HM Government (2011a) *No Health without Mental Health: A Cross-governmental Mental Health Outcomes Strategy for People of All Ages.* London: Department of Health.

HM Government (2011b) *No Health without Mental Health: A Cross-government Mental Health Outcomes Strategy for People of All Ages.* Analysis of the Impact on Equality. London: Department of Health.

Home Office (2009) *Together We Can End Violence against Women and Girls: A Strategy.* London: Home Office.

Kalikhat (2004) 'Paying the price for not fitting in.' *Asylum 14*, 3, 26–27.

Kimmel, M. (2008) *The Gendered Society. Third edition.* Oxford: Oxford University Press.

Magnusson, C. (2009) 'Gender, occupational prestige, and wages: a test of devaluation theory.' *European Sociological Review 25,* 1, 87–101.

Marmot, M. (2010) *Fair Society, Healthy Lives.* London: The Marmot Review. Accessed at www.marmotreview.org/.

Men's Health Forum (2010) *Untold Problems: A Review of the Essential Issues in the Mental Health of Men and Boys.* London: Men's Health Forum.

Men's Health Forum (2011) *Delivering Male: Effective Practice in Male Mental Health.* London: Men's Health Forum.

National Patient Safety Agency (2006) *With Safety in Mind: Mental Health Services and Patient Safety.* London: National Patient Safety Agency.

NIMHE (National Institute for Mental Health in England) (2008) *Informed Gender Practice.* London: NIMHE.

NMHDU (National Mental Health Development Unit) (2010) *Working towards Women's Well-being: Unfinished Business.* London: NMHDU.

NMHDU (2011) *Personalisation pages.* Accessed at www.nmhdu.org.uk/our-work/personalisation-in-mental-health-emerging-programme/paths-to-personalisation/what-is-personalisation/.

ONS (Office for National Statistics) (2011) *Statistical Bulletin: 2011 Annual Survey of Hours and Earnings.* Accessed at www.ons.gov.uk/ons/rel/ashe/annual-survey-of-hours-and-earnings/ashe-results-2011/ashe-statistical-bulletin-2011.html.

Phillips, L. and Jackson, A. (2012) 'Gender-specific Mental Health Care: the Case for Women-centred Care.' In P. Phillips, T. Sandford and C. Johnston (Eds) *Working in Mental Health: Policy and Practice in a Changing Environment.* Abingdon: Routledge.

Rose, D., Trevillion, K., Woodall, A., Morgan, C., Feder, G. and Howard, L. (2011) 'Barriers and facilitators of disclosures of domestic violence by mental health service users: qualitative study.' *British Journal of Psychiatry 198,* 189–194.

Royal College of Psychiatrists (2010) 'No health without public mental health: the case for action.' Position statement PS4/2010. London: Royal College of Psychiatrists.

Schaller, M. and Crandall, C. (2004) *The Psychological Foundations of Culture.* Mahwah, NJ: Lawrence Erlbaum Associates Inc. Publishers.

Stone, P. and Kuperberg, A. (2005) 'Anti-discrimination vs. anti-poverty? A comparison of pay equity and living wage reforms.' *Journal of Women, Politics & Policy 27,* 5, 23–39.

Taskforce (2010) *Responding to Violence against Women and Children – The Role of the NHS. The Report of the Taskforce on the Health Aspects of Violence against Women and Children.* Accessed at www.dh.gov.uk/en/Publicationsandstatistics/Publications/PublicationsPolicyAndGuidance/DH_113727.

United Nations (1979) *Convention on the Elimination of All Forms of Discrimination against Women.* New York: United Nations. Accessed at www2.ohchr.org/english/law/cedaw.htm.

Walker, C., (2009) 'New Dimensions of Social Inequality.' Postdoctoral Research Project carried out from April 2007 to April 2009. Accessed at www.ucl.ac.uk/ceelbas/research/socialinequality/#whyinequality.

WHO (World Health Organization) (2006) *Gender Equality, Work and Health: A Review of the Evidence.* Geneva: WHO Press.

WHO (2009) *Strategy for Integrating Gender Analysis and Actions into the Work of WHO.* Geneva: WHO. Accessed at www.who.int/gender/en.

Williams, J. (2005) 'Women's Mental Health – Taking Inequality into Account.' In J. Tew (Ed.) *Social Perspectives in Mental Health: Developing Social Models to Understand and Work with Mental Distress.* London: Jessica Kingsley Publishers.

Williams, J. and Keating, F. (2005) 'Social Inequalities and Mental Health: An integrative approach.' In A. Bell (Ed.) *Beyond the Water Towers: The Unfinished Revolution in Mental Health Services 1985-2005.* London: Sainsbury Centre for Mental Health.

Wolford, K.M. (2005) 'Gender discrimination in employment: wage inequity for professional and doctoral degree holders in the United States and possible remedies.' *Journal of Education Finance 31*, 1, 82–100.

Women's National Commission (2009) *Still We Rise: Report from WNC Focus Groups to Inform the Cross-government Consultation 'Together We Can End Violence Against Women and Girls'*. London: Women's National Commission.

Chapter 5

PREGNANCY AND MATERNITY

Sue Waterhouse

INTRODUCTION

The Equality Act 2010 introduced a number of new protected characteristics. Pregnancy and maternity is one such area. Although this area had, in part, been covered by the Sex Discrimination Act, the Equality Act 2010 strengthens legislation relating to it. Mental health during pregnancy and early motherhood, referred to as 'perinatal mental health', is a serious issue with 'potentially deleterious consequences for women's life-long mental health and the health and well-being of their children and families' (Edge 2011, p.5).

The aim of this chapter is to provide an overview of the issues related to perinatal mental health. It outlines the prevalence of mental health issues in pregnancy and perinatal period. It also summarises the consequences of mental disorder during the same period. The chapter concludes with an overview of recommendations for service delivery from the key policy documents.

LEGISLATION

The Equality Act 2010 protects women from discrimination on the grounds of pregnancy and maternity. In employment a women is protected from discrimination during the period of her pregnancy and during any period of compulsory or additional maternity leave. In cases outside the workplace, that involve the provision of services, goods and facilities, and the provision of recreational or training facilities, a woman is protected from discrimination during her pregnancy and subsequent 26 weeks, beginning with the day on which she gives birth.

The Act also protects a woman from direct discrimination because she is breastfeeding or due to illness suffered as a result of pregnancy; for example, a pregnant woman cannot be penalised if she misses work due to pregnancy-related illness or appointments. The Act does not, however, cover indirect discrimination or harassment on the grounds of pregnancy and maternity.

Perinatal mental health is also covered by other protected characteristics. Readers may benefit from reading, in conjuction, Chapters 3, 7 and 9.

PERINATAL MENTAL HEALTH

A common term that is used for this issue is 'postnatal depression'. Caution is needed in the use of this term, as there is concern that its misuse is widespread, with potentially serious negative consequences. (These include its misuse in clinical situations as a label for any mental illness occurring postnatally. This has been pointed out in the Confidential Enquiry into Maternal and Child Health (CEMACH) as a major concern because other serious illnesses fail to be identified as a consequence (Lewis and Drife 2004).) It also reinforces the view that postnatal depression is somehow different from depression at other times. Common false beliefs include: that the symptoms and effects are less severe, that it goes away by itself, that it is somehow associated with whether or not the woman is breastfeeding, that it is all due to hormones, that it has no risk of non-puerperal recurrence, that it carries inevitable risk of future postnatal recurrence, that depression is less common antenatally, or that depression that is already present before birth is not the same thing. All of these assumptions are misleading and can lead to disadvantageous and inappropriate responses by clinicians and by women themselves. In addition, they can lead to policy and service development focused on depression postnatally, to the exclusion of the full range of mental disorders occurring antenatally and postnatally, all of which have potentially serious and long-term effects on the woman, the infant and the family.

Prevalence

The majority of women who develop mental health problems during pregnancy or following delivery suffer from mild depressive illness, often with accompanying anxiety. Such conditions are equally prevalent in pregnancy and following delivery, and probably no commoner than at other times (O'Hara and Swain 1996). Pregnancy is not protective against relapses of pre-existing severe mental illness, and the rates are increased if, as commonly happens, the woman has stopped her usual medication at the beginning of pregnancy. The risk of developing bipolar illness and severe depressive illness is markedly elevated following childbirth, particularly during the first three months.

Women who have had a previous episode of a severe mental illness, either following childbirth or at some other time, are at increased risk of developing a postpartum onset illness, even if they have been well during pregnancy and for many years previously. This risk is estimated as at least one in two (Robertson *et al.* 2005; Wieck *et al.* 1991). Two previous CEMACH reports (Lewis and Drife 2001, 2004) found that over half of the women who died by suicide had a previous history of severe mental illness. It is also known that a family history of bipolar disorder increases the risk of a woman developing puerperal psychosis following childbirth (Robertson *et al.* 2005).

The risks and treatments of mental disorders occurring in the antenatal and postnatal period differ in a number of important areas.

BOX 5.1: DIFFERING RISKS AND TREATMENT OF MENTAL DISORDER

- There is a risk of pregnant women with an existing disorder stopping medication, often abruptly and without the benefit of an informed discussion, which can precipitate or worsen an episode.

- In women with an existing disorder (for example, bipolar disorder) there may be a substantially increased risk of developing an episode.

- The impact of such disorders requires more urgent intervention than would usually be the case, because of the severe and long-term effect on the foetus and developing child, and on the woman's physical health and care, and her ability to function and care for her family.

- Postnatal onset psychotic disorders have a more rapid onset, with more severe symptoms than psychoses occurring at other times (Wisner and Wheeler 1994).

- The shifting risk–benefit ratio in the use of psychotropic drugs in pregnancy and breastfeeding means that psychological treatments should be more readily available to this population, and within a maximum waiting time of one month.

(NICE 2007, p.55; Crown copyright 2007)

MATERNAL SUICIDE

Confidential Enquiries into Maternal Deaths in the United Kingdom reports (CEMACH) in 1997–1999 and 2000–2002 (Lewis and Drife 2001, 2004) found that maternal suicide was more common than previously thought, and was in fact the leading overall cause of death amongst women having a child in the UK. The CEMACH report for 2003–05 (Lewis 2007) showed a drop in the suicide rate and concluded that the decrease was just large enough to be unlikely to have occurred by chance. However, the latest report (Centre for Maternal and Child Enquiries (CMACE) 2011) shows an increase in the number of suicides in the six months following birth. There are some trends noted in the report, in that the women were older, married women in comfortable circumstances, with a previous psychiatric history, who were well during pregnancy.

Suicide during pregnancy is relatively uncommon (CMACE 2011). Overall, the suicide rate following delivery is no different to that amongst women in the general population, but for a subgroup of women, those suffering from severe mental illness, the suicide rate is substantially elevated (Appleby, Mortensen and Faragher 1998). This demonstrates the importance of targeting services on the detection and care of women with, or at risk of, severe mental illness at this time. This focus on the most severely ill is in line with policy relating to mental health services generally, but should not be at the expense of neglecting the support needs of the large number of women with less severe illnesses who require high-quality primary care and maternity care to meet their mental and physical healthcare needs (Department of Health (DoH) 2004).

Deaths related to substance misuse also represent a substantial group of women, in which there has been a small increase – although this not statistically significant and is compatible with random variation.

CONSEQUENCES OF MENTAL DISORDER DURING PREGNANCY AND THE POSTNATAL PERIOD

With mental disorder during pregnancy some treatments cause increased risk to the foetus, whilst risk in the general population of congenital malformation runs between two and four per cent (Brockington 1996). There is now extensive evidence that mental disorder during this period can also have a significant wider and long-term detrimental impact on the well-being of the woman, the foetus and the developing child. Severe depression is associated with an increased rate of obstetric complications, stillbirth, suicide attempts, postnatal specialist care for the infant, and low birth weight infants (Bonari *et al.* 2004; Lobel, Dunckel-Schetter and Scrimshaw 1992; Lou *et al.* 1994; Wadhwa *et al.* 1993). In schizophrenia and bipolar disorder, there is an increased rate of suicide and potentially significant exacerbation of the disorder if not treated, and poorer obstetric outcomes, including increased pre-term delivery (Hedegaard, Henriksen, Sabroe and Secher 1993; Lewis and Drife 2004; Nordentoft *et al.* 1996), low-birth-weight infants and infants who are small for gestational age (Howard 2005; Jablensky *et al.* 2005). Similarly, poor foetal outcomes have been associated with maternal eating disorders during pregnancy (Kouba, Hallstrom, Lindholm and Hirschberg 2005). Elevated risks of sudden infant death syndrome have also been reported in relation to postnatal depression (Mitchell *et al.* 1992; Sanderson *et al.* 2002) and to maternal schizophrenia (Bennedsen *et al.* 2001).

There is also evidence that untreated mental disorder in pregnancy and postnatally is associated with poorer long-term outcomes for children beyond the immediate postnatal period, including effects on cognitive development, as well as emotional and behavioural problems, which may be severe (Nulman *et al.* 2002). Schizophrenia in particular may also affect a woman's ability to care adequately for her children, with high rates of children being taken into care (Hipwell and Kumar 1996). Coupled with the direct effects of maternal mental illness on the infant, there are important indirect effects, such as the social isolation, exclusion and other disadvantages known to be associated with severe mental illness.

WIDER SOCIAL CONTEXT

There is a need to recognise the impact fear has on a women's perception of services, caused by a belief of negative involvement, such as children being taken into care. The disastrous consequences were evidenced in the *Saving Mothers' Lives* report (CMACE 2011), which described how a woman who had a complex social history refused treatment for a chest infection because she was concerned that her children would be taken into care. The ultimate outcome of this situation was that the women died after delivery. The report repeatedly makes the point of how fear inhibits not only help-seeking behaviour, but also mental health:

> It was apparent from their notes that fear that the child would be removed was a prominent feature of the women's condition and probably led them to have difficulties in engaging with psychiatric care. (CMACE 2011, p.137)

For those women who experience less disastrous outcomes, inequality develops in the use of services and the way services are received. This is damaging not only to the women but to the wider families. The fact that a parent has a mental health issue should not automatically indicate a risk; however, findings of research (Huntsman 2008) do identify a number of potential concerns, such as:

- irritability and diminished responsiveness during early infancy

- behavioural, developmental and emotional problems in children

- greater risk of developing mental health issues in later life.

Long-standing perinatal mental health problems can also impact on the bond between mother and baby (Mind 2006).

There is interplay between many forms of disadvantage, which compounds problems in maternity and pregnancy. For example, poverty, poor housing or a history of poor parenting or abuse, singly or cumulatively, can have adverse consequences on the experience of pregnancy and maternity. Ethnicity can be another compounding factor, either because of the negative impact of direct discrimination, or perhaps because of isolation that arises from language barriers or conventional norms about integration and family life.

The potential for inequalities to be played out is immense, and assessments in mental health must take account of the ways in which maternity creates or embeds inequalities, and steps must be taken to eliminate these.

Additionally the risk of inequalities increasing the likelihood of social services safeguarding children intervention needs to be understood and the possibility of entrenched inequalities taken into account; otherwise, as passive observers of inequalities, mental health services in effect fall into the role of active protagonists of disadvantage.

POTENTIAL SOLUTIONS

All key national policy documents highlight issues relating to perinatal mental health. All recommend that women should be asked at their early pregnancy assessment about their current mental health and any previous history of psychiatric disorder. Those at risk of developing a serious mental illness following delivery should be proactively managed. Key policy documents also recommend that specialised community perinatal teams should be established to manage women whose pregnancy or postpartum year is complicated by serious mental illness.

The following information has been taken from the key policy documents. The guidance offered by these documents has enabled significant improvements to be made in the approach taken with women in the perinatal phase. It is strongly believed that if the following solutions were implemented, 'not only would some mothers' lives be saved, but the care of those who live would be improved' (CMACE 2011, p.141).

Psychiatric deaths – specific recommendations

The *Saving Mothers' Lives* report (CMACE 2011) studies the deaths of women during and following pregnancy. One aspect of the report focuses on deaths arising directly from a psychiatric condition, suicide or accidental overdose of drugs of abuse. The following are the recommendations drawn from that report.

BOX 5.2: *SAVING MOTHERS' LIVES* SPECIFIC RECOMMENDATIONS

- All women should be asked at their antenatal booking visit about a previous history of psychiatric disorder as well as their current mental health. Women with a previous history of serious affective disorder or other psychoses should be referred in pregnancy for psychiatric assessment and management even if they are well. A minimum requirement for management should be regular monitoring and support for at least 3 months following delivery.

- Psychiatric services should have priority care pathways for pregnant and postpartum women. These will include a lowered threshold for referral and intervention, including admission and a rapid response time, for women in late pregnancy and the first 6 weeks following delivery. Care by multiple psychiatric teams should be avoided. Risk assessments of pregnant or postpartum women should be modified to take account of risk associated with previous history, the distinctive clinical picture of perinatal disorders and the violent method of suicide.

- All mental health trusts should have specialised community perinatal mental teams to care for pregnant and postpartum women. These should be closely integrated with regional mother and baby units so that all women requiring psychiatric admission in late pregnancy and the postpartum period can be admitted together with their infants.

> - Caution needs to be exercised when diagnosing psychiatric disorder if the only symptoms are either unexplained physical symptoms or distress and agitation. This is particularly so when the woman has no prior psychiatric history or when she does not speak English or comes from an ethnic minority.
>
> (CMACE 2011, p.134)

MENTAL HEALTH SERVICES

This section covers maternity and pregnancy in the routine work of mental health services and also specialist perinatal mental health services. In general mental health services workers need to:

- ensure that assessments take account of needs and context of women's lives

- ensure that services are accessible

- provide adequate facilities (e.g. privacy for breastfeeding)

- provide safety – women will not if they do not feel safe (and this includes psychological safety)

- be psychologically aware – many previous traumas are brought up by pregnancy and birth.

There is a need to ensure that these services facilitate collaboration between specialist and generalist services, thus reducing the degree of disruption faced by women needing to access many different elements of services.

BOX 5.3: PRINCIPLES THAT GUIDE THE CONFIGURATION OF SERVICES INCLUDE:

- Reduction of cross-agency/service barriers to a minimum and, where possible, their elimination. Women with mental health problems who are pregnant or have an infant will require care from several services, including primary care, mental health and maternity services. These need to be organised so that the woman's movement between various services should not interfere with, or limit access to, services. To ensure this, all relevant agencies and stakeholders, including service users, should be involved in the organisation of services.

- Accessible care (including access to expertise, the availability of relevant professionals, the provision of a prompt service

---

and appropriate geographical location). During pregnancy and the postnatal period, women need access to mental health services through a variety of contact points. The timeframe of pregnancy and the importance of the well-being of the child (see below) require that services should be available with a minimum of delay. This improved access should also extend to partners, carers and family members who have an important role in the care and support of the woman and infant, as well as having needs in their own right.

- Consideration of the well-being of the infant while providing appropriate care for the woman, the needs of the foetus/infant (and siblings) must be a central consideration in the organisation and delivery of services. This will often be best served by prompt and effective treatment of the woman's illness, but meeting the infant's needs and the needs of the mother–infant relationship should not be deferred while this is happening.

(NICE 2007, p.258; Crown copyright 2007)

Functions of specialist mental health services, including specialist perinatal services

Women requiring specialist care may be treated by general mental health services, mental health liaison services or specialist perinatal mental health services, and by combination of these services.

BOX 5.4: FUNCTIONS OF SPECIALIST MENTAL HEALTH SERVICES INCLUDING SPECIALIST PERINATAL SERVICES

- Assessment of women with moderate and severe mental disorder (or those with milder but treatment-resistant disorder) during pregnancy and the postnatal period, including assessment of the risk of relapse of existing disorder during pregnancy, childbirth or the postnatal period.
- Treatment of mental disorder during pregnancy and the postnatal period.
- Provision of intensive services, such as crisis, home treatment and inpatient services and, in the case of some specialist perinatal services, the provision of specialist inpatient beds Women who need inpatient care for a mental disorder within 12 months of childbirth should normally be admitted

to a specialist mother and baby unit (MBU), unless there are specific reasons for not doing so.

- Communication with primary care, maternity and obstetric services and, where appropriate, coordination and management of care pathways and service access.

- Provision of specialist consultation and advice to services providing treatment and care to patients with existing disorder who are planning a pregnancy or who become pregnant, and to services managing women with less severe disorders; this may include advice on care, treatment, mother-infant relationships, child protection issues and diagnosis.

- Liaison with primary care and maternity services concerning the care of women with moderate to severe mental disorders.

- Education and training for maternity and primary and secondary care mental health services.

(NICE 2007, p.253; Crown copyright 2007)

Implementing the managed network model

NICE guidance recommends a managed clinical (or care) network for perinatal mental health in all parts of the country. The networks are an effective way of improving access to services and ensuring that access is equitable. They ensure that there are good care pathways for women with perinatal mental health issues and help establish clear national standard for perinatal care services.

BOX 5.5: MANAGED NETWORK MODEL

Clinical networks should be established for perinatal mental health services, managed by a coordinating board of healthcare professionals, commissioners, managers, and service users and carers. These networks should provide:

- A specialist multidisciplinary perinatal service in each locality, which provides direct services, consultation and advice to maternity services, other mental health services and community services

- Access to specialist expert advice on the risks and benefits of psychotropic medication during pregnancy and breastfeeding

- Clear referral and management protocols for services across all levels of the existing stepped-care frameworks for mental disorders, to ensure effective transfer of information and continuity of care

> • Pathways of care for service users, with defined roles and competencies for all professional groups involved.
>
> (NICE 2007, pp.264–265; Crown copyright 2007)

CONCLUSION

This is an area of health where the extent of the issues has been ignored for many years, despite the devastating impact untreated mental health issues can have on all of the family. Perinatal mental health problems are common, and this chapter has set out the impact of mental health on women during pregnancy and the period following childbirth. It is important that the specific risks during this period are not overlooked. Women who have a history of mental health issues may well present differently following childbirth, and may act more impulsively. The assumption that pregnancy and motherhood is a protective factor must not be allowed to mislead.

It is essential that services work collaboratively and pay particular attention to early detection and a seamless approach to provision of services. There are clear policy documents which set out good practice that is widely acknowledged to have the potential to achieve positive outcomes if implemented. The argument is clear, that this will benefit not just the woman, but the wider family and the mental well-being of the next generation.

REFERENCES

Appleby, L., Mortensen, P.B. and Faragher, E.B. (1998) 'Suicide and other causes of mortality after postpartum psychiatric admission.' *The British Journal of Psychiatry 173*, 9, 209–211.

Bennedsen, B.E., Mortensen, P.B., Olesen, A.V. and Henriksen, T.B. (2001) 'Congenital malformations, stillbirths, and infant deaths among children of women with schizophrenia.' *Archives of General Psychiatry 58*, 674–679.

Bonari, L., Pinto, N., Ahn, E., Einarson, A., Steiner, M. and Koren, G. (2004) 'Perinatal risks of untreated depression during pregnancy.' *Canadian Journal of Psychiatry 49*, 726–735.

Brockington, I.F. (1996) *Motherhood and Mental Health*. Oxford: Oxford University Press.

CMACE (Centre for Maternal and Child Enquiries) (2011) 'Saving Mothers' Lives: reviewing maternal deaths to make motherhood safer: 2006–08. The Eighth Report on Confidential Enquiries into Maternal Deaths in the United Kingdom.' *BJOG 118*, Suppl. 1, 1–203.

DoH (Department of Health) (2004) *National Service Framework for Children and Young People, Standard 11: Maternity Services.*

Edge, D. (2011) *National Perinatal Mental Health Project Report: Perinatal Mental Health of Black and Minority Ethnic Women: A Review of Current Provision in England, Scotland and Wales.* London: National Mental Health Development Unit.

Hedegaard, M., Henriksen, T.B., Sabroe, S. and Secher, N.J. (1993) 'Psychological distress in pregnancy and preterm delivery.' *British Medical Journal 307*, 234–239.

Hipwell, A.E. and Kumar, R. (1996) 'Maternal psychopathology and prediction of outcome based on mother-infant interaction rating (BMIS).' *The British Journal of Psychiatry 169*, 655–661.

Howard, L.M. (2005) 'Fertility and pregnancy in women with psychotic disorders.' *European Journal of Obstetrics, Gynaecology and Reproductive Biology 119*, 3–10.

Huntsman, L. (2008) *Parents with Mental Health Issues: Consequences for Children and Effectiveness of Interventions Designed to Assist Children and their Families – Literature Review.* Ashfield, New South Wales, Australia: NSW Department of Community Services

Jablensky, A.V., Morgan, V., Zubrick, S.R., Bower, C. and Yellachich, L.-A. (2005) 'Pregnancy, delivery, and neonatal complications in a population cohort of women with schizophrenias and major affective disorders.' *The American Journal of Psychiatry 162*, 79–91.

Kouba, S., Hallstrom, T., Lindholm, C. and Hirschberg, A.L. (2005) 'Pregnancy and neonatal outcomes in women with eating disorders.' *Obstetrics and Gynaecology 105*, 255–260.

Lewis, G. (Ed.) (2007) *Saving Mothers' Lives 2003-2005: The Seventh Report on Confidential Enquiry into Maternal Death in the United Kingdom.* London: Confidential Enquiry into Maternal and Child Health.

Lewis, G. and Drife, J. (Eds) (2001) *Why Mothers Die 1997–1999: The Fifth Report of the Confidential Enquiries into Maternal Deaths in the United Kingdom.* London: RCOG Press.

Lewis, G. and Drife, J. (2004) *Why Mothers Die 2000–2002: The Sixth Report of Confidential Enquiries into Maternal Deaths in the United Kingdom.* London: Confidential Enquiry into Maternal and Child Health / Royal College of Obstetricians and Gynaecologists.

Lobel, M., Dunckel-Schetter, C. and Scrimshaw, S.C. (1992) 'Prenatal maternal stress and prematurity: a prospective study of socioeconomically disadvantaged women.' *Health Psychology 11*, 32–40.

Lou, H.C., Hansen, D., Nortdentoft, M., Pryds, O., Nim, J. and Hemmingsen, R. (1994) 'Prenatal stressors of human life affect fetal brain development.' *Developmental Medicine and Child Neurology 36*, 826–832.

Mind (2006) *Out of the Blue? Motherhood and Depression.* London: Mind Publications.

Mitchell, E.A., Thompson, J.M., Stewart, A.W., Webster, M.L., Taylor, B.J., Hassall, I.B., Ford R.P., Allen, E.M., Scragg, R. and Becroft, D.M. (1992) 'Postnatal depression and SIDS: a prospective study.' *Journal of Paediatrics and Child Health 28*, Suppl. 1, S13–S16.

NICE (2007) *Antenatal and Postnatal Mental Health. The NICE Guideline on Clinical Management and Service Guidance.* Leicester: British Psychological Society and Royal College of Psychiatrists.

Nordentoft, M., Lou, H.C., Hansen, D., Nim, J., Pryds, O., Rubin, P. and Hemmingsen, R. (1996) 'Intrauterine growth retardation and premature delivery: the influence of maternal smoking and psychosocial factors.' *American Journal of Public Health 86*, 347–354.

Nulman, I., Rovet, J., Stewart, D.E., Wolpin, J., Pace-Asciak, P., Shuhaiber, S. and Koren, G. (2002) 'Child development following exposure to tricyclic antidepressants or fluoxetine throughout fetal life: a prospective, controlled study.' *The American Journal of Psychiatry 159*, 1889–1895.

O'Hara, M.W. and Swain, A.M. (1996) 'Rates and risk of postpartum depression – a meta-analysis.' *International Review of Psychiatry 8*, 37–54.

Robertson, E., Jones, I., Haque, S., Holder, R. and Craddock, N. (2005) 'Risk of puerperal and non-puerperal recurrence of illness following bipolar affective puerperal (postpartum) psychosis: short report.' *The British Journal of Psychiatry 186*, 258–259.

Sanderson, C.A., Cowden, B., Hall, D.M., Taylor, E.M., Carpenter, R.G. and Cox, L. (2002) 'Is postnatal depression a risk factor for sudden infant death?' *The British Journal of General Practice 52*, 636–640.

Wadhwa, P.D., Sandman, C.A., Porto, M., Dunkel-Schetter, C. and Garite, T.J. (1993) 'The association between prenatal stress and infant birth weight and gestational age at birth: a prospective investigation.' *American Journal of Obstetrics and Gynaecology 169*, 858–865.

Webb, R., Abel, K., Pickles, A. and Appleby, L. (2005) 'Mortality in offspring of parents with psychotic disorders: a critical review and meta-analysis.' *The American Journal of Psychiatry 162*, 1045–1056.

Wieck, A., Kumar, R., Hirst, A.D., Marks, M.N., Campbell, I.C. and Checkley, S.A. (1991) 'Increased sensitivity of dopamine receptors and recurrence of effective psychosis after childbirth.' *The British Journal of Psychiatry 303*, 603–616.

Wisner, K.L. and Wheeler, S.B. (1994) 'Prevention of recurrent postpartum major depression.' *Hospital and Community Psychiatry 45*, 1191–1196.

Chapter 6

MARRIAGE AND CIVIL PARTNERSHIPS

Hári Sewell

INTRODUCTION

Of the nine protected characteristics identified under the Equality Act 2010, marriage and civil partnership is covered only in relation to employment. This chapter sets out to do two things. First, to enable readers who are 'dipping in' to see how the protected characteristic of marriage and civil partnership fits in alongside the eight other protected characteristics. Some readers will be aware that the Equality Act 2010 identifies nine protected characteristics, but may not be aware of the distinction made in relation to marriage and civil partnerships. Second, this chapter acknowledges that, despite the fact that service and education providers have no *duty* in relation to marriage and civil partnerships, inclusion in the Equality Act 2010 can promote some consideration of these issues within such contexts. This chapter is brief because of the status of the protected characteristic and the limited supporting literature on the subject in relation to service provision.

EMPLOYMENT

The Equality Act 2010 protects people who are married, or in a civil partnership, from discrimination in the workplace. There will clearly be implications for staff in mental health services who are married or in civil partnerships. Most important for consideration in this book is the experience of people who use mental health services, and who are being supported to maintain or secure employments. Staff in mental health services need to be aware of the protections for employees, and they will need to advocate where necessary to ensure that employer obligations are met. In practice this will mean ensuring that people in marital relationships or civil partnerships are not discriminated against. This is particularly important because mental health service users are known to experience significant discrimination in the workplace (Thornicroft 2006). Some employers will invoke strategies (whether consciously or not) to justify their decisions to exclude people with mental health problems. These strategies may include identifying barriers that are associated with being married or in a civil partnership. For example, a prospective employer may ask someone in a civil partnership questions about flexibility of working hours to provoke self-selecting out of a role, when in reality such flexibility may seldom be required, if ever. The interactions between different forms of discrimination can be complex, and the better equipped a worker is to understand how these may be manifested, the more effective they can be in challenging them.

SERVICE PROVISION

While there is no legal obligation to take marriage and civil partnership into account in service provision, some practitioners and leaders in organisations will wish to explore ways of tackling stigma and discrimination and being as inclusive as possible. In a predominantly heterosexist society it is more likely that staff will consider the needs of married people, in so far as these needs are consistent with the requirement to provide fair service. Responding to the needs of people in civil partnerships is a subset of the kinds of issues covered in Chapter 9 in relation to sexuality.

Societal attitudes to sexuality are changing – in 1806 more men were executed for homosexual acts than for murder (The Equalities Review 2007); at the time of writing the Coalition Government is consulting on equal marriage for same-sex couples. The absence of a legal duty is no excuse for failing to ensure fairness, with respect and dignity. There is not an established body of evidence or literature on civil partnership in relation to service provision. A few ideas are presented here for practitioners and service providers to consider.

TAKING HISTORIES

Staff need to use inclusive language when taking histories or asking about relationships. Assuming that partners are of the opposite sex can be alienating and cause people to be guarded and cautious in relationships with workers. For some this will invoke feelings of anger. Discussions about relationships with partners which may be long in duration and include references to the trappings of a shared life (such as holidays, extended families, etc.) can easily lead a worker to fall into making assumptions.

NEW UNIONS

From time to time people who use services form unions between themselves and sometimes wish to cement these relationships. Staff need to be mindful of the interest, support and flexibility that they show in relation to people who are embarking on civil partnerships. Though the Equality Act does not offer protections in service provision, it will be appropriate to consider wider issues of equality. These may arise in relation to:

- interest shown by a worker or staff team
- whether a gift is offered
- staff attendance if an invitation is made
- support in making plans
- leave or time off from work in a unit.

These are just examples of areas where workers may need to be vigilant that they are not giving differential treatment to individuals who are forming civil partnerships.

RESIDENTIAL SETTINGS

In circumstances that apply to large numbers of older people, special consideration needs to be given to the needs of people in civil partnerships who may need 24-hour care in residential settings. Attention needs to be paid to ensuring that couples who have formalised their partnership feel involved in decisions about care and treatment and life (and maybe even death) planning (National Mental Health Development Unit (NMHDU) 2011). Couples who might be comfortable with being open about their partnership in familiar social settings may feel cautious about disclosure in a mental health setting. Staff need to create safe environments so that people can feel more able to be true to themselves. This can avoid people who may be in a civil partnership referring to their partner as a friend and losing the benefits of staff awareness and understanding of their wishes for shared decision making as a couple.

EXERCISE 6.1: REFLECTION ON PRACTICE

Sandra is a social worker who attends a monthly 'Family Connections' workshop at her local mental health service, following a breakdown eight months ago. The workshop is designed to help people with mental health problems draw on their capacities, and for those close to them work with them as a team to achieve as much growth and recovery as possible. Some people attend with a parent, partner, sibling or offspring. Sandra is in a civil partnership with Judith, but did not disclose this when she first came into contact with mental health services and instead introduced Judith as a close friend. As a couple they agreed that, given the mental state Sandra was in, it would be better to avoid additional stress due to the kind of hostility and discrimination they were accustomed to experiencing in society outside their lesbian–gay–bisexual (LGB) circle.

During one of the 'Family Connections' workshops Sandra became upset and Judith comforted her by holding her hand, hugging her and stroking her face. Mary and Gabby, who ran the workshop, were visibly shocked. They carried on running the group as if nothing had happened. After this incident Sandra and Judith stopped attending the group.

Questions

- What might Mary and Gabby have done in organising, promoting and running the group to make it more likely that Sandra and Judith would have been more comfortable in sharing their status?

- What emotions do you suppose Mary and Gabby may have been feeling?

- What would have been a more appropriate set of responses from Mary and Gabby when Sandra broke down and Judith comforted her?

- What language and behaviours do you use to ensure that a service user in a civil partnership or same-sex relationship feels comfortable to disclose the nature of their primary relationship?

CONCLUSION

Marriage and civil partnership is the only one of the nine characteristics in the Equality Act 2010 to be protected in employment, but not for service provision. This chapter has briefly clarified this point and offered some considerations and illustrations for staff and providers who opt to respond to issues around civil partnerships in service provision.

REFERENCES

Equalities Review, The (2007) *Fairness and Freedom: The Final Report of the Equalities Review.* London: The Equalities Review.

NMHDU (National Mental Health Development Unit) (2011) 'Let's Respect Toolkit.' Accessed at www.nmhdu.org.uk/news/lets-respect-toolkit-for-care-homes-published/?keywords=older+people on 5 June 2006.

Thornicroft, G. (2006) *Shunned: Discrimination against People with Mental Illness.* Oxford: Oxford University Press.

Chapter 7

AGE EQUALITY

Barbara A. Vincent

Although age discrimination and inequality affects people of all ages, the weight of evidence suggests that older people are particularly disadvantaged. There have been numerous reports and reviews highlighting evidence that older people with mental health problems have been particularly discriminated against in the provision of mental health services in the UK (Age Concern/Mental Health Foundation (MHF) 2007; Centre for Policy on Aging (CPA) 2009); Royal College of Psychiatrists (RCPsych.) 2009, and a report to the Secretary of State by Sir Ian Carruthers and Jan Ormondroyd, *Achieving Age Equality in Health and Social Care* (Carruthers and Ormondroyd 2009). Older people have been doubly discriminated against, in terms of both age and mental health, and their needs have historically fallen into the gap between policy and services for mental health for adults of working age, and those for older people (Age Concern/MHF 2006). The stigma and negative attitudes surrounding both ageing and mental illness which have informed this discrimination have led to older people with mental health problems receiving poorer quality care in terms of access, provision and resources (Beecham *et al.* 2008). The very language used to describe this population has also served to reinforce the stigma and negative attitudes experienced by older people, with services historically using such terms as 'psycho-geriatric' and more recently 'elderly mentally ill' to describe their function. The use of such terms leads to older people with mental health problems being further discriminated against by consigning them to a category separate from the rest of the adult population. Mental health services to older people are therefore called 'older people' or 'older adult' services to counteract these views.

With an increasingly ageing population and higher life expectancy, it is not acceptable for health and social care providers to continue to provide care and treatment that discriminates on the basis of age. Modernisation of mental health services is therefore imperative, to ensure that older people receive an equitable, high-quality mental health service in the future. There has been some progress made since the 1980s when such terms as 'psycho-geriatric' were in common useage. However, the publication of the *National Service Framework for Older People* (Department of Health (DoH) 2001) marked a real watershed by enshrining anti-discriminatory practice in policy, culminating in the Department of Health publication *No Health without Mental Health* (HM Government 2011). However, as age-related sections of the Equality Act 2010 came into force in 2012, there has been no requirement on the public sector to address the indirect or 'hidden' discrimination inherent in current mental health service provision, and this has meant that older people have continued to receive poorer services (Audit Commission 2000; Carruthers and Ormondroyd 2009; DoH 2001; HM Government 2011; HM Government: Equalities Office 2011).

A CHANGING POPULATION

The character of the UK population is changing; we are living longer and having fewer children, which means the percentage of older people in the UK population is increasing (Age Concern/MHF 2006). In 2007 the percentage of people aged over 65 in the UK exceeded that of people under 16 for the first time, and is set to rise by 15 per cent by 2020. Of greater concern is the projected rise by 27 per cent of the number of people over 85, as the 'older old' experience a disproportionately greater number of mental health problems than younger people. The prevalence of mental illness in people aged over 65 is currently 20–25 per cent and the proportion of people in this group with dementia is approximately 25 per cent (RCPsych. 2009). The Department of Health estimates that mental health problems are present in 40 per cent of people over the age of 65 who attend their general practice (GP), in 50 per cent of older people admitted to general hospitals and in 60 per cent of all care home residents in the UK (Healthcare Commission 2009).

MENTAL HEALTH POLICY

The *National Service Framework for Mental Health* published in 1999 was the first mental health policy to set out standards and models of service delivery and came with funding to ensure these were met (DoH 1999). However, people over the age of 65 were excluded, and when a similar framework, *The National Service Framework for Older People*, was published in 2001, mental health for older people was relegated to a chapter sandwiched between 'falls' and 'health promotion'. While its stated aim was to decrease inequities in health and social care for older people, it came without the necessary dedicated resources and performance measures needed to achieve this (DoH 2001; Healthcare Commission 2009). This has resulted in the development of a mental health system that has disadvantaged older people and impacted negatively on their mental health (Age Concern/MHF 2006). Professor Ian Philp, in his report on the progress of the *National Service Framework for Older People, Better Health in Old Age*, observed that age discrimination in mental health services remained a problem, and advocated for the first time that services developed for working-age adults should be available to older adults on the basis of need and not age (DoH 2004).

This mandate was taken up by the Care Services Improvement Partnership (CSIP) in 2005 in its service guide *Everybody's Business. Integrated Mental Health Services for Older Adults: A Service Development*, which introduced the notion that mental health services should be 'age inclusive' by providing both access to adult mental health services and specialist older people's services (Bucks, Burley and McGuiness 2007; DOH/CSIP 2007). The suggestion that services should be 'age inclusive' led to a flurry of reports amid fears that older people's services would be lost once again in mainstream mental health services. In response, Age Concern, in conjunction with the Mental Health Foundation, raised the issue of 'indirect discrimination' in their report *Promoting Mental Health and Well-being in Later Life: A First Report from the UK Inquiry*, proposing that there were barriers inherent in the way mainstream mental health services were set up, which would prevent older people accessing them (Age Concern/MHF 2006). However, the publication of legislation covering age discrimination in October 2006, although not yet extending to age discrimination outside the workplace, has set the stage for addressing age inequality generally (HM Government 2006; Minshull 2007).

This spectre of older people's mental health specialist services disappearing galvanised the Royal College of Psychiatrists to articulate the specialist nature of older people's mental health services and the impact of age discrimination in their position paper and supporting evidence to the House of Commons: *The Need to Tackle Age Discrimination in Mental Health: A Compendium of Evidence* (RCPsych. 2009). This led to a series of reports for the Department of Health, calling for an end to age discrimination in mental health services and supporting the widespread implementation of the Equality Bill 2010 in health and social care organisations when it came into force in 2012 (Beecham *et al.* 2008; Carruthers and Ormondroyd

2009; CPA 2009; Healthcare Commission 2009; MHF 2009). The Equality Act 2010 replaces the existing anti-discrimination laws with a single Act and '…sets out a clear legal requirement to treat adults of all ages in a non-discriminatory manner when providing services, and bans both direct and indirect discrimination on the basis of age' (Carruthers and Ormondroyd 2009, p.16).

Within this Act is an 'Equality Duty' (set out in s149 of the Act) which ensures that all public bodies address discrimination and provide equality of opportunity for all. The new Equality Duty augments the three previous public sector equality duties – for race, disability and gender – to include age, disability, gender reassignment, and pregnancy and maternity. In particular, public bodies are required to have due regard for the need to advance equality of opportunity, consider the need to remove or minimise disadvantages suffered by people on account of their protected characteristics, and meet the needs of those people with protected characteristics (HM Government Equalities Office 2011).

MENTAL HEALTH IN LATER LIFE

Mental illness is not inevitable in old age, and there are considerable benefits in treating mental health problems, both for society and for older people themselves – yet older people continue to experience discrimination and inequality of access and availability of services, which can lead to their experiencing poorer quality of care than working age adults (Beeston 2006; CPA 2009). Although there is no specific point at which people's experiences of mental health problems changes, age does affect both the prevalence and nature of mental illness (RCPsych. 2009).

The incidence of schizophrenia declines in older age; however, psychosis is much more common in older people than in younger adults (RCPsych. 2009).

Hallucinations and perceptual symptoms in older adults are not generally classed as schizophrenia, and consequently that group's needs are poorly met. (Up to 20 per cent of people over the age of 65 experience hallucinations and paranoid thoughts and the great majority of these do not go onto develop dementia.) Charles Bonnet syndrome, characterised by complex visual hallucinations, is almost exclusively present in older people, and rates of psychotic symptoms remain high in people over 90 without dementia being present (RCPsych. 2009).

The prevalence of anxiety and depression in older people is high; at the same time older people are more likely to have physical health problems, and depression is approximately two to three times more common in people with a chronic physical health problem than in people who have good physical health (CPA 2009; National Institute for Clinical Excellence (NICE) 2009).

Depression is in fact the most common mental disorder in later life: the incidence of depression in people over 65 is three times more common than dementia, and increases with age (RCPsych. 2009). Between 13 and 16 per cent of older people will have depression that is severe enough to require treatment. Older people in residential care are at particularly high risk. Yet depression in older people often goes undiagnosed and untreated by primary care services, in care homes and in acute general hospital services (CPA 2009). The presentation of depression in later life differs from that in younger people. Presentation is often masked by complaints of anxiety and memory loss, with symptoms of depression in older people more likely to be expressed as tiredness and fatigue, sleep and appetite disturbance. Late onset depression also has different associations from early onset, particularly with physical ill-health, vascular brain disease, and multiple losses (Age Concern/MHF 2007; Beeston 2006; RCPsych. 2009).

Older people are more likely to experience multi-pathology that greatly affects their physical and mental well-being. Depression, late onset psychosis, visual hallucinations and alcohol misuse all increase the risk of dementia and other age-related conditions such as cardiovascular disease, stroke, Parkinson's disease or chronic obstructive pulmonary disease, all of which impact on the way older people experience depression and their response to treatment. It is therefore impossible to separate the treatment and care of people with dementia and those with functional mental health problems, is not recommended by current national policy (DoH 2001, 2009a, 2009b).

Dementia, although less common than depression, is a key issue for the older age group. Dementia affects five per cent of people aged over 65 and 20 per cent of those aged over 80, and some have depression as well as dementia. However, with prevalence rising to 32 per cent in people over 90, the number of people with dementia is set to increase significantly, with current estimates set at one million people by 2025 (Healthcare Commission 2009).

Delirium is also a significant mental health condition in older people. It is much more common in people over age 65 and people with dementia, increasing mortality, length of hospital stay, and disability, and yet it remains undiagnosed in over half of older patients in acute hospitals. Delirium affects up to 50 per cent of older people admitted to a general hospital (RCPsych. 2009) and on average it can double the length of hospital stay for older people affected, costing over £1000 per hospital patient in 2007 (Age Concern/MHF 2007).

THE IMPORTANCE OF SPECIALIST MENTAL HEALTH SERVICES IN LATER LIFE

Mental health problems are present in 40 per cent of older people who attend their GP, in 50 per cent of older adult inpatients in general hospitals and in 60 per cent of residents in care homes. Just over a quarter of admissions to mental health inpatient services involve people over the age of 65 (DoH/NHS South West 2010). Despite the high number of older people experiencing mental health problems, services for older people are characterised by under-detection and under-diagnosis, as well as under-provision. Under-detection of mental illness in older people is widespread due to the nature of the symptoms, the impact of ageism, and the fact that many older people live alone.

The mental health needs of older people from black and minority ethnic (BME) groups can be particularly difficult to identify and diagnose, especially in the case of dementia. The stigma associated with the condition may mean that few people from minority ethnic groups come forward for diagnosis.

As already discussed, depression in people aged 65 and over is a major problem, and suicide of older people is a cause for serious concern (Age Concern/MHF 2007; CPA 2009). The costs of failure to treat older people are high, particularly to the health and social care sector. Depression in old age increases the risk of physical health problems such as heart disease, diabetes and stroke, slows recovery from illness and increases the risk of re-admission to acute hospital following discharge (Age Concern/MHF 2007; DoH 2009; Healthcare Commission 2009).

Older people with mental health problems have an increased suicide risk compared to younger people. In addition, older people may often present as having mild to moderate depression, as opposed to a severe depression, but their level of risk is high. The suicide rate in people over 65 is double that of people under 25 in the general population, and between 1997 and 2006 increased, as a proportion of patient suicides (those in contact with mental health services within 12 months of death) from 12 per cent in 1997 to 15 per cent in 2006.

Depression is by far the most common mental illness associated with depression, and present in 80 per cent of people over the age of 74 who commit suicide (RCPsych. 2009).

WHAT COULD AN EQUITABLE SERVICE LOOK LIKE?

There is no single agreement as to how older people's mental health services should be provided in a non-discriminatory way, either as a separate service or as part of adult services. Discriminatory service provision cannot be addressed simply by reorganising services, as older people with mental health problems also experience indirect discrimination if they are treated in the same way as younger people. (Indirect age discrimination occurs if people from different age groups, with different needs, are treated in the same way, with the result that the needs of older people are not fully met.)

BOX 7.1: EXAMPLES OF INDIRECT AGE DISCRIMINATION IN OLDER PEOPLE ACCESSING AGE-INTEGRATED COMMUNITY MENTAL HEALTH SERVICES

1. *Older people were offered phone appointments for initial assessment following referral, and were turning down help.* Older people tend not to express psychological distress in terms of feeling 'depressed' or 'low in mood' and were denying any problems in response to such questioning (Age Concern/MHF 2007). Older people are generally not assessed in terms of a single presenting problem in isolation; they engage better at a home visit assessment which recognises the complexity of older people's mental health issues.

2. *Older people presenting at triage were either seen as being at low risk of self-harm, judged against younger adult criteria, or were not having the urgency of their needs appreciated.* Older people are more likely to complain of physical pain, anxiety and memory problems rather than depression. They are also less likely to act impulsively and more likely to use lethal methods (Beeston 2006).

3. *Older people presenting with depression and anxiety with some cognitive impairment were being referred straight to dementia services, without any consideration of their presenting problems and how appropriate this was.* Ageist assumptions make out that dementia is the mental illness of old age.

(Age Concern/MHF 2007)

While it is increasingly being recognised that older people have different mental health needs at times, the possibility of continuing to develop equitable but separate services is not financially viable in the current financial climate. In addition, the upcoming post-war generation of older people is not prepared to accept a second-class mental health service as their parents did, grateful for Bevan's NHS. This 'baby boomer' generation has higher expectations as consumers of goods and services, and less sense of deference than their parent's generation did (MHF 2009).

One possibility is a later life care pathway to ensure that care is directed to specifically meet the needs of older people (CPA 2009; DoH/ NHS South West 2010). A care pathway would impact positively on older people to ensure that their mental health needs were identified in a timely way, and appropriate interventions put in place to ensure that their specific mental health needs were addressed (in addition to the ability to access services available to younger adults). In order to deliver optimal care and respond appropriately to risk, older people presenting with mental health problems should be screened and have access to older people's mental health specialist clinicians (Age Concern/MHF 2006). At the same time, a later life care pathway needs to raise awareness and reflect the mental health needs of older people across the provision of health and social care, from GP surgeries to mental health crisis teams for older people allowing access to equitable mental health care.

Older people experiencing mental health problems for the first time are particularly disadvantaged by current service structures. Access to out-of-hours crisis services, psychological therapies and alcohol services have been noted to be particularly difficult for older people (Healthcare Commission 2009). Their problems have not up until now been recognised within primary and secondary care, or are considered to be just a normal part of ageing, not requiring a targeted intervention (CPA 2009). Primary care mental health teams and mental health liaison are ideally placed to raise awareness of older people's mental health needs. Under-detection and misdiagnosis are significant problems in older people's mental health care, and specialist screening is essential to prevent older people's mental health deteriorating to such an extent that they present a significant risk.

Under-diagnosis is a particular problem in primary care: two-thirds of older people with depression have never discussed this with their GP, and of the third that does discuss it, only half are diagnosed and treated and only six per cent receive specialist mental health care. GPs are ideally placed to pick up on and refer older people who present with mental health problems, but currently fail to detect depression and suicidality in older people. Assumptions are made and depression is often missed, with the ageing process being blamed for reported changes in mood, physical disability and social functioning (Age Concern/MHF 2007; CPA 2009). The role of primary care mental health workers in later life presentations should therefore also be focused on education and raising awareness of later-life mental health problems. Older people with depression are more likely to present with physical pain than low mood, and to report, in particular, chronic painful symptoms such as backache, joint pain, headaches and face pain. In fact, one study reported that 69 per cent of older people reported only somatic symptoms to their GP (Age Concern/ MHF 2007).

Up to 70 per cent of acute general hospital beds are currently occupied by older people, with levels of depression in hospital wards high, at around 30 per cent (DoH/NHS South West 2010). Current adult mental health liaison services focus on assessment and management of people in mental distress and crisis, primarily in accident and emergency departments. Older people with mental health problems, and depression in particular, are more likely to be inpatients of acute general hospitals, while showing no obvious mental distress, despite being at higher risk of suicide. Mental health liaison in later life therefore needs to focus on detection of mental health problems through the development of relationships with acute inpatient teams and raising awareness of older people's needs through educational initiatives in addition to these ongoing relationships. Co-morbidity of physical and mental health problems occurs frequently in older people.

There are important differences in the nature, treatment and care needs of mental health problems developing in later life – yet reference to the experience of depression of older people is made only in relation to medication and ECT (electroconvulsive therapy) in NICE guidance, *The Treatment and Management of Depression in Adults* (NICE 2009a, 2009b). Studies of efficacy of treatments for depression suggest that older people are just as responsive as younger people, but have different needs (Age Concern/ MHF 2007). However, psychological therapies need to take into account age-related needs: increased likelihood of chronic conditions, changes in cognitive capacity, and potential loss experiences, and may need to adapt the pace of therapy and socialise the older person to the therapy experience.

Older people make far fewer suicide attempts, but when they do attempt to commit suicide it is with much more serious intent, and the vast majority have a diagnosable mental illness; one in four attempted suicides by older people succeed, compared with one in 15 in the general population. Unfortunately, because depression in older people is frequently undetected, undiagnosed, untreated or inadequately treated, a failed suicide attempt may be the first presentation of a seriously depressed and high-risk older person to mental health services (Beeston 2006). Older people are more likely to experience their first episode of mental health problems after the age of 65. However, older people typically present with more complex needs, and multiple care needs for a range of co-existing problems: physical, mental health and social care needs, including different patterns of social care and family support (DoH/NHS South West 2010). Specialist older people's mental health practitioners should be involved at this level of complexity and risk, with recovery teams are set up to meet the needs of people with long-term mental illness, working towards recovery and relapse prevention. Meeting the complex needs of older people requires specific clinical skills and knowledge. Older people generally fare better with an ongoing case management approach in conjunction with discrete, time-limited interventions, so that services can respond to the complex mix of social, psychological, physical and biological factors that older people present with regardless of their mulitple needs (DoH/NHS South West 2010).

CONCLUSION

Older people's mental health services developed as a speciality in the mid-1980s because it was felt that older people were not receiving recognition of their different and specialist needs. However, the organisation of services into 'working age' and 'older adults', reinforced by policy divisions between the mental health and older people National Service Frameworks, has contributed to the position that older people have continued to receive an inequitable service. We cannot afford, in the interests of providing services accessible to all, run duplicate mental health services for both younger and older adults, nor would we wish to. What does need to be recognised, though, is that the way services are organised can prevent older people from accessing or gaining benefit from those services. The Equality Act 2010 is an important step towards achieving an age-equitable society, but a real cultural shift is now required to keep in step with older people's changing aspirations and expectations of a healthy old age (CPA 2009). Achieving age equality requires health and social care organisations not only to recognise and address discrimination hidden within services, but also to challenge the ageist assumptions inherent in health and social care provision (Carruthers and Ormondroyd 2009; CPA 2009).

REFERENCES

Age Concern/MHF (Mental Health Foundation) (2006) *Promoting Mental Health and Wellbeing in Later Life.* London: Age Concern/MHF.

Age Concern/MHF (2007) *Improving Services and Support for Older People with Mental Health Problems. The Second Report from the UK Inquiry into Mental Health and Well-being in Later Life.* London: Age Concern /MHF.

Audit Commission (2000) *Forget Me Not. Mental Health Services for Older People.* London: Audit Commission.

Beecham, J., Knapp, M., Fernandez, J.L., Huxley, P., Mangalore, R., McCrone, P., Snell, T., Winter, B. and Wittenberg, R. (2008) *Age Discrimination in Mental Health Services.* Personal Social Services Research Unit (PSSRU) Discussion Paper 2536. Canterbury: PSSRU.

Beeston D. (2006) *Older People and Suicide.* Stoke-on-Trent: Centre for Ageing and Mental health, Staffordshire University.

Bucks, R., Burley, C. and McGuiness, P. (2007) *To Merge Or Not to Merge? That Is the Question. A Survey of PSIGE Membership Regarding Pressure to Amalgamate Older Adult and Adults of Working Age Services in Their Localities.* On behalf of the PSIGE National Committee.

Carruthers, I. and Ormondroyd, J. (2009) *Achieving Age Equality in Health and Social Care. A Report to the Secretary of State for Health.* London: Department of Health.

CPA (Centre for Policy on Ageing) (2009) *Ageism and Age Discrimination in Secondary Health Care in the United Kingdom: A Review from the Literature.* London: CPA.

DoH (Department of Health) (1999) *National Service Framework for Mental Health: Modern Standards and Service Models.* London: DoH.

DoH (2001) *National Service Framework for Older People.* London: DoH.

DoH (2004) *Better Health in Old Age. Report from Professor Ian Philp, National Director for Older People's Health to Secretary of State for Health.* London: DoH.

DoH (2009a) *New Horizons: Toward a Shared Vision for Mental Health: Consultation.* London: DoH.

DoH (2009b) *Living Well with Dementia: A National Dementia Strategy.* London: DoH.

DoH/CSIP (Care Services Improvement Partnership) (2007) *Age Equality: What Does it Mean for Older People's Mental Health Services? Guidance Note on Age Equality.* London: DH/CSIP.

DoH/NHS South West (2010) *Achieving Age Equality in Health and Social Care: NHS Practice Guide.* London: DoH.

Healthcare Commission (2009) *Equality in Later Life: A National Study of Older People's Mental Health Services.* London: Commission for Healthcare Audit and Inspection.

HM Government (2006) *The Employment Equality (Age) (Amendment) Regulations 2006.* London: The Stationery Office.

HM Government (2011) *No Health without Mental Health: A Cross-government Mental Health Outcomes Strategy for People of All Ages.* London: Department of Health.

HM Government Equalities Office (2009) *Framework for a Fairer Future – The Equality Bill.* Accessed at www.equalities.gov.uk/PDF/FrameworkforaFairerFuture.pdf.

MHF (Mental Health Foundation) (2009) *All Things Being Equal – Age Equality in Mental Health Care for Older People in England.* London: MHF.

Minshull, P. (2007) *Age Equality: What Does it Mean for Older People's Mental Health Services? Guidance Note, Everybody's Business, Integrated Mental Health Services for Older Adults.* London: Care Services Improvement Partnership.

NICE (National Institute for Health and Clinical Excellence) (2009a) *The Treatment and Management of Depression in Adults. Clinical Guideline 90.* London: Department of Health.

NICE (2009b) *Depression in Adults with a Chronic Physical Health Problem, Clinical Guideline 91.* London: Department of Health.

RCPsych. (Royal College of Psychiatrists) (2006) Raising the Standard: Specialist Services for Older People with Mental Illness. *Report of the Faculty of Old Age Psychiatry.* London: RcPsych.

RCPsych. (2009) *The Need to Tackle Age Discrimination in Mental Health: A Compendium of Evidence.* Prepared by D. Anderson, S. Banerjee, A. Barker, P. Connelly, O. Junaid, H. Series and J. Seymour on behalf of the Faculty of Old Age Psychiatry.

Chapter 8

MENTAL HEALTH AND DISABILITY

Hári Sewell

INTRODUCTION

This chapter considers inequality from two main perspectives: first, people who have mental health problems and who are disabled in relation to another condition; second, mental health problems considered as a disability. Issues, implications and solutions are presented.

Within the Equality Act 2010 disability had a particular place. It is the one protected characteristic for which there is a discrete form of discrimination. Further, the Act places a requirement on public bodies to make reasonable adjustments for disabled persons (see Chapter 1). Mental health service providers will wish to assure themselves that they are making reasonable adjustments for the people who use services. Commissioners will wish to be sure that they are commissioning for equality.

Traditionally disability has been conceptualised as a condition, or conditions, possessed by the individual. Various terms evolved which maintained the language and perspective that people suffer from a disability in their bodies. In 1976 a coalition of radical voices in the United Kingdom, called the Union of Physically Impaired Against Segregation (UPIAS), produced a statement which is seen as the foundation of the shift to what is referred to as the social model of disability:

> In our view, it is society which disables... Disability is something imposed on top of our impairments, by the way we are unnecessarily isolated and excluded from full participation in society. Disabled people are therefore an oppressed group in society. (UPIAS, cited in Equalities National Council 2012, p.16)

> The social model of disability rejects the notions of impairment as problematic, focusing instead on discrimination as the key obstacle to a disabled person's quality of life. (Crow 2010, p.132)

Disabled people in society may also be covered by other protected characteristics, and if so, they will find that the challenges or discrimination they face may be in relation to one aspect of their identity more than another at different times. People with mental health problems sometimes have disabilities, and these are not always appropriately catered for by services. Data on disability has not been routinely captured by mental health service providers. The otherwise data-rich report *How Fair is Britain?* stated:

> A lack of disaggregated data for disabled people means that we have a general association between poor mental health and disability but no more detailed information of the particular impairments that may be associated with poor mental health. (Equality and Human Rights Commission (EHRC) 2010, p.270)

The Count Me In census of psychiatric inpatients, which ran from 2005–2010, captured data on disability and found the following:

> About 75% of patients said they did not have a disability, and 25% said they had one or more disabilities. Of these, 7% were blind or visually impaired, 1% were deaf or had a hearing impairment, 1% had Autistic Spectrum Disorder, 2% had a learning disability, 4% had a mobility impairment and 2% used a wheelchair. The remaining 8% had more than one disability. (Care Quality Commission (CQC) 2011, p.20)

The national mental health strategy identified that 25–40 per cent of people with learning disabilities have mental health problems (HM Government 2011). There is evidence that people with physical disabilities are at more risk of mental health problems (Thurer and Rogers 1984).

It seems clear that mental health services have not just a legal responsibility but also a moral one to respond proactively to the inequalities disabled persons face. The first response by mental health services is often the estates management function, ensuring that sites are physically accessible in line with the law and supplementary guidance, or in the procurement of new builds or refurbishments. In mental health front-line practice there are a number of issues that need to be considered. These are set out below.

CONSIDERATIONS IN PRACTICE

This section covers implication in front-line practice under these headings:

- physical accessibility for service users to sites and buildings for meetings and events

- communication – sensory impairments

- the possible role of physical conditions in mental health problems

- the role of other professionals in responding to need

- social and psychological consequences.

Physical accessibility for service users to sites and buildings for meetings and events

Technical guidance on the design and management of National Health Service (NHS) estates is provided by the Department of Health via the website www.spaceforhealth.nhs.uk. Various guides include clarification on how to ensure that the physical design of a building complies with the requirements of the Equality Act 2010 to ensure that buildings are accessible. Reasonable adjustments have to be made to ensure that barriers are removed. As case law develops, mental health services will become clearer as to what constitutes a reasonable adjustment. A number of factors can be taken into account when considering what is reasonable:

- how effective the change will be in assisting disabled people in general or a particular customer, client, service user or member

- whether it can actually be done

- the cost, and

- the organisation's resources and size.

(EHRC 2012)

In practice a mental health worker will need to ensure that assessments are effective in ascertaining whether the individual service user is disabled. It is not acceptable to assume that by observing the service user a decision can be made about whether they are disabled, nor is it acceptable to assume that service users will feel comfortable about discussing their disability.

CASE STUDY 8.1: PHYSICAL DISABILITIES OVERLOOKED IN ASSESSMENT

William was asked a lot of questions during his assessment following his referral to the community mental health team: his full name, date of birth, address with the accurate postcode, etc. Claire, the community psychiatric nurse (CPN) assessing him, asked about what triggered his overdose, and they spoke about his upbringing; he had been born in London then taken back to Uganda in his early teens. William started a conversation about 'something private' on several occasions, but broke down in tears each time. Claire did not get to the bottom of this even after four meets.

William was diagnosed with HIV eight months ago. He immediately ended his relationship with his girlfriend without telling her why, and just hoped that she was not infected. He had become withdrawn and spoke to no one about his diagnosis. His health had deteriorated rapidly; he lost a lot of weight and his eyesight was rapidly failing. This information had not been passed on by the GP. Claire was interested in the psychological concerns that William had, and did not ascertain information about his disabling HIV.

William was too embarrassed and ashamed to discuss his condition and eventually killed himself. Claire became depressed and was off work for four months, because with hindsight she felt there were cues that she had missed. The GP maintained that patient confidentiality was paramount and that William had specifically requested that the GP did not divulge his HIV condition.

Whilst corporate managers are responsible for alterations to the organisation's buildings, it is important to remember that front-line workers also need to be alert to other physical barriers for the individual service users with whom they work, and to find ways to overcome these – as the following example illustrates.

CASE STUDY 8.2: PHYSICAL DISABILITIES OVERLOOKED FOLLOWING ASSESSMENT

Calvin reported at his initial assessment that he was asthmatic. Calvin's condition is well controlled and Vince, his then social worker in the community mental health trust (CMHT), was not mindful of his asthma and the need to take this into account. When Calvin attended the CMHT base for a meeting, Vince booked into a meeting room where there was a stockpile of latex gloves waiting to be moved to the storeroom. Calvin's chest became tight and he became anxious that he was about to have an asthma attack. He alerted Vince and they explored what the trigger might be. Upon realising that the latex gloves could have had a role in the onset of an asthma attack, they discussed how Calvin's asthma was considered. Vince said that he never thought about it because it never seemed to be an issue. Calvin said that it might not seem to be an issue because he takes it into account in his life, and that Vince needed to do the same.

Communication – sensory impairments

In 2002 the then Labour Government embarked on a consultation about responding to the needs of Deaf and Deafblind people with mental health problems. This generated a massive response and a guidance document called *Mental Health and Deafness: Towards Equity and Access* (Department of Heath (DoH) 2005). The document highlighted the fact that an above average number of Deaf people experience mental health problems. The use of the term Deaf, with an initial capital letter, was used in both the consultation document and the guidance, in response to Deaf people's request that this was done in line with their convention of signifying a community of people whose primary method of communication was British Sign Language (BSL) (DoH 2002). It takes only a cursory thought to realise the challenge for workers and service users who do not share a common language (such as BSL) in a field where the communication of feeling, thoughts, ideas and perceptions is the foundation of assessments and relationships. Though the consultation and guidance documents related to the defined group of Deaf people, the guidance was explicit in stating the requirement of services to respond to *all* disabled people, including Deaf people with sensory impairments such as hearing loss in older age. Exploring how to meet the needs of Deaf people provides a useful illustration as to why responding to the equalities agenda requires more than just a general openness to individual need. The guidance *Mental Health and Deafness: Towards Equity and Access* points to some very specific considerations, such as whether a service user would prefer to receive communications by text or fax. The possibility of requiring a BSL interpreter needs to be considered, and also the consequence on the length of a session. If a worker has not considered allowing a longer session to allow for interpreting, service users will immediately face indirect discrimination by way of having less time to communicate, and potentially having needs or other vital information missed (DoH 2002). Some knowledge of how disabled people face inequalities is essential.

Working effectively with people who are blind or have other sensory impairments requires knowledge and careful planning. For example, a Deaf person may rely on lip reading to augment a mechanical aid to hearing. Positioning will be important – for example, a window or bright backlight behind a speaker will make lip reading very difficult, if not impossible in some scenarios.

These are just examples of facts that need to be known when working with people with sensory impairments. Not every person working in mental health will be fully equipped with all they need to know in order to work with Deaf people or people with sensory impairments. There are three reasonable requirements to be made of all mental health workers (Crown 2005).

BOX 8.1: DEAF AND SENSORY IMPAIRMENTS – FUNDAMENTAL REQUIREMENTS OF MENTAL HEALTH WORKERS

- Be conscious of barriers and possible inequality; be aware that being disabled is likely to mean that barriers are faced, and be keen to take active steps to remove or reduce these.

- Know the basics; person-centred approaches will go a long way, but know enough to make it easier for service users to ask for what they need. If you are already taking steps to remove barriers and make someone feel valued, it will be easier for them to be vocal about what will help. A worker who seems to know nothing, or who is oblivious, communicates a lack of interest in the individual. This erects a barrier.

- Know where to get more information or expert involvement; a core skill of any professional is to know when they reach the limit of their capability. Workers should, for example, know how to contact the local social services disability services to get expert help and involvement.

The possible role of physical conditions in mental health problems

People have various ways of explaining the causes of their mental health problems (DoH 2007). Some people see their disability and mental health issues as causally linked in a way that may seem less obvious to someone else, while in other cases the link might be more obvious. The broad definition of disability under the Equality Act 2010 means that there are medical conditions which are covered, and for some people there will be a relationship between their disabling condition and their mental health problems. It is important for workers to provide a supportive environment for service users who wish to make the connection between being disabled and having mental health problems, and for this to be incorporated into the care plan. Velthorst *et al.* (2010) identified that for people in high-risk groups for psychosis, the presence of a disability appears to increase the likelihood.

A traditional, purely biological approach to psychiatry is dying out but statutory mental health services are still built around a concept of mental illness as a disease. Often the human dimension is subordinated in the search for symptoms and pathology (Bentall 2003). A more humane approach is required.

The role of other professionals in responding to need

The Disability Rights Commission report *Equal Treatment: Closing the Gap* (Disability Rights Commission 2006), believed to be the biggest study of its kind, highlighted that people with a diagnosis of schizophrenia or bipolar affective disorder are likely to die 5–10 years younger than those without such a diagnosis. The study looked at long-term disabling conditions. Some powerful statistics that pointed to the role of professionals were revealed. Twenty-eight per cent of people who had had a stroke and also had a diagnosis of schizophrenia died, compared with 12 per cent of people who had no serious mental health diagnosis. The figure for people who had a stroke and who were also diagnosed diagnosed with bipolar affective disorder was 19 per cent.

Twenty-eight per cent of people with respiratory disease, chronic obstructive pulmonary disorder (COPD), who had schizophrenia died, compared with 15 per cent of people with no serious mental health problems. The figure for people who had COPD and were also diagnosed with bipolar disorder was 24 per cent.

Mental health professionals need to be aware that a serious mental health diagnosis can affect the way people are viewed, and aware of the potential consequence for them of developing conditions that leave them disabled (that is, within the social definition of 'disabled').

Studies show that sexual violence against disabled people, especially those with mental health problems, is often not treated as a crime (EHRC 2010).

Reducing inequality is likely to mean, at times, that a worker has to challenge other professionals to take seriously the needs of people with mental health problems, and to be an active advocate for the service users with whom he or she works. Without such action, mental health workers are tacitly colluding in a system that harbours prejudices against people with mental health problems, and causes some people to become disabled or die prematurely.

Social and psychological consequences

The guidance on Deaf people and mental health draws links between the social consequences of being disabled (such as reduced access to education and leisure opportunities, and higher rates of unemployment) and the impact on mental health.

The social consequences of being disabled range from harassment to fewer qualifications and higher rates of offending. Further, only 27 per cent of people with a disability or limiting long-term illness have confidence that the criminal justice system will meet the needs of victims, compared with 39 per cent in the general population. Twenty to thirty per cent of adult offenders are believed to have learning disabilities. Disabled people may rely on benefits and other publicly funded services (EHRC 2010). Mental health workers need to appreciate the importance of these issues for disabled people with whom they work. These inequalities reinforce the point made by Perkins (2012) about the role of mental health services:

> Recovery-focused mental health policy requires a shift from a primary focus on problem/symptom removal to helping people to live the lives they want to lead, to do the things they want to do and to participate as equal citizens. (Perkins 2012, p.21)

CONCLUSION

The social model of disability identifies the problem as barriers people face, rather than conditions that people have. People who use mental health services may have increased need of mental health services as a result of being disabled. Being disabled whilst in receipt of mental health services, or disabled by having a mental health diagnosis, may lead to greater inequalities and discrimination. Mental health workers need to understand the ways in which people who are disabled face barriers. Workers must also know what is required in order to assist in overcoming obstacles and discrimination, including advocating with some professionals and challenging others to ensure fairness and equality for disabled mental health service users.

REFERENCES

Bentall, R. (2003) *Madness Explained: Psychosis and Human Nature*. London: Penguin Books.

Crow, L. (2010) 'Renewing the Social Model of Disability.' In J. Rix et al. (Eds) *Equality, Participation and Inclusion 1: Diverse Perspectives*. Abingdon: Routledge.

CQC (Care Quality Commission) (2011) *Count Me In 2010: Results of the 2010 National Census of Inpatients and Patients on Suspended Community Treatment in Mental Health and Learning Disability Services in England and Wales*. London: CQC.

DoH (Department of Health) (2002) *A Sign of the Times: Modernising Mental Health Services for People Who Are Deaf. Consultation*. London: DoH.

DoH (2005) *Mental Health and Deafness: Towards Equity and Access. Guidance*. London: DoH.

DoH (2007) *Consultation on Guidance on 'Finding a Shared Vision of How People's Mental Health Problems Should Be Understood.'* London: DoH

Disability Rights Commission (2006) *Equal Treatment: Closing the Gap. Formal Investigation into Physical Health Inequalities Experienced by People with Learning Disabilities or Mental Health Problems*. London: Disability Rights Commission.

Equalities National Council (2012) *Stop, Look and Listen*. London: Equalities National Council.

EHRC (Equality and Human Rights Commission) (2010) *How Fair is Britain? Equality, Human Rights and Good Relations in 2010. The First Triennial Review*. London: EHRC.

EHRC (2012) *'What is meant by reasonable?'* Accessed at www.equalityhumanrights. com/advice-and-guidance/service-users-guidance/the-duty-to-make-reasonable-adjustments-to-remove-barriers-for-disabled-people/what-is-meant-by-reasonable/ on 17 May 2012.

HM Government (2010) *No Health without Mental Health: A Cross-government Mental Health Outcomes Strategy for People of All Ages*. Analysis of the Impact on Inequality. London: Department of Health. Accessed at www.dh.gov.uk/prod_consum_dh/groups/dh_digitalassets/documents/digitalasset/dh_123989.pdf on 15 May 2012.

Perkins, R. (2012) 'UK Mental Health Policy: A Counter-argument.' In P. Phillips, T. Sandford and C. Johnston (Eds) *Working in Mental Health: Policy and Practice in a Changing Environment*. Abingdon: Routledge.

Thurer, S. and Rogers, S. (1984) 'The mental health needs of physically disabled persons: their perspective.' *Rehabilitation Psychology 29*, 4, 239–249.

Velthorst, E., Nieman, D., Linszen, D., Becker, H., de Haan, L., Dingemans, P., Birchwood, M., Patterson, P., Salokangas, R., Heinimaa, M., Heinz, A., Juckel, G., von Reventlow, H., French, F., Stevens, H., Schultze-Lutter, F., Klosterkötter, J. and Ruhrmann, S. (2010) 'Disability in people clinically at high risk of psychosis.' *British Journal of Psychiatry 197*, 278–284.

Chapter 9

OUT AND EQUAL

Towards Mental Health Equality for Lesbian, Gay and Bisexual (LGB) People[2]

Sarah Carr

INTRODUCTION

This chapter gives an overview of the situation for lesbian, gay and bisexual (LGB) people using or needing to use mental health services in the UK. The exploration is written in the context of the Equality Act 2010, in which 'sexual orientation' (including people who are attracted to those of the same sex) is a 'protected characteristic'. All mental health services should be developed and delivered in accordance with the Equality Act 2010, so it is important to examine what this means for LGB people. The aim is to equip the reader with some of the core knowledge about LGB mental health, good practice, and achieving equality for LGB people in mental health service provision.

This chapter provides a summary of the current situation, using the best available research evidence and some of the underpinning adult mental health and social care policy and guidance. The chapter includes a discussion on the prevalence of mental health problems among LGB people and explores why rates of mental distress might be so high. Part of the exploration looks at the historical pathologisation of same-sex attraction in psychiatry to see what this legacy might mean for contemporary mental health practice. The chapter also looks at the implications of some of the newer policies and approaches to mental health that sit alongside the legal equality framework, such as the personalisation agenda and the recovery model, as well as some of the evidence-based practice.

---

2   This chapter is written in a personal capacity and does not necessarily represent the views of the Social Care Institute for Excellence.

DEFINING THE FOCUS ON LGB PEOPLE

Sexual orientation as a 'protected characteristic' under the Equality Act 2010

Since 1967, when the Sexual Offences Act decriminalised male homosexuality in England, the civil rights of LGB people have slowly come to be recognised in law (Cant 2009; Cocker and Hafford-Letchfield 2010; Fish 2009), with one of the most significant pieces of anti-discrimination legislation being the Equality Act 2010. It replaces previous anti-discrimination laws (such as the Equality Act [Sexual Orientation] 2007) with a single Equality Act. This Act defines sexual orientation as a 'protected characteristic' and places a duty on public sector bodies and providers to account for the needs of LGB people when designing and delivering services. The Act covers mental health and social care services provided by statutory, voluntary, private and community sector organisations. It not only prohibits direct discrimination but also indirect discrimination (discrimination against someone because of their association with a person who has a protected characteristic), harassment or victimisation. The Act 'requires public bodies and those carrying out public functions to have due regard to the need to eliminate unlawful discrimination, advance equality of opportunity and foster good relations between people from different equality groups. This is called the "public sector equality duty"' (Social Care Institute for Excellence (SCIE) 2011, p.1). Mental health services are subject to this equality duty.

The Equality Act 2010 provides a vital underpinning legal framework for the design and delivery of accessible, acceptable and effective mental health services to people from LGB communities. The Government Equalities Office (GEO) issued a cross-government work plan to support the implementation of the Act for LGB people (GEO 2010, 2011). The plan is clear that 'public bodies such as hospitals and local councils…need to involve the LGB and T [transgender] communities when planning their work and priorities' under the Public Sector Equality Duty (GEO 2011, p.2). Further, the work plan specifically acknowledges the progress for LGB people to be made in health and social care, as well as on the part of voluntary, community and independent providers.

Prevalence of mental health problems and inequalities among LGB people

Despite the fact that not all mental health strategies yet recognise LGB people as a high-risk group (see, for example, Royal College of

Psychiatrists (RCPsych.) 2011), there is now some compelling evidence to show that there are higher rates of certain mental health problems among LGB communities, and this is gradually being recognised (Department of Health (DoH) 2007a, 2007b; HM Government 2010). It is important to be very clear from the outset that same-sex attraction is *not* a mental health problem in itself, and was removed from the World Health Organization *International Classification of Diseases* in 1992 (Smith, Bartlett and King 2004), although mental health services are still dealing with a legacy of the historical pathologisation of LGB people (see relevant section below). However, LGB people often experience higher degrees of mental distress than heterosexual people, which is why a specific focus on health inequalities for LGB people, particularly in mental health, is required. To demonstrate the potential elevated mental health risk and health inequalities, below is a broad comparative table of indicative mental health outcomes, based on a systematic review of UK research on LGB health.

Table 9.1: Comparative mental health outcomes

Mental health issue	LGB people	General population
Anxiety	18%	5%
Depression	28%–40%	6%
Eating disorders	5%–20%	2%
Self-harm	20%–25%	2.4%
Suicide attempts (lifetime)	20%–40%	4.4%

Source: Meads et al. *2009*

Another systematic review conducted in the UK, this time focusing specifically on LGB mental health, concluded that: 'LGB people are at higher risk of mental disorder, suicidal ideation, substance misuse, and deliberate self-harm than heterosexual people' (King *et al.* 2008, p.1). Finally, recent findings from the UK Adult Psychiatric Morbidity Survey found that:

> self-reported identification as non-heterosexual [8% of the 7,403-person sample] was associated with a significantly elevated prevalence of unhappiness, any neurotic disorder, depressive episodes in the previous week, generalised anxiety disorder, obsessive-compulsive disorder, phobic disorder, probable psychosis, suicidal thought and acts and

self-harm, alcohol dependence and drug dependence. (Chakraborty *et al.* 2011, p.146)

Therefore there is an increasingly robust and growing evidence base to show that LGB people are at higher risk of certain mental health problems, compared to their heterosexual counterparts, and experience greater health inequalities in relation to mental health and well-being.

Understanding the social impacts on LGB mental health

There is now a wealth of evidence to show that LGB mental health is very likely to be affected by experiences of fear, prejudice, familial and social ostracism and discrimination (including verbal and physical attacks), often over a lifetime (Carr 2005; Chakraborty *et al.* 2011; King *et al.* 2008), with childhood bullying being a significant early factor (Imperial College 2004; Rivers and Carragher 2003), and isolation and fear in older age also having an impact (Knocker 2012; Stonewall 2011). The Department of Health has recognised the social impact of discrimination on LGB mental health (including the mental health of LGB people from black and minority ethnic (BME) communities) (DoH 2007a, 2007b). Researchers analysing the findings of the UK Adult Psychiatric Morbidity Survey concluded that:

> this study corroborates international findings that people of non-heterosexual orientation report elevated levels of mental health problems and service usage, and it lends further support to the suggestion that... discrimination may act as a social stressor in the genesis of mental health problems for this population. (Chakraborty *et al.* 2011, p.143)

Further, the authors refer to a conceptual framework for understanding 'minority stress' for LGB people and the risk it poses to mental health:

> stigma, prejudice and discrimination create a hostile and stressful social environment that causes mental health problems...[the sexual minority stress model] describes processes, including the experience of prejudice events, expectations of rejection, hiding and concealing, internalised homophobia and ameliorative coping processes. (Chakraborty *et al.* 2011, p.147)

Sexual minority stress is a very useful model for gaining insight into the nature of LGB mental health problems (Meyer 2003), and more generally for understanding the psychological effects of social discrimination or stigma (Goffman 1990) and appreciating social perspectives on mental health (Tew 2005). Meyer's detailed paper on the sexual minority stress framework and LGB mental health and identity formation argues that:

> minority identity is linked to a variety of stress processes; some LGB people, for example, may be vigilant in interactions with others (expectations of rejection), hide their identity for fear of harm (concealment), or internalize stigma (internalized homophobia). (Meyer 2003, p.677)

One US study of LGB people and their heterosexual siblings who grew up in exactly the same family environment identified minority stress factors as having a negative impact on the LGB participants' mental health (this was generally worse than that of the heterosexual brothers and sisters):

> LGBs still use mental health services more and are at higher risk for suicidal ideation, suicide attempts, and self-injurious behaviour than are heterosexual siblings. One potential explanation is that although familial factors impact mental health for all siblings in a family, LGB siblings must also contend with 'minority stress' associated with their sexual orientation. (Balsam, Rothblum and Beauchaine 2005, p.474)

Mental health services themselves have added to and may still impact on this sexual minority stress, as explored in the next section.

THE CURRENT PICTURE FOR LGB PEOPLE IN ADULT MENTAL HEALTH SERVICES

Historical overview of psychiatric and mental health service practice with LGB people

Research, survivor testimony and accounts of the history of psychiatry provide undeniable evidence that LGB people have been pathologised and mistreated in psychiatric and mental health services since the advent of psychiatry in the nineteenth century (Carr 2005; Foucault 1990; Porter 1997; Smith *et al.* 2004). As noted earlier, 'homosexuality' as a disease, under s302 – 'sexual deviations and disorders' – was only removed from the World Health Organization's *International Classification of Diseases* (ICD-10) in 1992. Researchers have argued that 'mental health professionals in Britain should be aware of the mistakes of the past. Only in that way can we prevent future excesses and heal the gulf between gay and lesbian patients and their psychiatrists' (King and Bartlett 1999, p.106).

Therefore, it is vital for people working in mental health services to understand that during the mid to latter part of the twentieth century,

National Health Service (NHS) psychiatric hospitals continued to treat LGB people for 'homosexuality' (King and Bartlett 1999; King, Smith and Bartlett 2004; Smith *et al.* 2004), with gay men often being referred for treatment via the criminal justice system, instead of being sent to prison as happened before the 1967 decriminalisation (Jivani 1997; Smith *et al.* 2004). Treatments from the 1950s until the 1970s 'included behavioural aversion therapy with electric shocks, oestrogen therapy, religious counselling, electroconvulsive therapy, and psychoanalysis, and often had a negative impact on patients' sense of identity and place in society' (Smith *et al.* 2004, p.3). As this research quote suggests, it is important to note that these extreme and often violent interventions had little or no impact on the individual's sexual orientation, but 'the definition of same-sex attraction as an illness and the development of treatments to eradicate such attraction have had long-term impacts on individuals' (Smith *et al.* 2004, p.1). It is reckoned that this historical legacy continues to influence the way mental health services and some individual practitioners treat LGB people (Carr 2005, 2010b; King *et al.* 2004).

Contemporary LGB user experience of mental health and social care services

The first UK study of the experiences of LGB people who use mental health services was carried out in 1998 and indicated that pathologisation of same-sex attraction was still a problem. It concluded that 'lesbian, gay and bisexual mental health service users are discriminated against and oppressed, not only by the attitudes and behaviour of society at large, but also from within mental health services' (McFarlane 1998, p.117). When the Department of Health conducted research into LGB people and mental health services nearly ten years later, the situation was much the same: a third of gay men, a quarter of bisexual men and over 40 per cent of lesbians reported negative or mixed reactions from mental health professionals when they disclosed their sexual orientation; 20 per cent of lesbians and gay men and a third of bisexual men stated that a mental health professional made a causal link between their sexual orientation and their mental health problem (DoH 2007a). Other research has shown that 'in mental health provision, lesbians and gay men have reported insensitive and sometimes hostile treatment by professionals despite being proportionally greater users of services' (Fish 2009, p.47).

Historically, same-sex sexual orientation was treated as a mental illness and experts have decisively warned 'against the use of mental health services to change aspects of human behaviour that are disapproved of on social, political, moral, or religious grounds' (Smith *et al.* 2004, p.3). Although psychiatric classification and practice has changed, there are still issues for LGB people using psychotherapeutic or counselling services (Bartlett, King and Phillips 2001; King *et al.* 2008). Contemporary investigations have shown that LGB people are still being referred, or may be subject, to 'reparative therapy', a psychoanalytic or psychological intervention which attempts to change their same-sex attraction (Bartlett, Smith and King 2009). Often this has strong religious overtones, with some practitioners using the faith-oriented language of 'healing' rather than conventional clinical terminology (Forstein 2004; Bartlett *et al.* 2009; Carr 2011; Strudwick 2010). Researchers associated with the Royal College of Psychiatrists found that:

> a significant minority of mental health professionals are attempting to help lesbian, gay and bisexual clients to become heterosexual. Given lack of evidence for the efficacy of such treatments, this is likely to be unwise or even harmful. (Bartlett *et al.* 2009, p.1)

Such 'reparative therapy' has recently been discredited as harmful by major professional bodies, such as the British Medical Association and the UK Council for Psychotherapy (UKCP), with the latter calling on the mental health establishment to 'work more energetically and in partnership to prevent the re-pathologisation of LGB...people' (UKCP 2010). The Equality Act 2010 should provide a legal framework to challenge this trend and the type of discrimination that LGB people can still encounter in mainstream services if they seek help for mental health problems.

Finally, there is emerging evidence to show that affirmative approaches can result in positive mental health outcomes for LGB people:

> affirmative talking therapies appear to help LGB...people to normalise their day-to-day experiences, face and counteract the homophobic nature of their early development and receive therapy that is appropriately focused on issues brought to therapy, rather than on their sexual identity. (King *et al.* 2008, p.3)

Such affirmative, person-centred approaches would be more appropriate for mental health services providing supportive and accessible care to LGB people experiencing mental distress.

WHAT DOES 'GOOD' LOOK LIKE FOR LGB PEOPLE USING MENTAL HEALTH SERVICES?

A brief examination of the research for evidence-based good practice with LGB people

Formal research and practice evidence as well as service user, carer and community knowledge are providing an increasingly clear indication of good practice for people from LGB communities who use mental health services. Therefore there is an evidence base for adult mental health service improvement to provide accessible and safe support to LGB people in line with the Equality Act 2010. This section is a brief summary of some of the evidence-based good practice points, and there is additional signposting to useful training and development resources at the end of this chapter.

A systematic review of qualitative literature on LGB healthcare practice has highlighted important issues for improving service user and practitioner relationships (Pennant, Bayliss and Meads 2009). Among these were:

- avoiding homophobia and heterosexism

- improving practitioner knowledge

- improving patient trust

- being perceptive to terminology use

- understanding embarrassment

- reducing over-caution

- importance of affirmation of sexual identity.

Institutional-level changes, particularly improvement of protocols, confidentiality, LGB-friendly resources and training, were also identified as important for improving health service provision. Elsewhere research has shown that on an institutional level there may be some issues with LGB people achieving equal recognition in participation initiatives, equalities training and development programmes (Carr 2008; Commission for Social Care Inspection (CSCI) 2008; Fish 2009; McNulty, Richardson and Monro 2010). One UK study concluded that:

> Well-designed and inclusive equalities training programmes were identified as crucial to reducing people's levels of discomfort and fear

and improving their understanding of how people who are [LGB] experience inequalities. (McNulty *et al.* 2010, p.15)

The authors of a systematic review conclude that an empathetic, holistic, person-centred approach is particularly vital: 'approach patients with an open mind, listen to them and engage with their experience' (Pennant *et al.* 2009, p.198). This is echoed for social work practice with LGB people:

> we need each lesbian and gay man to be seen as a unique individual within his/her own context, and an understanding that this will include her/his social and political current and historical context. (Brown 2008, p.270)

In understanding the individual and their history 'attention needs to be paid to the fact that LGB people are from diverse cultural, racial and social backgrounds, and can often encounter quite complex forms of multiple discrimination' (Ross and Carr 2010, p.213), and that LGB people who are refugees or seeking asylum may have significant and specific mental health needs relating to the trauma of homophobic violence in their country of origin (Carr 2010b; UK Lesbian and Gay Immigration Group (UKLGIG) 2010).

A person's spirituality has been cited as being important for mental health and recovery (Gilbert 2011; Swinton 2001), and the same is true for LGB people: 'the spiritual needs of sexual minorities are not different from [those] of the sexual majority' (Macaulay 2010, p.11). There is emerging evidence to show that an LGB person's mental health may have been affected by rejection from family or community on grounds of faith or belief, and so this may need to be recognised as part of mental health care and support (Carr 2010b, 2011). Research by the Lesbian and Gay Foundation (LGF) shows that 'many LGB…people feel alienated from their faith, with some having experienced rejection by organised religious groups, leading to general spiritual needs being forgotten' (LGF 2011, p.1). Although not all people from BME communities are religious, BME LGB people from certain religious backgrounds may be at greater risk of fearing or experiencing ostracism from their faith and faith community, yet faith and belonging is still important to their identity and mental health (Galop 2001; Keogh, Dodds and Henderson 2004; Safra Project 2003). For example, based on his pastoral experience, Rowland Jide Macaulay, the founder of an LGBTI (lesbian, gay, bisexual, transgender and intersex)-affirmative African Christian ministry, has recommended that there needs to be a tailored, holistic approach 'to support the journey for reconciliation of sexuality and spirituality' (Macaulay 2010, p.9), particularly for LGB African Christians.

Research suggests that:

> training to improve mental health practice with LGB people and to enable staff to work with them holistically and with due regard to religious or spiritual needs as appropriate...means allowing practitioners 'a safe context' in which they can ask 'potentially difficult questions' [Peel 2008]. (Carr 2011, p.339)

Such difficult questions may relate to practitioner views, moral or religious principles, and social prejudice that could result in discriminatory practice towards LGB people if not explored and addressed (Aymer and Patni 2011; Brown and Cocker 2011; Carr 2008; Smith *et al.* 2004). Service user, carer and LGB community organisations have been identified as having an essential role to play in designing and delivering training to health and social care staff: 'user involvement...with LGB people [is an] essential tool in the design and delivery of services' and training programmes (Fish 2009, p.58).

The evidence for good practice with LGB people in mental health points to the importance of a person-centred, empathetic, holistic approach which is capable of engaging with and accommodating individual identity, difference, complexity and self-determination: 'mental health practitioners need to be able to offer support in a way that is led by the individual person rather than by professional or personal assumptions' (Carr 2011, p.338). This is, of course, what good practice should be for anyone using mental health services.

Understanding LGB diversity

As implied in the section above, it is important for those involved with the development and delivery of mental health services to understand that LGB communities in the UK are as diverse as UK society itself. The LGB&T Consortium of Voluntary and Community Organisations has succinctly described the diversity of LGB people:

> LGB...people are diverse; they can be young, old, women, men, BME, disabled, of any class and any faith. LGB...people may be homeless, living in poverty, asylum seekers, refugees and/or prisoners. Their living situations may vary in terms of whether they are in civil partnerships and if they have children... (LGB&T Consortium 2010, p.9)

One of the challenges of working in a person-centred way that accounts for an individual's whole self and history is recognising that LGB people may have other identities, or may come from different cultural, ethnic or religious backgrounds (Carr 2010b, 2011; DoH 2007a, 2007b; Fish 2008). Furthermore, sexual orientation may not be a person's primary identity even, if they are attracted to the same sex – because, for example, their racial or cultural rather than sexual identity may be of primary importance to their self-concept (Carr 2010b; Fish 2008). Therefore approaches to support planning should not rely on simple categorisations, and effective, individually tailored support will probably not be achieved by relying on 'box-ticking' that does not necessarily capture a person's needs and preferences in an integrated way, or reflect the fullness of who they are (Brown and Cocker 2011; Carr 2010b; Cocker and Hafford-Letchfield 2010; Cronin *et al.* 2011; Fanshawe and Sriskandarajah 2010; Fish 2008).

The implications of personalisation and recovery for LGB mental health service and support development

Support planning and mental health management led by the person rather than the service or practitioner is part of personalisation in adult social care mental health (Carr 2010a; HMG 2007; National Mental Health Development Unit (NMHDU)/DoH/National Development Team for Inclusion (NDTi) 2010). Such user-led support also fits with the type of approach to recovering identity, life, independence and self-determination inherent in the recovery approach in mental health (DoH 2001; Shepherd, Boardman and Slade 2008):

> A central tenet of recovery is that it does not necessarily mean cure (clinical recovery). Instead it emphasises the unique journey of an individual living with mental health problems to build a life beyond illness (social recovery). Thus a person can recover their life, without necessarily recovering from their illness. (Shepherd *et al.* 2008, p.2)

The aims of the personalisation agenda in adult social care and mental health and the recovery approach are shared ones, as these two selected quotes show:

> Personalisation means recognising people as individuals who have strengths and preferences and putting them at the heart of their own care and support... Personalised approaches like self directed support and personal budgets involve enabling people to identify their own needs

and make choices about how and when they are supported to live their lives... Personalisation is also about making sure there is an integrated, community-based approach for everyone. (SCIE/LGB&T Consortium 2011)

If we want to develop recovery-oriented services for people with serious mental illness, we need to offer systematically organised and personally tailored collaborative help, treatment and care in an atmosphere of hope and optimism. (Lester and Gask 2006, p.402)

Mental health services based on social recovery, self-determination, self-management, person-centred support and service user choice and control should be available to everyone. In the context of the Equality Act 2010 this approach is particularly important for LGB people using mental health services. As already discussed, fear or experience of discrimination in statutory, mainstream mental health services can make them difficult to access or even damaging for LGB people. In order to ensure that LGB people have choice and control over their mental health support, statutory services need to be seen and experienced as 'safe spaces' (Gildersleeve and Platzer 2003; McFarlane 1998) which welcome LGB people:

mainstream services are not always welcoming to LGB people and yet personalisation is about being able to choose appropriate mainstream... care and support if you want to... LGB people are more likely to come out to services [and therefore get the appropriate personalised support] if they feel safe and comfortable to do so. (SCIE/LGB&T Consortium 2011, p.4)

In addition to making mainstream services more safe, welcoming and inclusive for LGB people, giving service users choice and control also means that they should be able to opt for available community-based specialist services if that type of support is most likely to result in better outcomes for them. Building community capacity and developing the support provider market is part of the wider aims of personalisation in adult social care and mental health (DoH 2010; Think Local Act Personal (TLAP) 2011). LGB communities have a history of establishing specialist and peer support services, including mental health and sexual health services (see, for example, PACE 2011 or www.naz.org.uk), when statutory mainstream services have been discriminatory or inaccessible so:

commissioning for personalisation [and recovery in mental health] means understanding the profile and needs of the local population and nurturing the type of peer support, community and voluntary activity that happens in LGB communities. (SCIE/LGB&T Consortium 2011, p.4)

Personalisation and recovery are therefore key components for developing mental health services and support that are safe, accessible and effective for LGB people, but it is important to remember that:

> Rather than treating everybody in a uniform way which ignores difference, commissioners, providers and practitioners should be aiming to treat every individual with the same level of dignity and respect. This means listening, understanding and responding to their unique needs. (SCIE/LGB&T Consortium 2011, p.2)

National strategies, guidance and quality standards for mental health and social care to support good practice with LGB people

As well as the specific obligations under the Equality Act 2010 and the associated GEO LGB&T work plan, there are a number of generic national mental health and social care strategies, frameworks and quality standards which aim at improving services for all people who experience mental health problems. These apply to LGB people and communities and can be used to drive the development and implementation of the good practice evidenced and described above. Three of the current key strategies and standards for mental health and social care are outlined here.

Government strategy: No Health without Mental Health

First, the cross-government *No Health without Mental Health* (HM Government 2011) strategy outlines the need to account for LGB people when planning and providing mental health services, and identifies LGB people as a group whose mental health outcomes need to be improved. In order to promote equality and reduce inequality in mental health services, the Government is clear that 'a priority action for securing improved outcomes is to achieve routine local monitoring of access to services, experience and outcome by sexual orientation' (HM Government 2011, p.61). The NHS in partnership with LGB organisations has produced useful resources to inform and support accurate and sensitive sexual orientation monitoring (NHS North West/LGF 2011).

NICE Guidance and Quality Statement: Service user experience in adult mental health: Improving the experience of care for people using adult NHS mental health services

Recent user-informed National Institute for Clinical Excellence (NICE) guidance and quality statement to improve the experience of people using adult NHS mental health services (NICE 2011) specifically states that mental health services should 'take into account the requirements of the Equality Act 2010 and make sure services are equally accessible to, and supportive of, all people using mental health services' (NICE 2011, p.16). The NICE guidance embeds this legal framework throughout and emphasises the need for services and staff to be aware and respectful of diversity and difference (p.11). NICE also requires that NHS mental health services measure themselves by a set of 15 quality statements based on the guidance. The following are of particular relevance to improving mental health services and outcomes for LGB people:

- People using mental health services, their families or carers, feel optimistic that care will be effective.

- People using mental health services, their families or carers, feel they are treated with empathy, dignity and respect.

- People using mental health services are actively involved in decision-making and supported in self-management.

- People using community mental health services are normally supported by staff from a single, multidisciplinary community team, familiar to them, and with whom they have a single, continuous relationship.

- People using mental health services understand the assessment process, their diagnosis and treatments options, and receive emotional support for any sensitive issues.

- People using mental health services jointly develop a care plan with mental health and social care professionals, and are given a copy with an agreed date to review it.

(NICE 2011, p.7; Crown copyright 2011)

In addition, the guidance clarifies some of the essential elements of mental health services that are accessible, inclusive and effective for everyone, including LGB people:

1.1.22 Service managers should routinely commission reports on the experience of care across non-acute and acute care pathways, including the experience of being treated under the Mental Health Act… These reports should:

- include data that allow direct comparisons of the experience of care according to gender, sexual orientation, socioeconomic status, age, background (including cultural, ethnic and religious background) and disability. (NICE 2011, p.15; Crown copyright 2011)

1.2.5 Local mental health services should work with primary care and local third sector, including voluntary, organisations to ensure that:

- All people with mental health problems have equal access to services based on need, irrespective of gender, sexual orientation, socioeconomic status, age, background (including cultural, ethnic and religious background) and disability

- Services are culturally appropriate.

(NICE 2011, p.16; Crown copyright 2011)

1.4.10 Mental health and social care professionals inexperienced in working with service users from different cultural, ethnic, religious and other diverse backgrounds should seek advice, training and supervision from health and social care professionals who are experienced in working with these groups. (NICE 2011, p.20; Crown copyright 2011)

Social care improvement: Think Local Act Personal markers of progress towards personalised, community support

The Think Local Act Personal (TLAP) partnership is a sector-led improvement organisation which is continuing the implementation of personalisation and community-based support in adult social care and mental health. With service users and carers, the partnership has defined some 'citizen-led' key markers of progress to support all those working towards personalisation and improved outcomes. Again, these progress markers emphasise the legal and social importance of 'ensuring that support is culturally sensitive and relevant to diverse communities across age, gender, religion, race, sexual orientation and disability' (TLAP 2011, p.5). For people who are using personal budgets, there should be 'a market of diverse and culturally appropriate support and services that people…can access. People have maximum choice and control over a range of good value, safe and high quality supports' (TLAP 2011, p.11). Finally, community-based support, such as the type offered by local LGB mental health and peer support organisations, is recognised as being important: 'people are supported to access a range of networks, relationships and activities to maximise independence, health and well-being and community connections' (TLAP 2011, p.7).

GOOD PRACTICE EXAMPLE
MindOut LGB&T Mental Health
Project, Brighton and Hove

MindOut (www.mindout.org.uk) is a specialist voluntary sector organisation based in Brighton which provides support to LGB&T people who have mental health concerns. It won the 2010 Stonewall Community Group of the Year award. The organisation offers free, confidential, one-to-one meetings with trained lesbian or gay mental health workers and provides a safe space for group work and peer support where LGB&T people can meet and share their experiences and problems. As part of the support choices on offer, they run a peer support group for Black, Asian and minority ethnic people who are LGB&T who have emotional or mental health issues. MindOut provides information, advice and advocacy about accessing appropriate mental health services and social care and support. They also provide LGB&T awareness training for mainstream mental health service providers so that the quality of local services is improved.

EXERCISE 9.1: HIDING AN IMPORTANT PART OF YOURSELF

This is a very simple exercise, but it can give an idea of the stress of monitoring what you say all the time in order to hide an important part of yourself. This can be done in pairs or in a small group. Taking turns, over five or ten minutes talk about someone who is very important to you *without* using the 'gendered pronoun' – that is, *without* saying 'he, she, him, her, his, hers'. This is what it can be like for a lesbian, gay or bisexual person if they're talking about their same-sex partner in a situation where they do not feel safe to be open – and this could include a mental health service.

CONCLUSION

This chapter has outlined some key aspects for understanding and promoting positive mental health for LGB people, particularly through awareness of the particular mental health impacts and good practice for LGB communities. Some of the contributors to negative impacts on LGB mental health have been psychiatric treatments and mental health systems. The challenge of the Equality Act 2010 is to develop welcoming, sensitive and safe mental health services to and with LGB people from diverse backgrounds. Within the broader context of achieving personalisation, choice and control for people who use mental health services, this means responding to every person as an individual; respecting their preferences; focusing on their human rights; supporting them to live the lives they want to; understanding their histories and social contexts; and safeguarding their human dignity.

REFERENCES

Aymer, C. and Patni, R. (2011) 'Identity, Emotion Work and Reflective Practice: Dealing with Sexuality, Race and Religion in the Classroom.' In P. Dunk-West and P. Hafford-Letchfield (Eds) *Sexual Identities and Sexuality in Social Work: Research and Reflections from Women in the Field.* Farnham: Ashgate.

Balsam, K., Rothblum, E. and Beauchaine, T. (2005) 'Victimization over the life span: a comparison of lesbian, gay, bisexual, and heterosexual siblings.' *Journal of Consulting and Clinical Psychology 73*, 3, 477–487.

Bartlett, A., King, M. and Phillips, P. (2001) 'Straight talking: an investigation of the attitudes and practice of psychoanalysts and psychotherapists in relation to gays and lesbians.' *British Journal of Psychiatry 179*, 12, 545–549.

Bartlett, A., Smith, G. and King, M. (2009) 'The response of mental health professionals to clients seeking help to change or redirect same-sex sexual orientation.' *BMC Psychiatry 9*, 11.

Brown, H.C. (2008) 'Social work and sexuality, working with lesbians and gay men: what remains the same and what is different?' *Practice 20*, 265–275.

Brown, H.C. and Cocker, C. (2011) *Social Work with Lesbians and Gay Men.* London: Sage Publications.

Cant, B. (2009) 'Legal outcomes: reflections on the implications of LGBT legal reforms in the UK for health and social care providers.' *Diversity in Health and Care 6*, 1, 55–62.

Carr, S. (2005) '"The Sickness Label Infected Everything We Said": Lesbian and Gay Perspectives on Mental Distress.' In J. Tew (Ed.) *Social Perspectives in Mental Health.* London: Jessica Kingsley Publishers.

Carr, S. (2008) 'Sexuality and religion: a challenge for diversity strategies in UK social care service development and delivery.' *Diversity in Health and Social Care 5*, 2, 113–122.

Carr, S. (2010a) *Personalisation: A Rough Guide. Second revised edition.* London: Social Care Institute for Excellence.

Carr, S. (2010b) 'Seldom heard or frequently ignored? Lesbian, gay and bisexual (LGB) perspectives on mental health services.' *Ethnicity and Inequalities in Health and Social Care 3*, 3, 14–25.

Carr, S. (2011) 'Mental Health and the Sexual, Religious and Spiritual Identities of Lesbian, Gay, Bisexual and Transgender (LGBT) People.' In P. Gilbert (Ed.) *Spirituality and Mental Health.* Brighton: Pavilion.

Charkraborty, A., McManus, S., Brugha, T. and Beggington, P. (2011) 'Mental health of the non-heterosexual population of England.' *British Journal of Psychiatry 198,* 143–148.

Cocker, C. and Hafford-Letchfield, P. (2010) 'Out and proud? Social work's relationship with lesbian and gay equality.' *British Journal of Social Work,* 1–13.

Cronin, A., Ward, R., Pugh, S., King, A. and Price, E. (2011) 'Categories and their consequences: understanding and supporting the caring relationships of older lesbian, gay and bisexual people.' *International Social Work 54,* 3, 421–435.

CSCI (Commission for Social Care Inspection) (2008) *Putting People First: Equality and Diversity Matters 1. Providing Appropriate Services for Lesbian, Gay and Bisexual and Transgender People.* London: CSCI.

DoH (Department of Health) (2001) *The Journey to Recovery: The Government's Vision for Mental Health Care.* London: DoH.

DoH (2007a) *Briefing 9: Mental Health Issues within Lesbian, Gay and Bisexual (LGB) Communities.* London: DoH.

DoH (2007b) *Briefing 12: Lesbian, Gay and Bisexual (LGB) People from Black and Minority Ethnic Communities.* London: DoH.

DoH (2010) *A Vision for Adult Social Care: Capable Communities, Active Citizens.* London: DoH.

Fanshawe, S. and Sriskandarajah, D. (2010) *You Can't Put me in a Box: Super-diversity and the End of Identity Politics in Britain.* London: Institute for Public Policy Research.

Fish, J. (2008) 'Navigating Queer Street: researching the intersections of lesbian, gay, bisexual and trans (LGBT) identities in health research.' *Sociological Research Online 13,* 1.

Fish, J. (2009) 'Invisible no more? Including lesbian, gay and bisexual people in social work and social care.' *Practice 21,* 1 47–64.

Forstein, M. (2004) 'Pseudoscience of sexual orientation change therapy.' *British Medical Journal 328,* 7445, E287–E288.

Foucault, M. (1990) *The History of Sexuality, Volume I: An Introduction.* London: Penguin.

Galop (2001) *The Low Down: Black Lesbians, Gay Men and Bisexual People Talk about their Experiences and Needs.* London: Galop.

GEO (Government Equalities Office) (2010) *Working for Lesbian, Gay, Bisexual and Transgender Equality.* London: HM Government.

GEO (2011) *Working for Lesbian, Gay, Bisexual and Transgender Equality: Moving Forward.* London: HM Government.

Gilbert, P. (Ed.) (2011) *Spirituality and Mental Health.* Brighton: Pavilion.

Gildersleeve, C. and Platzer, H. (2003) *Creating a Safe Space: Good Practice for Mental Health Staff Working with Lesbians, Gay Men and Bisexuals.* Brighton: Pavilion.

Goffman, I. (1990) *Stigma: Notes on the Management of Spoiled Identity.* London: Penguin.

HM Government (2007) *Putting People First: A Shared Vision and Commitment to the Transformation of Adult Social Care.* London: HM Government.

HM Government (2010) *No Health without Mental Health: A Cross-government Mental Health Outcomes Strategy for People of All Ages.* London: Department of Health.

Imperial College (2004) Imperial College Press Release 1 December 2004: 'Discrimination against gay men, lesbians and bi-sexual men and women could lead to mental health problems.' Accessed at www.imperial.ac.uk/college.asp?P=5802 on 31 March 2012.

Jivani, A. (1997) *It's Not Unusual: A History of Lesbian and Gay Britain in the Twentieth Century.* London: Michael O'Mara Books Ltd.

Keogh, P., Dodds, C. and Henderson, L. (2004) *Migrant Gay Men: Redefining Community, Restoring Identity.* London: Sigma Research.

King, M. and Bartlett, A. (1999) 'British psychiatry and homosexuality.' *British Journal of Psychiatry 175*, 8, 106–113.

King, M., Semlyen, J., Tai, S.S., Killaspy, H., Osborn, D., Popelyuk, D. and Nazareth, I. (2008) *Mental Disorders, Suicide and Deliberate Self-harm in Lesbian, Gay and Bisexual People*. London: National Institute for Mental Health in England.

King, M., Smith, G. and Bartlett, A. (2004) 'Treatments of homosexuality in Britain since the 1950s – an oral history: the experience of professionals.' *British Medical Journal 328*, 7437, 429.

Knocker, S. (2012) *Perspectives on Ageing: Lesbians, Gay Men and Bisexuals*. York: Joseph Rowntree Foundation.

Lester, H. and Gask, L. (2006) 'Delivering medical care for patients with serious mental illness or promoting a collaborative model of recovery?' *British Journal of Psychiatry 188*, 401–402.

LGB&T Consortium (2010) *Building the Case for LGB&T Health*. London: LGB&T Consortium.

LGF (Lesbian and Gay Foundation) (2011) *Faithbook*. Manchester: LGF.

Macaulay, R.J. (2010) '"Just as I am, without one plea": a journey to reconcile sexuality and spirituality.' *Ethnicity and Inequalities in Health and Social Care 3*, 3, 6–13.

McFarlane, L. (1998) *Diagnosis Homophobic: The Experiences of Lesbians, Gay Men and Bisexuals in Mental Health Services*. London: PACE.

McNulty, A., Richardson, D. and Monro, S. (2010) *Lesbian, Gay, Bisexual and Trans (LGBT) Equalities and Local Governance: Research Report for Practitioners and Policy Makers*. Newcastle: University of Newcastle.

Meads, C., Pennant, M., McManus, J. and Bayliss, S. (2009) *A Systematic Review of UK Research on Lesbian, Gay, Bisexual and Transgender Health*. Birmingham: Unit of Public Health, Epidemiology & Biostatistics, West Midlands Health Technology Assessment Group. Accessed at www.wmhtac.bham.ac.uk/postersx/LGBTHealth.pdf on 31 March 2012.

Meyer, I. (2003) 'Prejudice, social stress, and mental health in lesbian, gay, and bisexual populations: conceptual issues and research evidence.' *Psychological Bulletin 129*, 5, 674–697.

NHS North West/LGF (Lesbian and Gay Foundation) (2011) *Everything You Always Wanted to Know about Sexual Orientation Monitoring...But Were Afraid to Ask*. Manchester: NHS North West/LGF.

NICE (National Institute for Clinical Excellence) (2011) *NICE Clinical Guideline 136: Service User Experience of Adult Mental Health Services*. London: NICE.

NMHDU (National Mental Health Development Unit)/DoH (Department of Health)/ NDTi (National Development Team for Inclusion) (2010) *Paths to Personalisation*. London: NMHDU.

PACE (2011) *The RaRE Study: Risk and Resilience Explored – Understanding Health Inequalities in Sexual Minorities*. Accessed at www.pacehealth.org.uk/The-RaRE-Study(2340454). htm on 3 September 2012.

Pennant, M., Bayliss, S. and Meads, C. (2009) 'Improving lesbian, gay and bisexual healthcare: a systematic review of qualitative literature from the UK.' *Diversity in Health and Care 6*, 3, 193–203.

Porter, R. (1997) *The Greatest Benefit to Mankind: A Medical History of Humanity*. London: HarperCollins.

RCPsych. (Royal College of Psychiatrists) (2010) *No Health without Public Mental Health. The Case for Action. Position Statement PS4/2010*. London: RCPsych.

Rivers, I. and Carragher, D. (2003) 'Social-developmental factors affecting lesbians and gay youth: a review of cross-national research findings.' *Children and Society 17*, 5, 374–385.

Ross, P.D.S. and Carr, S. (2010) '"It shouldn't be down to luck": training for good practice with LGBT people – Social Care TV.' *Diversity in Health and Care 7*, 3, 211–216.

Safra Project (2003) *Identifying the Difficulties Experienced by Muslim Lesbian, Bisexual and Transgender Women in Accessing Social and Legal Services.* London: Safra Project.

SCIE (Social Care Institute for Excellence) (2011) *At a Glance 41: Personalisation Briefing: Implications of the Equality Act 2010.* London: SCIE.

SCIE/LGB&T Consortium (2011) *At a Glance 42: Personalisation Briefing: Implications for Lesbian, Gay, Bisexual and Transgender (LGB&T) People.* London: SCIE.

Shepherd, G., Boardman, J. and Slade, M. (2008) *Making Recovery a Reality.* London: Centre for Mental Health.

Smith, G., Bartlett, A. and King, M. (2004) 'Treatments of homosexuality in Britain since the 1950s – an oral history: the experience of patients.' *British Medical Journal 328*, 7437, 4297.

Stonewall (2011) *Lesbian, Gay and Bisexual People in Later Life.* London: Stonewall.

Strudwick, P. (2010) 'The ex-gay files: The bizarre world of gay-to-straight conversion', *The Independent,* 1 February. Available at www.independent.co.uk/life-style/health-and-families/features/the-exgay-files-the-bizarre-world-ofgaytostraight-conversion-1884947.html on 31 March 2012.

Swinton, J. (2001) *Spirituality and Mental Health Care: Rediscovering a 'Forgotten' Dimension.* London: Jessica Kingsley Publishers.

Tew, J. (Ed.) (2005) *Social Perspectives in Mental Health.* London: Jessica Kingsley Publishers.

TLAP (Think Local Act Personal) (2010) *Think Local, Act Personal: Next Steps for Transforming Adult Social Care.* London: Department of Health.

TLAP (2011) *Making it Real: Marking Progress towards Personalised, Community Based Support.* London: TLAP.

UKLGIG (UK Lesbian and Gay Immigration Group) (2010) *Failing the Grade: Home Office Initial Decisions on Lesbian and Gay Claims for Asylum.* London: UKLGIG.

UKCP (United Kingdom Council for Psychotherapy) (2010) UKCP Statement on the 'Reparative' Therapy of Members of Sexual Minorities. Accessed at www.psychotherapy.org.uk/reparative_therapy_statement.html on 31 March 2012.

Chapter 10

BLACK PEOPLE AND MENTAL HEALTH

Marcel Vige and Hári Sewell

INTRODUCTION

The title of this chapter, 'Black People and Mental Health', is really shorthand for 'Racialised People and Mental Health'. The process of racialisation operates through a conscious or unconscious belief in a binary world where people are either white or black. The one-drop rule has been discussed elsewhere (see Sewell 2009) and applies to the notion that people are either (pure) white or black. Although Asian people with various ethnicities may not feel comfortable with the notion of being considered as black, in reality the themes of this chapter relate to the impacts of being racialised as being other than white, with all the prejudices and stereotypes that are associated with this. An indication of the impact of racialisation is the fact that poorer racial outcomes in mental health are the most extreme for African and African Caribbean people. These groups, traditionally considered to be black, are given focus in this chapter and provide a case example of extremes of inequalities that affect all racialised groups to a greater or lesser extent.

Any attempt to understand social trends is inevitably influenced by the position of whoever is doing the interpreting. When dealing with highly politicised issues such as race, the influence of how one is positioned relative to the issue is particularly pronounced. When linked with mental health, itself a highly politicised issue, it becomes nigh-on impossible to arrive at a widely agreed position. The best one can do is marshal the available evidence and bring a degree of intuitive interpretation to present a case for others to judge. This is particularly true of the various efforts to understand the reasons why black people seem to suffer particularly high levels of severe mental illness (Care Quality Commission (CQC) 2011), which is the focus of this chapter.

Throughout this chapter we explore the development of current thinking on why such trends persist. We also see that each subsequent explanation emerges from a critique of the former. Of course, all of this has implications for how policymakers and mental health practitioners respond to apparent racial differences in the profile of mental illness. We begin by exploring the various ways in which the elevated propensity for mental illness amongst black people has been understood – from a genetic predisposition to develop psychosis, to culturally rooted stereotypes and institutionalised discrimination that lead to a conflation of 'blackness' deviancy, threat and mental instability, ultimately expressed as psychosis – and which influences the expectations of professionals and wider society, including black people's own identity/self-concept. This is followed by a reflection on recent policy developments that relate to race and mental health, and specifically on how various conceptualisations of the issues explored earlier have shaped mental health policy. Finally the focus shifts to considering where this is leading, including the emergence of 'the single equalities approach', where the focus shifts away from specific areas of inequality such as race or gender, to a focus on equality in a more general sense.

A word on terminology

Throughout this chapter, we have used the terms 'race', 'racialised', 'black', 'mental illness'. We are conscious of the nature of these terms, and that in various ways they can be seen as reinforcing assumed group differences based in biology and/or social categories that position one group as 'normal', and therefore desirable in contrast to another. How language frames our thoughts and perceptions is a serious issue which one must never lose sight of. Therefore, when reading this chapter, you are advised to continually question the legitimacy of such terms. Whilst we have used them to aid communication (given that most readers will be familiar with them, and, we hope, will find them useful in grasping what we are trying to convey), we are aware that by doing so, we are also affirming their legitimacy. It's for this reason, in an attempt to counter this, that we suggest that even as you read what is to come, you retain an active scepticism about these terms, rather than taking them as givens.

THE PERSPECTIVES – UNDERSTANDING RACIAL INEQUALITY IN MENTAL HEALTH

It is not surprising, given the biomedical focus of psychiatry, that early explanations of racial difference in the prevalence of mental illness were based in physiology and genetics. This was simply an extension of the broader mission of psychiatry to establish physiological (including genetic) causes of the clusters of behavioural symptoms representative of various forms of psychosis (schizophrenia and bipolar disorder). Of course, it did not take long for this rather binary explanation to be challenged, not least by those with expertise in genetics and genetic expression. A cursory understanding of the concept of genotype/phenotype (see Box 10.1) contradicts the notion of strict genetic determinism, whereby particular genes are seen as leading to particular types of behaviour. Therefore, even before the full weight of sociological perspectives is brought to bear, environment is already acknowledged as determining how genetic propensity is expressed. The implication is that, whether or not particular groups of people are genetically predisposed to develop psychosis, its manifestation ultimately depends on environmental influences.

BOX 10.1: GENOTYPE/PHONOTYPE INTERACTION

An organism's *genotype* is the set of genes that it carries. An organism's *phenotype* is all of its observable characteristics – which are influenced both by its genotype and by the environment. An example of this interaction is seen in the colour of flamingos, which are generally pink. However, this colour is a consequence of the food they eat. Therefore, their colour emerges from their genetically determined physiology, which results in their ability to metabolise food, and the environmentally determined food that results in their pink hue.

A similar process is seen in relation to body shape, which is determined by the interaction of genetically based physiology, the availability of food, and consumption behaviours. In relation to humans, both genetic and environmental aspects result in the variation in body shapes (fat, thin, short, tall) that we see around us.

What this reveals is the difficulty of ascribing genetic causality to observed physical characteristics. This is further complicated where, as with mental illness, there also a high degree of interpretation, making inferences from observed behaviour. One is never entirely certain of the extent to which observed behaviour is a consequence of genetic propensity or environmental contingency. Indeed, to presume a clear distinction between both drivers is to misunderstand them. In terms of behaviour (or physical characteristics related to behaviour, e.g. body shape determined by calorie intake, or flamingo colour determined by food intake), genetic propensity is always situated within environments, so the consequences of both can never really be isolated when seeking to understand behaviour in a real-world setting.

Another explanation that has gained prominence in the mid/late 2000s is the notion that disproportionately high rates of mental illness amongst black people is a consequence of maladapted/maladjusted communities, specifically the conditions in which black people exist: communities with high rates of absentee fathers, restrictive family dynamics where women and young people have their freedoms curtailed, poor levels of understanding of and response to mental health issues, and culturally-based stigma attached to mental illness (Fearon 2006). Taken together with the relatively high levels of poverty and urbanisation of minority ethnic communities, such factors conspire to produce high levels of stress, thwarted ambition, and a lack of productive coping strategies, all of which lead to increased incidence of psychosis.

The consideration of environmental factors in the 'maladaptive communities' thesis may be seen as a development from previous biomedical explanations. The emphasis on stressful life events acknowledges the interaction between an individual's mental health and the conditions in which they live. That said, in many ways the analysis can still be seen as incomplete. Aside from the rather major value-laden assumption that non-white communities are indeed maladaptive, and to a greater extent than white communities, the analysis does not consider the interaction between black communities and the wider society in which they are based. Nor does it consider the role of mental health professions themselves, and specifically how they engage with differing ethnicities and cultures. It will be important for mental health professionals to reflect on their assumptions about the causes of existing disparities, such as the higher rates of detention for African and African Caribbean people.

EXERCISE 10.1: EXPLORING PERSONAL VIEWS ABOUT
CAUSES

Imagine you were asked these questions by the person you most trust; write down the answers you would give.

- What do you really think the reasons are for the over-representation of black people in psychiatric hospitals?
- Think about family life, lifestyles and habits. What part do you think they play?
- What about genetics?
- If you had to give a percentage to show the balance of contributory factors for all the causes you believe to be true, how would you score them?

A key question to consider following such an exercise is how your views affect the way you work with black people. For each causal factor you identified, think about how you incorporate it into your practice and consider how this helps or hinders the service user's experience of recovery.

The shift away from strict biomedical explanations has coincided with increased challenge to the validity of psychiatric diagnosis. Academics such as Fernando published extensively on the origin of mental illness as an expression of Western culture, which characterised non-Western cultures as primitive, underdeveloped, even threatening (e.g. Fernando 2003). Pathologising the beliefs and behaviours of non-white people as expressions of mental illness is but one example. The propensity for black people to be seen as mentally ill is rooted in how 'blackness' and 'mental illness' are constructed. The notion of abnormality and the threat or danger this implies are themes shared by both. This reflects the cultural stereotype of 'dangerous other' that has characterised representations of black people and people with mental illness over the centuries. So racial disparity in diagnosis and compulsory treatment is revealed as an outcome of the normal functioning of benign professionals working to professional precepts and practices that are inherently discriminatory.

Another approach to understanding racial disparity in mental health is provided by toxic interaction theory (a term coined by Sewell). The theory suggests that black people suffer psychological traumas as a consequence of living in close proximity with white people who exercise power, complicity or explicitly, by defining acceptable norms (Sewell 2009). What Sewell offers is a perspective on the psychological consequences of the broader social forces explored by Fernando (1996) for black people, white people and interactions between them. The history of discriminatory power differences serves to frame individual perceptions and expectations of what is possible and permissible in normal social relations. The psychological implications for black people of negotiating their socially disempowered position are elevated stress and frustration, manifest as mental illness. One of the advantages of toxic interaction theory is that it fills the gap between explanations that focus on mental illness within black people, and discriminatory social dynamics that associate 'blackness' with 'non-normal' cultures, beliefs and behaviours. In effect, the predisposition of black people to developmental health problems is itself a consequence of the social forces which presuppose that black people are more likely to be mentally ill.

Despite the shift in understanding which now sees environmental dynamics as essential to explaining racial differences in rates of mental illness, there remains a lack of clear consensus about precisely which environmental factors it is legitimate to include in the explanation, and their relative influence. The point on which the debate twists seems to be the extent to which cause is attributed to dynamics within communities, or the impact of an unbalanced, racialised society on its constituent groups and individuals. Toxic interaction theory emphasises the manifestation of these broader societal dynamics in the interaction between individuals. It focuses on the interaction between what have so far been referred to as communities in which black people exist, and wider society. The essential point here is that any attempt to seek reasons for increased levels of mental illness within maladjusted communities, for racism in wider society, or for discriminatory practices inherent in mental health professions, can only ever give part of the story. What needs to be considered is the way these various dynamics interact with each other. This approach reveals that these various causal factors are mutually reinforcing.

The variety of explanations of racial disparity within mental health diagnosis is indicative of the fact that it remains a highly politicised issue. Part of the drive amongst campaigners and others to develop explanations that take account of historically-rooted inequality is as a response to what are often observed as non-therapeutic consequences for black people of being labelled mentally ill. Conflating 'blackness' and mental illness is taken as an expression of the exploitation of particular racialised groups, which is a cornerstone of Western culture and society; characterisation of the 'oppressed other' as deviant from 'the norm' is expressed as a propensity to conflate those identified as 'non-normal' with mental abnormality. Whether such deviance is located in the genetic makeup of black people, or in the cultures and interpersonal relationships in which they exist, it is ultimately about problematising racialised groups. This is seen since around 2011 surrounding the amendment of the Mental Health Act in 2007, and attempts to respond to this disparity through health and social policy.

POLITICISATION OF THE DEBATE – POSITIONS OF CAMPAIGNERS, PROFESSIONALS AND POLICYMAKERS

During debates about the amendment of mental health legislation some of the key issues of contention amongst campaigners, including ourselves, were around expanding the definition of what constitutes mental illness, lowering the threshold of what is defined as treatment, and the effective expansion of compulsion from hospital to community settings. In addition, campaigners argued for the need to incorporate principles of equality on the face of the Act, rather than simply the codes of practice (which is what was actually done by decision of the Government). What was significant about these debates was the extent to which they revealed how much what are deemed by policymakers to be legitimate explanations of disparity are determined by the prevailing political climate.

From the early to mid 2000s, there occurred a major shift in thinking around inequality within health, largely driven by campaigns around the deaths of black men in psychiatric settings, most notably Orville Blackwood and David Rocky Bennett. Campaigns by the family of the latter gained traction with the change of government in 1997, resulting in the inquiry into the death of David Rocky Bennett (Norfolk, Suffolk and Cambridgeshire Strategic Health Authority NSCSTHA) 2003).

The Government's response to the inquiry came in the form of *Delivering Race Equality* (DRE), the Government's five-year national strategy to tackle ethnic inequality within mental heath (Department of Health (DoH) 2005).

DRE emerged in an era of increased willingness amongst policymakers to accept that the UK is indeed racialised, that there are dynamics within society at large that disadvantage particular ethnic groups. This shift in awareness was initiated by the acknowledgement of institutional racism by the Macpherson Inquiry into the murder of Stephen Lawrence (Macpherson 1999). After being refused an inquiry by Michael Howard, the previous Home Secretary, the Lawrence family were finally granted a public inquiry by new Home Secretary Jack Straw following the 1997 Labour landslide general election victory. In effect, the Macpherson Report was official acknowledgment that racial inequality was indeed about the *modus operandi* of institutions throughout society, rather than genetic or cultural deficiencies within racialised groups and individuals. This affirmed what mental health campaigners had been advocating for years. It also created the conditions from which DRE emerged.

With the ending of DRE in 2010 coinciding with another change of government, there was again a shift in political thinking around inequality. This represented the culmination of a growing backlash against the concept of institutional racism as an explanation for racial disparity in mental health. Explanations emphasising maladaptive subcultures in which minority ethnic people exist gained ascendance. Whilst various academics advocating this explanation still acknowledged the influence of racism in wider society, in essence this represents a return to earlier partial explanations, which fail to consider the role of conceptualisations of, and responses to mental ill-health by mental health professions themselves (*The Guardian* 2009). This shift coincided with the a new mental health strategy, *No Health without Mental Health* (HM Government 2011), which focused on developing the capacity of communities to respond better to mental health needs by engaging with some of the negative factors such as low educational attainment, stigma assisted in mental health, etc. This was entirely in keeping with the decentralised 'big society' advocated by the Coalition Government.

EXERCISE 10.2

The term 'institutional racism' both describes the type of culture and practice that propagate racism within institutions, and prompts a remedial response intended to reduce or eradicate the problem.

- Is the term 'institutional racism' accurately applied to the mental health profession and services?
- What are the consequences for mental health professionals of acknowledging or rejecting the term?

FUTURE DIRECTIONS – TOWARDS A SINGLE EQUALITIES APPROACH?

The shift in emphasis away from institutional racism and back to 'maladaptive communities' matches the broader shift in understanding away from the history of racial inequality and its role in the development and maintenance of Western culture, to emphasis on inequality in a generic sense. In this regard inequality itself is the focus – identified as a general theme that finds various forms of expression, be it race, gender, sexuality or class. In this sense, the target of the response is inequality itself, rather than its specific manifestations, which are seen as variations on this general theme. This is a profound shift away from previous perspectives.

The shift towards a combined approach to equality is, to a degree, indicative of the successes of various struggles against oppression, not least gains made on race equality during the civil rights era of the 1960s, 1970s and beyond. Such campaigns serve as an inspiration for other campaigns for social justice. However, for organisations and institutions charged with responding to such issues, expediency leads to convergence on the simplest way of understanding them – which often amounts to seeing all forms of social inequality as one-and-the-same thing. This is also a way of developing a common language that generates engagement from various quarters. In campaigning terms, if the targets of influence have difficultly understanding, say, racial inequality, then framing the issue in terms of, say, gender or sexuality, can aid understanding. That said, in developing this 'single equalities' approach, campaigners have also identified possible challenges, not least of which is the fact that the emphasis on a single approach reconfigures our perception of inequality in such a way that the particular issues pertinent to each area of inequality (e.g. race, gender) are at best downplayed, and at worst rendered insignificant. In this regard, the 'single equalities' approach is a strategy to avoid the challenge of engaging meaningfully with inequality.

It is also the case that previous challenges to discrimination have been intellectually and practically rooted in grassroots, 'bottom-up' campaigning, ultimately driving policy change (Fernando 2003). By contrast, the shift towards a 'single equalities' approach springs from the intellectual and policy domain. For those campaigning against racial discrimination, this is a reason for mistrust and suspicion that racial discrimination is being redefined by a section of society that has long resisted the social change that campaigners have called for. In this respect, the single equalities approach reflects a reaction against the challenge to racial inequality, on the part of the very power structures that challenge seeks to confront; an answer that co-opts and reworks the rationale behind the challenge in such a way as to undermine its potency.

It is important to emphasise that what is being argued here is not that one form of inequality is somehow more or less important than another, nor that there are no thematic connections between them. As with various explanations of racial inequality referred to earlier, the point of contention is that in terms of challenging inequality, the single equalities approach becomes counterproductive when it is used to obscure the particular drivers of inequality in a specific domain. This is commonly seen in attempts to understand issues around racial inequality by viewing them through a generic inequalities lens. This is not necessarily a problem if the intention is to engage with equality issues *per se*. However, this is often not the case. The danger that lies in the ascendancy and widespread acceptance of this generalist approach as the principle frame of reference in social policy is the obliteration of a particular focus on specific areas such as race, which by contrast are cast as archaic and passé. In this regard, what could be happening is an unravelling of intellectual gains achieved in previous eras, where comprehensive explanations of racial inequality were increasingly gaining traction.

EXERCISE 10.3: VISION AND REALITY

Think about either the mental health profession that you belong to, or a mental heath setting that you have worked in. Write a vision statement that captures how the profession/organisation seeks to respond to the effects of racial inequality. Then write a statement that captures the way such issues are actually dealt with. Note reasons for any disparity between the vision and the reality.

Having completed the exercise, consider it:

a) as a response to the issues covered in this section; and

b) in terms of its potential role in the process of addressing those issues.

CONCLUSION

A key theme to emerge is the challenge of understanding issues of ethnic inequality, both generally and in relation to mental health. Such issues are part of our shared history and culture, infused in interactions between individuals and groups. Consequently, the way such issues are understood reveals as much, if not more, about the individual holding the position, as about the issue itself. The question then becomes 'whose perspective will be accepted as the legitimate basis from which these issues will be understood?' Our position is that those directly affected by the issues at hand should be the principle source of how to frame how the issues will be understood. This means basing our understanding of racial discrimination on the views and perspectives of black people, and basing our understanding of racial disparity within mental health on the views/ perspectives of black service users. This is about more than establishing a frame of reference for understanding this issue. It is also about validating the views and experience of black service users, which in itself is the first step in challenging racial disparity.

This chapter has merely scratched the surface of debates about the origins of and responses to racial disparity in mental health. The politicised nature of such debates means that in all likelihood positions will continue to reflect broad differences between mental health professionals, policymakers, and those Black communities directly impacted by the way key issues are conceptualised and responded to. The real challenge, then, for all involved in the development and provision of mental health services, lies in deconstructing such distinctions, to establish a truly shared understanding of mental health.

REFERENCES

CQC (Care Quality Commission) (2011) *Count Me In 2010: Results of the 2010 National Census of Inpatients and Patients on Supervised Community Treatment in Mental Health and Learning Disability Services in England and Wales.* London: CQC.

DoH (Department of Health) (2005) *Delivering Race Equality in Mental Health Care: An Action Plan for Reform Inside and Outside Services and the Government's Response to the Death of David Bennett.* London: DoH.

Fearon, P. (2006) Incidence of Schizophrenia and Other Psychoses in Ethnic Minority Groups: Results from the MRC AESOP Study. Accessed at http://cambridge.academia.edu/JamesKirkbride/Papers/530023/Incidence_of_schizophrenia_and_other_psychoses_in_ethnic_minority_groups_results_from_the_MRC_AESOP_Study on 5 June 2012.

Fernando, S. (1996) 'Black people working in white situations: lessons from personal experience.' *Human Systems: The Journal of Systematic Consultation & Management 7*, 23, 143–154.

Fernando, S. (2003) *Cultural Diversity, Mental Health and Psychiatry: The Struggle Against Racism.* London: Routledge.

Guardian, The (2009) 'Schizophrenia "epidemic" among African Caribbeans spurs prevention policy change.' *Guardian Society*, p.3.

HM Government (2011) *No Health without Mental Health: A Cross-government Mental Health Outcomes Strategy for People of All Ages.* London: Department of Health.

Macpherson, W. (1999) *The Stephen Lawrence Inquiry.* London: HMSO.

NSCSTHA (Norfolk, Suffolk and Cambridgeshire Strategic Health Authority) (2003) *Independent Inquiry into the Death David Bennett.* NSCSTHA.

Sewell, H. (2009) 'Leading race equality in mental health.' *International Journal of Leadership in Public Services 5*, 2, 19–16.

Chapter 11

GENDER REASSIGNMENT

Scott Durairaj and Jourdan Durairaj

Neglecting people's human rights is bad for their health. In contrast,
the protection and promotion of their human rights is not only good
for individuals' health, it also makes better services for everyone.

(Department of Health (DoH) 2008a)

INTRODUCTION

This chapter explores the emotional and mental health needs and preferences of transsexual people using mental health services in the United Kingdom. This exploration is set against the relevant civil rights context, including the Equality Act 2010 definition of 'gender reassignment' as a 'protected characteristic' for the purposes of anti-discrimination. The chapter includes a discussion about labels and use of the more inclusive term 'trans'.

The aim is to provide the reader with essential information about trans-inclusive practice across the entire mental health pathway: prevention, assessment, diagnostics, care, treatment, rehabilitation and ongoing care. The chapter will be useful for all practitioners and managers working within mental health care settings and seeking to improve equality of access, experience and outcome for trans people.

This exploration includes putting 'gender reassignment' within a wider discussion about 'gender identity'. The chapter summarises some of the best available research evidence and policy drivers and guidance for adult mental health and social care policy.

DEFINING GENDER IDENTITY

The language surrounding gender reassignment has developed and evolved, just as it has in other protected characteristic areas such as race and disability.

A modern history

- Magnus Hirschfeld, a German physician and sex researcher, coined the term 'transvestite' (1910). He went on to found the *Institut für Sexualwissenschaft* (Institute for Sexual Science) in Berlin and supervised one of the first known operations for sex reassignment surgery. A contemporary definition of the term 'transvestite' was offered by the Equality and Human Rights Commission (EHRC) (2011a) as referring 'to people who wear, for short periods of time, the clothes associated with people of the opposite sex'.

- In 1949 David O. Cauldwell published an article, 'Psychopathia Transexualis', in the journal *Sexology* (1949), and is often wrongly credited with creating the term 'transexual'. However, Hirschfeld (1923) first used the term '*seelischer Transsexualismus* (psychic transsexualism)'.

- 'Gender dysphoria syndrome' as a published diagnostic term was popularised in 1973 (Fisk 1974).

- 'Trans' was a term 'adopted in the late 1990s by the UK Government, now commonly used by members of the UK cross dressing and transsexual community to refer to themselves' (Whittle, Turner and Al-Alami 2007, p.85).

- According to the Oxford English Dictionary, the first use of 'androgyne' was recorded in 1552, but it is only since around the year 2000 that people have claimed it for themselves to describe a state of being in-between, or having, both genders. 'Polygender' is a late 1990s Californian invention used to describe a state of having multiple genders (Whittle 2010).

In addition to the larger categories of transgender and transsexual, there is a wide range of gender expressions and identities that are contrary to the mainstream male–female binary. These include terms such as cross-dressers, drag queens, drag kings, transvestites, gender queer.

This is not an exhaustive list of words used by people to describe their sense of being or gender identity. Long before Hirschfeld coined the term 'transvestite' (1910), almost all cultures around the world had developed their own terminologies to describe 'trans' people. From the Hijra of India to the Fa'afafine of Polynesia and the Takatāpui of New Zealand, there are a myriad of words used by trans people to describe themselves (Whittle 2010).

'Gender reassignment' as a protected characteristic for a 'transsexual' person under the Equality Act 2010

The Equality Act came into force on 1 October 2010 and extends to transsexual people who have the protected characteristic of gender reassignment, the earlier legal protection from direct discrimination, indirect discrimination, gender reassignment discrimination, cases of absence from work, and harassment.

More generally this new 'protected characteristic' must be considered in connection by most public authorities in the UK (including government departments, health regulators and National Health Service (NHS) organisations) to exercise a general duty to have due regard to the need to advance equality of opportunity for transsexual persons as compared to those who are not transsexual.

Unlike previous equality law, the Act does not require a person to be under medical supervision to be protected from discrimination, but does require that a person is 'proposing to undergo, is undergoing or has undergone a process (or part of a process) for the purpose of reassigning the person's sex, by changing physiological or other attributes of sex' (s7, Equality Act 2010).

This non-medical definition emphasises a person's intent to reassign their gender identity; however, that intent is not irrevocable – for example, it may change as a result of psychiatric counselling; or the personal process may be indicated simply through manifestations such as mode of dress – for example, where a person is too young to make a final decision to reassign their sex (EHRC 2011b).

Some trans service users resident in the UK may not meet the broader criteria of the new definition because they have no intention to undergo gender reassignment. There are nonetheless some potential protections from discrimination provided for such people within the Equality Act 2010 and the European Convention on Human Rights.

Direct discrimination by association

Protection from direct discrimination by association benefit a person with a route to justice if they are treated less favourably by a mental health service because of their association with a 'transsexual' person.

BOX 11.1: ILLUSTRATION OF DISCRIMINATION BY ASSOCIATION

A carer with power of attorney for his transsexual life partner is excluded from participating in a decision to move his partner onto a single-sex ward that is discordant with his partner's gender identity. An attorney for a different, non-transsexual patient would always be involved in a decision to change accommodation. This is likely to be less favourable treatment ('direct discrimination') of the carer because of his association with his transsexual partner's 'gender reassignment', and the carer may be able to claim protection through the courts.

Direct discrimination by perception

Similarly there is protection from direct discrimination by perception, i.e. someone who is perceived to be 'transsexual' can claim protection.

BOX 11.2: ILLUSTRATION OF DISCRIMINATION BY PERCEPTION

A transvestite service user is asked by a member of staff to stop attending a regular support group because the other service users find 'transsexual' people offensive. The transvestite person may have no intention of reassigning their gender, but this type of exclusion could be interpreted as evidence of discrimination by perception. The person would be able to claim protection and have possible recourse to remedy through the courts.

Gender reassignment discrimination: cases of absence from work

Section 16 of the Equality Act 2010 introduced a new class of anti-discrimination protection for transsexual workers, called 'Gender reassignment discrimination: cases of absence from work'. This does not offer mental health service users any further legal protections against gender reassignment discrimination in the provision of mental health services, but it is important to recognise that the achievement of additional protections within the workplace may have an impact upon wider organisational culture. Colleagues working alongside a team member who is going through the transition process may increase their understanding of gender identity by osmosis and apply this new understanding within their practice.

A transsexual person is discriminated against if – in relation to their absence from work because of gender reassignment – they are treated less favourably by their employer than they would have been if either: (a) their absence had been due to sickness or injury, or (b) their absence had been for some other reason and it was not reasonable for them to be treated less favourably.

For example, a transsexual employee asks her manager if she can compress her hours and finish early every Friday once a fortnight for three months to attend a course of speech and language therapy. The manager refuses her request because he believes that since she is not actually sick or injured she is not entitled to flexible working. This would be gender reassignment discrimination.

Harassment

The scope of protection from harassment related to gender reassignment within a mental health service is far-reaching. There are three broad types of harassment: harassment related to gender reassignment; sexual harassment; and less favourable treatment of a service user or worker because they submit to, or reject, harassment related to gender reassignment.

BOX 11.3: ILLUSTRATION OF HARASSMENT RELATED TO GENDER REASSIGNMENT

Following on from the example of discrimination by association (see Box 11.1), a member of staff overhears the manager who made the discriminatory decision referring to the transsexual patient as a 'freak'. This language was unwanted behaviour related to gender reassignment, and the staff member feels it had the purpose or effect of violating the staff member's dignity and creating a hostile work environment. She may be able to obtain protection through the harassment provisions contained in s26(1) of the Equality Act, regardless of her own gender identity, and take a claim for harassment related to gender reassignment against her employer mental health organisation to an employment tribunal.

In the above example, a service user in the same area who also overhears the manager's comments could also take a claim for harassment related to gender reassignment, not an employment tribunal, but to the county court.

BOX 11.4: ILLUSTRATION OF LESS FAVOURABLE TREATMENT OF A SERVICE USER OR WORKER BECAUSE THEY SUBMIT TO, OR REJECT, HARASSMENT RELATED TO GENDER REASSIGNMENT

Following on from the example in Box 11.3 above, the patient's carer also overhears the transphobic remark made by the manager and immediately challenges her. Later that night, at home, the carer is telephoned and told that his partner has been waiting for some time and needs transport home. The carer is dismayed to discover that his partner has been discharged, which was not part of the plan discussed previously with the care team. The carer believes that because he rejected the manager's behaviour earlier in the day, his partner has been discharged without proper regard for his safety. The carer may have protection through s26(3) of the Equality Act 2010 and be able to make *another* claim against the mental health service provider.

Discrimination: Miscellaneous

It is unlawful for an employer to instruct, cause or induce a worker to discriminate, harass or victimise another person, or to attempt to do so. The person who is instructed, caused or induced to discriminate against a transsexual person can take a claim against the person giving the instruction if they suffer loss or harm as a result.

BOX 11.5: ILLUSTRATION OF INSTRUCTION TO DISCRIMINATE

Following on from the example in Box 11.1, a porter who is instructed to move a patient onto a single-sex ward against the patient's presentation refuses to do so. Later the porter is disciplined for failing to perform duties. The porter could bring a claim against the manager for instruction to discriminate because of gender reassignment.

Medical definitions

In the UK it is estimated that one in 4000 people is receiving medical help for gender dysphoria. However, there may be many more people with the condition who have yet to seek help. On average, men are diagnosed with gender dysphoria five times more often than women (*NHS Choices* 2010).

The term '*gender dysphoria*' is commonly used as a diagnosis by medical professionals to describe the discomfort that arises when the experience of oneself as a man or as a woman is incongruent with the sex characteristics of the body and the associated gender role. In transsexual people the discomfort is extreme, and they have to deal with it by transitioning, usually with medical assistance, to a gender role inconsistent with the sex assigned to them at birth. Transsexualism is not a lifestyle choice. A person has to be experiencing 'gender dysphoria' in order to obtain gender reassignment treatment in the NHS (EHRC 2011a).

The provision of gender reassignment services is relevant to a number of legal obligations that apply to public authorities under the Equality Act 2010 and the Human Rights Act 1998, and to the principles set out in the NHS Constitution.

The diagnosis of gender dysphoria is often misinterpreted as meaning that simply because of being transgender, a person suffers from *gender identity disorder* (GID), which is not the case. This has caused much confusion to transgender people and those who seek to either criticise or affirm them. Transgender people who are comfortable with their gender, whose gender does not directly cause inner frustration or impair their functioning, do not suffer from GID. Moreover, GID is not necessarily permanent, and is often resolved through therapy and/or transitioning. GID does not apply to people who simply feel oppressed by the negative attitudes and behaviours or others, including legal entities. (For the sake of comparison, racist institutions do not create a 'race disorder'.) Neither does GID imply an opinion of immorality; the psychological establishment holds the position that people with any kind of mental or emotional problem should not be stigmatised. The solution for GID is whatever will alleviate suffering and restore functionality; this often, but not always, consists of undergoing a gender transition (Brown and Rounsley 1996).

GID and disability

The EHRC states in the statutory code of practice for services:

> Where an individual has been diagnosed as having 'Gender Dysphoria' or 'Gender Identity Disorder' and the condition has a substantial and

long-term adverse effect on their ability to carry out normal day-to-day activities, they will also be protected under the disability discrimination provisions of the Act. (EHRC 2011, para. 2.25)

In practice this means that a person with gender dysphoria or GID might be able to bring any of the discrimination claims described above, but under the protected characteristic of disability. This opens up routes to justice by potentially allowing eligibility to bring claims under two disability-specific classes of contraventions of the Equality Act 2010:

- discrimination arising from disability

- failure to make reasonable adjustments.

The importance of the first class, discrimination, is that in bringing a claim, a person with GID would only need to show that they were treated unfavourably. There is no need for them to prove less favourable treatment compared to a non-disabled person. This is a lower threshold than a transsexual person would need to demonstrate, if they were to bring a direct discrimination claim because of their 'gender reassignment' protected characteristic, where a comparator would be necessary.

BOX 11.6: ILLUSTRATION OF DISCRIMINATION ARISING FROM DISABILITY

A receptionist prevents a person with GID from using a female-only toilet within a mental health unit because the person does not produce a copy of their Gender Recognition Certificate (GRC) when requested. The person could bring a claim saying that they were treated unfavourably, because failing to produce a GRC arose in consequence of the GID-related disability. There is no need for the person to demonstrate that their treatment was less favourable in comparison with a person who is not transsexual. In this example there may be additional criminal liability under contraventions of the Gender Recognition Act upon the person who shared the information with the receptionist in the first place, that the person even had a GRC.

A mental health service provider is able to justify certain types of discrimination arising from disability if they meet a very high legal threshold called 'objective justification'. However, the EHRC's statutory code of practice for services goes on to say: 'If a service provider has failed to make a reasonable adjustment which would have prevented or minimised the unfavourable treatment, it will be very difficult for them to show that the treatment was objectively justified' (EHRC 2011b).

This ties into the second disability-specific contravention, which is failure to make reasonable adjustments. There is no prohibition within the Equality Act against mental health service providers and employers treating disabled people *more* favourably than a non-disabled person (sometimes called 'positive discrimination'). Indeed, mental health service providers may be required to discriminate positively in favour of a disabled person as part of complying with a duty to make a 'reasonable adjustment' to allow them to overcome a substantial disadvantage (*Archibald v. Fife Council 2004*).

This means that mental health service providers should take reasonable steps, and provide alternative methods or auxiliary aids, to avoid a substantial disadvantage being experienced by a disabled person compared with a person who is not disabled.

BOX 11.7: ILLUSTRATION OF FAILURE TO COMPLY WITH A DUTY TO MAKE REASONABLE ADJUSTMENTS

A reasonable adjustment may mean that a patient with GID who is staying in an open single-sex dormitory is offered the opportunity to stay in a separate side-room. These types of discussion should be handled sensitively, respecting the dignity and privacy of the individual with GID, and conducted in compliance with the Data Protection Act 1998 and the Gender Recognition Act 2004.

Human rights definitions

The European Court of Human Rights has ruled that member states which are signatories to the European Convention on Human Rights (including the UK) are required to recognise legally the gender change of post-operative transsexuals (*L. v Lithuania 2007*). The Court stated in a previous case (*Christine Goodwin v. the United Kingdom 2002*):

> …the very essence of the Convention was respect for human dignity and human freedom. Under Article 8 of the Convention in particular, where the notion of personal autonomy was an important principle underlying the interpretation of its guarantees, protection was given to the personal sphere of each individual, including the right to establish details of their identity as individual human beings. In the twenty-first century the right of transsexuals to personal development and to physical and moral security in the full sense enjoyed by others in society could no longer

be regarded as a matter of controversy requiring the lapse of time to cast clearer light on the issues involved.

Within the convention document itself (Convention for the Protection of Human Rights and Fundamental Freedoms as amended by Protocols No. 11 and No. 14, 1950), Article 14 sets forth:

> The enjoyment of the rights and freedoms set forth in this Convention shall be secured without discrimination on any ground, such as sex, race, colour, language, religion, political or other opinion, national or social origin, association with a national minority, property, birth or other status.

This unlimited definition of grounds for discrimination in the enjoyment of the rights laid forth in the Convention by any and all trans people is in contrast to the approach within UK domestic law with the more limited definitions set forth within the Equality Act 2010.

GENDER IDENTITY AND HEALTHCARE

The discussion about gender identity in healthcare is not restricted to gender reassignment services only, as there are general and wider issues and concerns related to the provision and quality of care for trans people. For example, there are issues around gender-specific treatments such as mammograms and cervical smears, because post-operative females are not identifiable as such, even on cursory gynaecological examination (Ettner 2007). Another example concerns the medical risks associated with hormone use and smoking, which require attention because patients who smoke and take oestrogen face a significantly higher risk of thromboembolic complications than those who do not. The risk of polycythaemia (a blood condition) and polycythaemic stroke is also increased by androgen supplementation with concurrent smoking (Darby 2005). Gender reassignment services are, however, the priority health issue identified by most trans advocacy groups (EHRC 2011a).

Within a research project and report titled *Engendered Penalties* (Whittle *et al.* 2007) 42 per cent of trans people said that they were unable to go through the transition process at work, and therefore unable to comply with any specific requirement of the gender identity clinic. The report went on to report that 34 per cent of adult trans respondents reported having attempted suicide at least once as an adult.

The acknowledgement of differential access, experiences and outcomes for trans service users and patients is the first step towards developing individual practice and transforming mental health services. Care needs to be designed, provided and regularly reviewed to address disadvantage suffered by trans people, to meet needs related to gender identity and to encourage participation in activities where it is disproportionately low.

For services the next step might be to get a better sense of the local picture – for instance, by the introduction of voluntary monitoring of the gender identity of clients accessing services, to improve emotional well-being. This should be done in conjunction with local trans service users wherever possible, and will help to establish where disadvantage and discrimination might be occurring.

For individual nurses, doctors and therapists the next steps might be to consider how they can improve their own understanding of trans people's needs and how this can be applied in practice. For example, the sensitive and dignified assessment of service users' gender identity may improve the delivery of their care and help ensure their safety whilst in care.

Sharing 'protected information'

Under s22 of the Gender Recognition Act 2004 it was made an offence to disclose 'protected information' regarding (a) someone's application for a GRC or (b) his or her gender before a GRC was granted. The offence only occurs if one of a number of exclusions does not apply, including if the person agrees to the information being shared, or if the information does not make it possible to identify that person. If it is necessary for professionals to know someone's gender identity, then it is recommended that the trans person be asked to provide permission in writing.

Anyone who, in their professional capacity, acquires knowledge of a transsexual person's gender history and knows, or is able to surmise, that the person has a GRC or new birth certificate, and passes on that information to a third party without the consent of the person concerned, and for any reason apart from the exceptions above, can be prosecuted and fined up to £5000 and/or be jailed for up to six months (Gender Recognition Act 2004).

Disclosure for medical purposes

The Gender Recognition Act was later amended to include further limitations of the offence for those disclosing 'protected information' for certain medical purposes:

1. It is not an offence under section 22 of the Act to disclose protected information if:

- the disclosure is made to a health professional;

- the disclosure is made for medical purposes; and

- the person making the disclosure reasonably believes that the subject has given consent to the disclosure or cannot give such consent.

2. 'Medical purposes' includes the purposes of preventative medicine, medical diagnosis and the provision of care and treatment.

3. 'Health professional' means any of the following:

   - a registered medical practitioner;

   - a registered dentist within the meaning of section 53 (1) of the Dentists Act 1984 (1);

   - a registered pharmaceutical chemist within the meaning of section 24 (1) of the Pharmacy Act 1954 (2) or a registered person within the meaning of article 2 (2) of the Pharmacy (Northern Ireland) Order 1976 (3);

   - a registered nurse;

   - a person who is registered under the Health Professions Order 2001 (4) as a paramedic or operating department practitioner;

   - a person working lawfully in a trainee capacity in any of the professions specified in this paragraph.

(The Gender Recognition Act (Disclosure of Information) (England, Wales and Northern Ireland) Order 2005; Crown copyright 2005)

The process for changing a patient's gender within the Personal Demographic Service (PDS) – the national electronic database of NHS patient demographic details – is handled by the patient's general practitioner (GP) or primary care trust with a request to the PDS National Back Office. A new NHS number is generated for the person, with the old number withdrawn from use (National Information Governance Board for Health and Social Care 2011).

Gender identity monitoring

The issue of gender identity monitoring is a rather contentious one, in that there is not one single preferred way to record gender recognition in

NHS services. The Department of Health has not yet published a standard within the NHS Data Model. There are commonly two main methods being used in practice to ask questions on patient equality monitoring forms or computer systems – *either*:

- Are you the gender that you were assigned at birth? *or*

- Are you now or have you ever considered yourself as trans?

The problem in both cases is that in the rush to monitor, mental health services are not necessarily giving adequate consideration to the reason why they are monitoring, and how that information will be used to improve the care they are providing. Mental health services should not collect any information about service users' protected characteristics if they only intend to report it *without* considering whether there needs to be a development plan to address any patterns or trends indicating discrimination, disadvantage or lack of equality of opportunity for transsexual people. A person's gender identity is a key determinant of the way they need services to be delivered to them and their care to be provided sensitively.

A trans person choosing or accessing a service needs to be assured of dignity in care and treatment from day one. The monitoring of gender identity should lead to improved treatment and experience, and could lead to enhanced clinical safety outcomes for individuals – for example, reducing the risk of misdiagnosis by considering the side effects of hormone treatment, or interpreting diagnostics and the metabolism of drugs using sex-based test markers.

There is a requirement, formed originally under the Gender Reassignment Regulations 1999, for individuals to live as a member of the acquired sex before going through surgical procedures. Living as a different gender will obviously include using single-sex facilities. The issue of when this will begin is something that needs to be decided by the individual and supported by the appointed advisor and those around him or her. This will involve open discussion, education and understanding. Trans people (like everyone else in Britain) can use toilets or changing facilities appropriate to their gender presentation, with or without a GRC. (Usually it is acceptable in a work or health setting to do this on presentation of a letter from a GP or gender specialist confirming that the individual is undergoing gender reassignment with the intention of living permanently in the new gender.) As mentioned previously, people are protected by the Equality Act 2010 as soon as they start the gender reassignment process.

The Durairajs' top recommendations
for improving practice

1. Provide care to trans people with respect for their dignity. Like everyone else, trans people have individual care needs and preferences shaped by a very broad range of different experiences and social influences. Trans patients, service users and visitors just want a friendly and comforting experience while in care.

2. Make waiting areas and clinical areas trans-friendly. Display information about the standards of care equality that trans people are entitled to. Update patient, visitor and health promotion information to include advocacy and support groups, local or national.

3. Identify and record patient name, title and preferred form of address on their documentation during booking or initial assessment, e.g. Mr, Mrs, Miss, Ms, other, or none. Refer to supporting care passports, such as 'This is Me' for dementia patients, where this information may already be recorded.

4. Accommodate trans people according to their presentation: the way they dress, and the name and pronouns that they use. Differences in sex characteristics, e.g. genitals, chest, larynx ('Adam's apple'), should be disregarded. It is good practice, in agreement with an individual, to maintain their privacy and dignity, to offer accommodation in side-rooms. However, this should not be used to segregate trans people.

5. Remember that being trans is not a mental health condition. The experience of transphobic prejudice, discrimination and related isolation, as well as knock-on social factors such as poor housing and low income, may be contributory factors towards developing mental health conditions.

6. Trans people who spend prolonged periods within mental health services need their physical health needs met. Appropriate access to care will need to be provided, e.g. endocrinological emergencies or cancer screening. It is good practice to seek consent before sharing a person's gender history with another medical professional for medical reasons, including between referring agencies.

7. Unless requested, do not comment on a trans person's appearance and consequent ability to pass in their gender identity.

8. Trans people, like everyone, can have a wide range of attractions and sexual orientation: heterosexual, lesbian, gay or bisexual. For many these 'labels' about their identity are fixed points on a wider social spectrum, which has varied at different stages during their life and/or transition.

9. Avoid using terms such as 'disorder' or 'choice'. People who transition align their biological sex towards their true gender identity. There is no 'choice' in that gender identity; they are not changing the gender they want to be.

10. Raise awareness about trans people's experiences and needs in relation to your service. Commission or engage local trans people within your service's patient surveys and involve them within relevant clinical audits and research areas.

11. Include trans people within staff learning and development. Deconstructing trans stereotypes and misconceptions will help reduce prejudice and promote understanding.

12. Update your skills to effectively challenge transphobia, and update your knowledge of your employer's procedures to handle transphobic complaints and incidents.

ANNEX A
DISCUSSION OF TERMINOLOGY USED BY THE EHRC
Trans and transgender

The terms 'trans people' and 'transgender people' are often used as umbrella terms for people whose gender identity and/or gender expression differs from their birth sex, including transsexual people (those who intend to undergo, are undergoing or have undergone a process enabling them to live permanently in their acquired gender). Other self-descriptions include androgyne, polygender, pangender or gender queer. 'Gender variant' is also a widely used term to cover any gender expression that is not typical, and in particular it is used for young people who may not ultimately undertake gender reassignment.

Whittle, Turner and Al-Alami (2007) note that 'trans' is an inclusive term 'adopted in the late 1990s by the UK Government, now commonly used by members of the UK cross-dressing and transsexual community to refer to themselves' (p.85). The term 'transgender' is also widely used to denote this population. Whittle *et al.* (2007) state that 'transgender' is:

> a very broad term to include all sorts of trans people. It includes cross-dressers, people who wear a mix of clothing, people with a dual or no gender identity, and transsexual people. It is also used to define a political and social community which is inclusive of transsexual people, transgender people, cross-dressers (transvestites), and other groups of 'gender-variant' people'. (p.85)

Non-gendered people may prefer not to be considered under the 'trans' umbrella. The trans community is also subject to common myths and confusion around sexual orientation and gender identity – for example, that trans people are mostly lesbian, gay or bisexual, which is not the case. As with the general population, there is a variety of sexual orientation across the heterosexual, lesbian, gay and bisexual spectrum.

Transsexual

The term 'transsexual' is used to describe people who seek gender reassignment treatment, which may include gender constructive surgery. Transsexual people generally identify with the opposite sex from a young age (Fish 2007b). Most people who have transitioned permanently regard themselves, and wish to be regarded by others, as men and women (Burns, for the DoH 2008b). Such people may consider themselves for all intents and purposes to be members of that gender and not transsexual, a fact recognised by the Gender Recognition Act 2004. Where reference to a past gender role is unavoidable, the term 'man or woman of transsexual history' is sometimes used.

Gender dysphoria

'Gender dysphoria' is the term that is often used to describe the extreme discomfort that arises when the experience of oneself as a man or as a woman – that is, 'gender identity' – is incongruent with the sex characteristics of the body (phenotype) and with the gender role (the social role) typically associated with that phenotype. Whittle *et al.* (2007, p.86) state that this is 'the term used by psychiatrists and psychologists to describe the condition transsexual people have – that is, not feeling well or happy with their gender as assigned at birth, in terms of both their social role and their body'. A 'diagnosis' of gender dysphoria is required before gender reassignment treatment.

Transvestite or cross-dresser

These terms refer to people who wear, for short periods of time, the clothes associated with people of the opposite sex. Some may do this because they identify with the opposite sex, and may decide to transition full-time at some point. Others may cross-dress for a variety of reasons but wish to remain within their natal sex.

Male-to-Female (MtF) and Female-to-Male (FtM)

Alternative terms for MtF and FtM are (but are not always considered polite) 'trans woman' and 'trans man' respectively. These are used to describe the direction of the person's 'transition', which marks the stage when trans individuals start to live in the gender role that accords with their innate gender identity. There is disagreement over whom these terms include. Whittle *et al.* (2007) and Aston and Laird (2003) apply them to all trans people, but Fish (2007b) appears to apply them more specifically to transsexual people.

Intersex conditions

There are a number of intersex conditions (recently renamed disorders of sex development), some of which lead to physical genital anomalies. Those born with them may experience inconsistency between their gender identity and the gender role assigned at birth. The developmental anomalies that fall under the intersex umbrella may be associated with atypical sex chromosomes, as in Klinefelter syndrome (XXY) or Jacob's syndrome (XYY), or mosaicism (a mix of chromosome configurations) or other genetic anomalies, such as androgen insensitivity syndrome or congenital adrenal hyperplasia, in which unusual hormone levels are present in the foetus (Gender Identity Research and Education Society (GIRES) 2011).

REFERENCES

Archibald v. Fife Council [2004] IRLR 651, 2004 GWD 23-505, [2004] UKHL 32, [2004] ICR 954, 2004 SLT 942, [2004] 4 All ER 303 (House of Lords 2004).

Aston, L. and Laird, N. (2003) *Participatory Appraisal Transgender Research.* London: Stonewall.

Christine Goodwin v. the United Kingdom, Application Number 28957/95 (European Court of Human Rights July 11, 2002).

Brown, M.L. and Rounsley, C.A. (1996) *True Selves – Understanding Transsexualism.* San Francisco, CA: Jossey-Bass.

Cauldwell, D.O. (1949) 'Psychopathia Transexualis.' *Sexology 16,* 274–280.

DoH (Department of Health) (2008a) *Human Rights in Healthcare: A Framework for Local Action. Second edition.* London: DoH.

DoH (2008b) *Trans: A Practical Guide for the NHS.* London: DoH.

EHRC (Equality and Human Rights Commission) (2011a) *A Review of Access to NHS Gender Reassignment Services (England Only).* London: EHRC.

EHRC (2011b) *Services, Public Functions and Associations Statutory Code of Practice.* London: EHRC.

Ettner, R. (2007). *Principles of Transgender Medicine and Surgery.* London: Routledge.

Fish, J. (2007) *Trans People's Health, Briefing II.* Gender Identity Advisory Group, London: Department of Health.

Fisk, M.N. (1974) 'Gender Dysphoria Syndrome: the conceptualization that liberalizes indications for total gender reorientation and implies a broadly based multi-dimensional rehabilitative regimen.' *Western Journal of Medicine 120,* 5, 386–390.

GIRES (Gender Identity Research and Education Society) (2011) Collecting Information on Gender Identity. Accessed at www.gires.org.uk/assets/workplace/CollectingInfo. pdf.

Hirschfeld, M. (1910) *Die Transvestiten: Eine Untersuchung über den erotischen Verkleidungstrieb, mit umfangreichem kasuistischem und historischem Material.* Berlin: Alfred Pulvermacher.

Hirschfeld, M. (1923) 'Die intersexuelle Konstitution.' *Jarhbuch fuer sexuelle Zwischenstufen,* 3–27.

L. v Lithuania, Application 27527/03 (European Court of Human Rights September 11, 2007).

NHS Choices (2010) *Gender dysphoria.* 28 April.

National Information Governance Board for Health and Social Care (2011) *Advice: Process for Changing Name and Gender in Primary Care.*

Whittle, S. (2010) 'A brief history of transgender issues.' *The Guardian,* 2 June. Accessed at www.guardian.co.uk/lifeandstyle/2010/jun/02/brief-history-transgender-issues on 29 May 2012.

Whittle, S., Turner, L. and Al-Alami, M. (2007) *Engendered Penalties: Transgender and Transsexual People's Experiences of Inequality and Discrimination.* London: The Equalities Review.

Chapter 12

SPIRITUALITY AND EQUALITIES

Peter D. Gilbert

INTRODUCTION

This chapter highlights the potential inequalities that arise in mental health services in relation to religion and belief, as defined within the Equality Act 2010. Potential solutions are considered, within the context of national policy, guidance and best practice.

RELIGION, BELIEF AND SPIRITUALITY IN MENTAL HEALTH

Religion, belief and spirituality can be seen as having particular relevance for mental health service users as people search for meaning in their experiences. As Cook, Powell and Sims (2009) state:

> ... the spiritual perspective reminds us that 'negotiating terms' with pain and suffering is a universal and primarily spiritual task for human beings, which offers evidence of spiritual health, not psychopathology. (p.xiii)

Chapter 1 set out the definitions, within the Equality Act 2010, of 'religion and belief' and explains (with reference to explanatory guidance) the protections afforded to this characteristic. The definitions of religion (requiring a structure and belief system) and the inclusion of philosophical beliefs are inclusive, despite the strict criteria determining their coverage by the Act.

Many attempts have been made to define spirituality. The Royal College of Psychiatrists defines spirituality as:

> a distinctive, potentially creative and universal dimension of human experience arising both within the inner subjective awareness of individuals and within communities, social groups and traditions. (Cook *et al.* 2009, p.4)

The spiritual dimension, in harmony with mind, heart and body, strives to reach out beyond the material world to values which encompass a relationship and a responsibility for the human condition, the natural world and a sense of the transcendent and supernatural. Spirituality has to do with meaning, the significance of life, and how we make sense of life situations, especially in a crisis. It is about people's inner motivating force and sense of value and values, and how people travel forward in this world; and for some people a connection with an afterlife. Genuine spirituality cannot be a purely '*me*' perspective; it must be experienced through relationships, and comes to the fore, perhaps most powerfully, at times of loss and challenge.

Inequalities in mental health that emerge in relation to religion and belief may arise through:

- discrimination against people holding religious or other beliefs

- a failure to fully take account of religious or other beliefs or the spirituality of people in services

- assumptions made about people, based on stated or perceived religion or belief and the consequent erosion of a person-centred approach.

There are other important considerations in relation to religion and belief in mental health that fall outside of the scope of this chapter – for example, the possibility that people extend the precepts of their faith to the point that they cause themselves physical harm (e.g. fasting to a point that causes serious ill-health).

EVIDENCE AND EXPERIENCE

The 'Count Me In' annual census of inpatients revealed that over 60 per cent of inpatient service users stated that they had a religion (Care Quality Commission (CQC) 2010).

A significant number of service users and carers have said that, in the field of mental health, their spiritual dimension, whether related to a religious faith or not, is of vital importance to their recovery (see Cook *et al.* 2009; Gilbert 2007, 2011). If spirituality is partly about connection to oneself, to other people, to nature and to some sense of 'the other' (God, the cosmos), then mental health services need to respond to what Sacks (2011) describes as our universal human condition, and also to our uniqueness as individuals. The challenge, for some facets of organised religion, is also to recognise a person's individuality, which may encounter problems with some of the institutional responses; and for a person whose spirituality is highly individualistic, the challenge is more to do with how they connect as a 'social animal' with other people and the community around them. Census surveys such as 'Count Me In' demonstrate that more people from diverse ethnic backgrounds find religious beliefs an essential element of their mental well-being (HM Government 2011, para. 6.36/7 and Sewell 2011, p.141). Research demonstrates that a nation's mental health is directly related to levels of societal inequality (see Wilkinson and Pickett 2009, and Sewell 2009).

BOX 12.1: A PERSONAL STORY (CONTRIBUTED BY TRACEY HOLLEY)

My 'religion' is spirituality, which equates to companionship, love and friendship, nature, genius of place, self-acceptance and mindfulness, my work to keep humanity within professionalism – all give me hope.

For me, Spirituality infuses all our beings. We may not be aware of it at a conscious level, or we may even be in denial about it. But for me the bottom line is that we are all Spiritual Beings – it is the very root and essence of our existence...

Three is a magic number. For me the 'holy trinity' consists of mind, body and soul. Or nature, place and people, i.e. humanity.

I needed someone to guide me through the fog of despair and self-doubt to find out that life still was meaningful. I had closed the door of life and entered into a dark place. The 'Light of the World' gently knocked at the threshold of my soul and lit up those dark days with a lantern of hope – those professionals who believed in me did more than ease my troubled mind; they gently rocked my soul awake.

I found the faith and strength in myself via those emotionally capable professionals who showed me they had faith and belief in me – those temporary custodians of hope. They have even been temporary custodians of my soul – their intervention of humanity was that powerful.

Such human intervention using a recovery approach would have *helped find out what is meaningful to me much more quickly*.

This, combined with occupational therapy intervention, was needed, from day one.

I did not get someone to push open that door of self-imprisonment and to come into my home to help me in structuring my day – morning, noon and night and everything in between, i.e. the grey areas of time and space, like the area between joy and sadness. I am thankful that my therapist helped me with the latter.

But I needed a humane professional to encourage me out of my physical prison, my home, and to rediscover the great outdoors *with* them. I needed them to cross the physical threshold of my home so that they could then see me as a person, and so make a connection with me on a human level and literally 'lift my spirits' and faith in humanity.

'Holy communion' for me involves communing with people, (companionship); with certain architecture and with music, particularly when they play to the aesthetics of the soul, with nature and with my man [Tracey's partner].

The communion of people apart from my significant others (especially professional health practitioners) is just as important for my recovery. Very few connected with me and saw the problem – diagnosis only. I needed to accept me, so it was vital others did. Those who did believed in me when I didn't. They gave me *hope*, and still do. They were my temporary custodians of hope.

My spirituality = accepting who I am (including my own vulnerability), and discovering the compassionate self, through the compassion of others – and unexpectedly becoming more understanding of people who seem angry and resentful, given that everyone expresses despair in their own way.

Tracey Holley is a mental health survivor and freelance consultant. My thanks to Tracey for the narrative of her personal journey.

'WHO DO YOU THINK YOU ARE?' PERSONALISED MENTAL HEALTH CARE, SPIRITUALITY AND IDENTITY

Professor Kamlesh Patel, Chief Executive Officer of the former Mental Health Act Commission, stated:

> If you don't know who I am, how are you going to provide a package of care for me to deliver something? When you do not know how important my religion is to me, what language I speak, where I am coming from, how are you going to help me cope with my mental illness? And that is what I am trying to get over to people; the first step is about *identity*. It is absolutely fundamental to the package of care we offer an individual. (Mulholland 2005, p.5, quoted in Gilbert 2011, p.35; emphasis added)

This statement should perhaps appear on the front of every assessment form.

Knowing oneself can, however, sometimes be elusive.

BOX 12.2: AUTHOR'S PERSONAL STORY

Following an intensive social work qualification course, I went, several years later, on a residential course studying the enneagram, a psychological programme approach adapted from Sufism (Hampson 2005) – and was intrigued to find that there were aspects of my personality that I really didn't understand at all. Again, when I experienced a serious episode of mental illness in 2000–2001 (see Basset and Stickley 2010, Chapter 9) it changed me radically, though not so as to change my fundamental identity. To understand it I came up with the phrase 'travelling identity', to try to describe the pilgrimage that we journey on, which is fundamental to who we are.

Being aware of the impact of spirituality on identity can enable practitioners more readily to appreciate the spiritual aspect in the lives of service users with whom they work.

EXERCISE 12.1: WHO DO YOU THINK YOU ARE?

Please take some time to think through, or discuss with a friend or colleague, issues of identity and spirituality, and how these affect your work.

Social worker Zobia Arif has written of research that she undertook amongst first generation British-born Pakistani Muslims, and how the participants identified more with their religion, which traverses cultural and geographical boundaries, rather than from a purely ethnic stance (Arif 2011).

The recent position statement by the Royal College of Psychiatrists (RCPsych. 2011) states that whatever disagreements there might be around the definition of spirituality and religion, we are talking about the essential values and experiences of human beings. Therefore spiritual practices, whether within the framework of organised religion or more individualised spirituality, 'have the potential to influence a course of mental illness and attitudes towards people with mental illness, for good or ill' (p.5).

Tracey Holley's vivid description of her spirituality (in Box 12.1) captures both of these aspects.

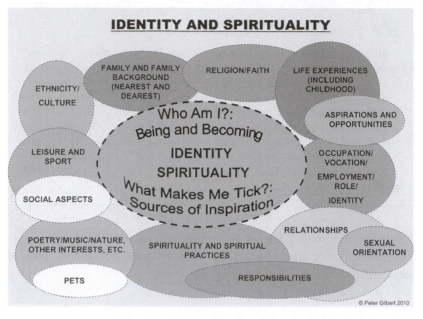

Figure 12.1: Identity and spirituality
Source: Gilbert 2008, p.9

POSITIVE ROLE OF RELIGION

Belonging to a faith community as part of an *organised religion* may bring additional advantages of:

- the feeling that a benevolent and more powerful entity is looking after one

- the provision of specific coping resources, not least through the signs, symbols, rituals and narratives which faith communities provide to give a framework and meaning for life

- the generation of positive emotions, e.g. love and forgiveness (this links strongly with the Foresight research of 2008)

- a sense of belonging

- a trust in God and in the faith community

- a sense of altruism towards others.

(Armstrong 2009; Koenig, McCullough and Larson 2001; Parkes with Gilbert 2010, 2011; RCPsych. 2011; and Sacks 2011)

Potentially negative aspects of religion

Clearly, organised religion also has its downside, in that it can be:

- over-controlling, and a 'straightjacket' rather than a 'framework'

- paternalistic, repressive and homophobic

- overly concerned with the needs of the organisation and not the individual or group.

(Carr 2011 and Gilbert 2011)

It is interesting that the philosopher Alain de Botton (2012), writing from an atheistic perspective, suggests that human beings need some form of 'religion' to promote community harmony and combat selfish individualism, and also to help us cope with some of the pain inherent in human life.

The Department of Health in its 2009 policy statement *Religion or Belief* (DoH 2009), and an increasing number of statements from professional bodies, make it clear that 'religious and spiritual beliefs are powerful forces' (RCPsych. 2011, p.5). These, whether forces for good or impeding mental and physical heath, must be taken into account in assessment, treatment and ongoing care.

WORKING WITH PEOPLE TOWARDS SOLUTIONS

Not only is the spiritual dimension important to people who use services and to their informal carers, but it is now part of the policy imperative under the Human Rights Act and Equalities Act 2010 (see Chapter 1) and policy documents issued by Government (see Box 12.4.). Recent publications, focusing on the service user experience, have highlighted the importance of spirituality in the lives of people who use mental health services (e.g. Bassett and Stickley 2010).

BOX 12.4: NATIONAL POLICY – GUIDANCE AND KEY PUBLICATIONS ON SPIRITUALITY, RELIGION AND BELIEF

- Personalisation – through the White Paper *Our Health, Our Care, Our Say* (DoH 2006), the 2007 Commissioning Framework for Health and Well-being, *Putting People First* (December 2007), the Government concordat to transform adult social care and *Religion or Belief: A Practical Guide for the NHS* (2009).

- The need to meet the aspirations recorded by service users and carers in surveys, research and through inspection reports.

- The 2001 revised Patient's Charter (DoH 2010) states that NHS staff will respect your privacy and dignity. 'They will be sensitive to and respect your religious, spiritual and cultural needs at all times' (p.29).

- Clear evidence from research that membership of faith communities can improve physical and mental health. (e.g. Koenig *et al.* 2001).

- The importance of ethnicity and of faith in individual and group identity (Mulholland 2005). Note: university research (Wohland *et al.* 2010) indicates a rise of ethnic diversity from 8 per cent in 2010 to 20 per cent in 2051.

- Increased cost–benefit analysis achieved through working with the motivations of individual service users, carers and community groups (Gilbert and Parkes 2011; Parkes with Gilbert 2011).

- The recovery approach, as set out in (for example) the Care Services Improvment Partnership (CSIP)/RCPsych/Social Care Institute for Excellence (SCIE) document of 2007. Links with the Royal College of Psychiatrists' policy paper on spirituality (RCPsych. 2011).

- The need for health and social care to be sensitive to user, carer and staff belief systems (DoH 2009). Links across to Scottish guidance (The Scottish Government 2009).

DEVELOPING THE WORKFORCE

The National Spirituality and Mental Health Forum (see Coyte 2011) has been working with mental health trusts across England and has found considerable recognition among staff concerning the importance of the spiritual dimension, but a concomitant uncertainty as to how to recognise spiritual strengths and meet spiritual needs (see Parkes and Gilbert 2011; Parkes, Milner and Gilbert 2010). In this uncertainty the role of the spiritual and pastoral care/chaplaincy team will be of vital importance. This is primarily a consultancy, training and coordination role, as well as providing direct pastoral care, so as to enable staff to have the confidence to respond appropriately to spiritual needs that are being articulated by a service user, and to offer specialist advice and referral where necessary (see Aris and Gilbert 2007; Raffay 2010).

Education for all staff should encapsulate recognition of the importance of a whole-person, whole-systems approach. Staff should also be equipped to identify how they themselves or others may be discriminating on the basis of religion or other beliefs (for example, through judgemental or pejorative language). The skills of mental health workers in tackling blatant discrimination may need to be employed in situations where there are verbal or physical attacks against service users or property on the basis of religion or belief.

For many people the interaction between their culture, spirituality and belief system will be complex, interactive and often changeable (see Figure 12.1).

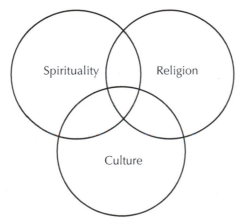

(Circle size and position varies for each individual)

Figure 12.2: The conceptual relationship between religion, spirituality and culture
Source: Parkes with Gilbert 2011, p.5

For staff to have the confidence to address this vital aspect of equality, they need to feel that they have support from their organisation. If the support is not forthcoming, then situations such as that described in the case study in Box 12.5 may well occur.

CASE STUDY 12.1: SERVICE RESPONSE TO SERVICE USER WHO BELIEVES THEY ARE POSSESSED

A young South Asian woman was admitted to an acute ward. She was in great distress, and both medication and a period of restraint were used to calm her down and ensure her safety. During this period of distress she mentioned that she thought she might be possessed by a *jinn* (spirit).

Several of the nurses on the ward were from the same ethnic and cultural group as the young service user, and later the chaplain asked them whether they thought that she was experiencing a period of 'spiritual distress'. The nursing staff agreed that they felt she was, and that they had not responded in a way that addressed her spiritual needs. But they were concerned that a more spiritual approach might not have been viewed favourably by the organisation if they had attempted it.

(Gilbert 2008)

INFORMED PRACTICE

For people in touch with mental health services over the longer term, it may be appropriate for a spiritual history to be taken (see Culliford 2007), but in the first instance, most important may be to ask a simple but vital question, such as: 'What is important to you?' Responses to this might vary, including personal relationships, family, religion, nature, exercise, art, pets, etc. No single answer to such a question can be in any sense definitive. Staff need to be continually thinking to themselves: 'What makes this person tick? What is the meaning and purpose of life for them?'

Very helpful commentaries are now available on assessing a person's spiritual needs (e.g. Eagger and McSherry with Gilbert and Wharmby 2011; McSherry and Ross 2010).

A number of assessment tools have been developed, but a cautionary note must be sounded, that merely importing a model from outside may not elicit ownership from service users, carers and staff within the service. Probably a sounder, long-term approach is to discuss forming of an approach that meets the needs of a specific service.

At the heart of assessment of spiritual strengths and needs is recognition of complementarity: that we all love as human beings and we need each other, but recognising our similarities and differences can be helpful.

CONCLUSION

Taking account of needs arising from religious or other beliefs, protected by the Equality Act 2010, enhances the experience of people who use services and increases the possibility of recovery. Getting to the heart of people's beliefs and their inner meaning and purpose – and the possible relationship between these and mental health problems – takes little more than the prime interviewing skill used in the caring professions: relating with openness and empathy.

REFERENCES

Arif, Z. (2011) 'Do we have faith in our practice?' *OpenMind, November and December,* pp.12–13.

Aris, S. and Gilbert, P. (2007) 'Organisational Health: Engaging the Heart of an Organisation.' In M.E. Coyte, P. Gilbert and V. Nichols (Eds) *Spirituality, Values and Mental Health: Jewels for the Journey.* London: Jessica Kingsley Publishers.

Armstrong, K. (2009) *The Case for God: What Religion Really Means.* London: The Bodley Head.

Basset, T. and Stickley, T. (Eds) (2010) *Voices of Experience: Narratives of Mental Health Survivors.* Chichester: Wiley-Blackwell.

Carr, S. (2011) 'Mental Health and the Sexual, Religious and Spiritual Identities of Lesbian, Gay, Bisexual and Transgender (LGBT) People.' In P. Gilbert (Ed.) *Spirituality and Mental Health.* Brighton: Pavilion.

CQC (Care Quality Commission) (2011) *Count Me In 2010 Census.* London: CQC.

CSIP (Care Services Improvement Partnership)/RCPsych. (Royal College of Psychiatrists)/ SCIE (Social Care Institute for Excellence) (2007) *A Common Purpose: Recovery in Future Mental Health Services. SCIE Position Paper 08.* London: SCIE.

Culliford, L. (2007) 'Taking a spiritual history.' *Advances in Psychiatric Treatment 13,* 212–219.

Cook, C., Powell, A. and Sims, A. (2009) *Spirituality and Psychiatry.* London: Royal College of Psychiatrists.

Coyte, M.E. (2011) 'Promoting spirituality in mental health.' *OpenMind, November/ December,* pp.20–21.

De Botton, A. (2012) *Religion for Atheists.* London: Hamish Hamilton.

DoH (Department of Health) (2006) *Our Health, Our Care, Our Say. Cm 6737.* London: DoH.

DoH (2009) *Religion or Belief: A Practical Guide for the NHS.* London: DoH.

DoH (2010) *The NHS Constitution for England, 2010: The NHS Belongs to Us.* London: DoH.

Eagger, S. and McSherry, W. with Gilbert, P. and Wharmby, S. (2011) 'Assessing a Person's Spiritual Needs in a Healthcare Setting.' In P. Gilbert (Ed.) *Spirituality and Mental Health.* Brighton: Pavilion.

Gilbert, P. (2007) 'The Spiritual Foundation: Awareness and Concepts for People's Lives Today.' In M.E. Coyte, P. Gilbert and V. Nichols (Eds) *Spirituality, Values and Mental Health: Jewels for the Journey.* London: Jessica Kingsley Publishers.

Gilbert, P. (2008) Guidelines on Spirituality for Staff in Acute Care Services. Leeds: National Institute for Mental Health in England/Care Services Improvement Partnership/Staffordshire University.

Gilbert, P. (Ed.) (2011) *Spirituality and Mental Health.* Brighton: Pavilion.

Gilbert, P. and Parkes, M. (2011) 'Faith in one city: exploring religion, spirituality and mental wellbeing in urban UK.' *Ethnicity and Inequality in Health and Social Care 4,* 1.

Hampson, M. (2005) *Head Versus Heart and Our Gut Reactions: The 21st Century Enneagram.* Hampshire: O-Books.

HM Government (2011) *No Health without Mental Health.* London: Department of Health.

Koenig, H.G., McCullough, N.E. and Larson, D.E. (2001) *Handbook of Religion and Health.* Oxford: Oxford University Press.

McSherry, W. and Ross, L. (Eds) (2010) *Spiritual Assessment in Healthcare Practice.* Keswick: M&K Publishing.

Mulholland, H. (2005) 'Counting on change.' *The Guardian,* 7 September.

Parkes, M. and Gilbert, P. (2010) 'Gods and Gudwaras: the Spiritual Care Programme at the Birmingham and Solihull Mental Health Foundation NHS Trust.' *Mental Health, Religion and Culture 13,* 6, September, 569–583.

Parkes, M. and Gilbert, P. (2011) 'Professionals calling: mental healthcare, staff attitudes to spiritual care.' *Implicit Religion 14,* 1, 23–45.

Parkes, M. with Gilbert, P. (2011) Report on the Place of Spirituality in Mental Health. London: NSMHForum. Accessed at www.mhspirituality.org.uk.

Parkes, M., Milner, K. and Gilbert, P. (2010) 'Vocation, vocation, vocation: spirituality for professionals in mental health services.' *The International Journal of Leadership in Public Services 6,* 3, September, 14–26.

Raffay, J. (2010) 'Training the workforce for spiritual care.' *Mental Health, Religion and Culture 13,* 6, September, 605–615.

RCPsych (Royal College of Psychiatrists) (2011) *Recommendations for Psychiatrists on Spirituality and Religions. Position statement PS03/2011.* London: RCPsych.

Sacks, J. (2011) *The Great Partnership: God, Science and the Search for Meaning.* London: Hodder & Stoughton.

Scottish Government, The (2009) *Confidence in Spiritual Care in the NHS in Scotland.* Edinburgh: The Scottish Government.

Sewell, H. (2009) *Working with Ethnicity, Race and Culture in Mental Health.* London: Jessica Kingsley Publishers.

Sewell, H. (2011) 'Ethnicity and Spirituality.' In P. Gilbert (Ed) *Spirituality and Mental Health.* Brighton: Pavilion.

Wilkinson, R. and Pickett, K. (2009) *The Spirit Level: Why More Equal Societies Almost Always Do Better.* London: Allen Lane.

Wohland, P., Rees, P., Norman, P., Boden, P. and Jasinka, M. (2010) *Ethnic Population Projections for the UK and Local Areas: 2001 to 2051.* Leeds: University of Leeds.

PART
III

ESSENTIAL CONSIDERATIONS

Chapter 13

THE PREVALENCE OF TRADITIONAL PSYCHIATRIC MODELS AND INHERENT DRIVERS OF INEQUALITY

Hári Sewell

INTRODUCTION

Increasingly the expressed needs and wishes of mental health service users are for services to take account fully of their identities and experiences (including experiences of discrimination). The evidence in Chapters 4 to 12 illustrates that a model of service that focuses on symptoms and cure rather than on the individual is likely to have particularly adverse implications for people from the groups protected by the Equality Act 2010. Traditional psychiatric models, based on the assumption of an illness with a biological cause, are more likely to have such a focus.

This chapter explores what is meant by 'traditional psychiatric models' and also examines the extent to which mental health services are shaped by the models of psychiatry that defined the profession for a century. Policies, and even new laws, have attempted to drive a shift away from a biological model towards a biopsychosocial model (McCulluch and Lawton-Smith 2012). Increasing attention is being given to recovery approaches in mental health service provision. This includes a focus on hope, capacities and strengths that people have (Repper and Perkins 2012).

There is not always consensus in literature about the extent to which the shifts in policy and political rhetoric have resulted in lived experiences of mental health services that are substantively different from those at a time when biological psychiatry was largely accepted within the profession.

WHAT IS MEANT BY 'TRADITIONAL PSYCHIATRIC MODELS'?

In this chapter the term 'traditional psychiatric models' is used to mean adherence to the original way in which mental health problems were conceptualised, diagnosed and treated, including professional relationships with service users and ultimately the system that supported these. It is possible to point to concrete changes in mental health services. Treatments have shifted from exorcisms, cold baths and straitjackets (Bentall 2003; Read, Mosher and Bentall 2004) to combined biological, psychological and social intervention (Tang 2012). The mental health inpatient estate has been significantly upgraded. Service users are invited to be co-signatories to their care plans, and individual budgets are available via social services. The initiative 'Improving Access to Psychological Therapies (IAPT)' has made therapy more widely available and has popularised the idea that people with mental health problems can have access to 'talking therapies'. These areas of progress certainly point to a departure from the old ways, but it is worth considering some key issues:

- whether the language, concepts and idioms from the foundations of psychiatry are still heard in current mental health services, and if so, how?

- the extent to which the positive changes are experienced by the majority of service users

- the extent to which the power balances between professionals and service users have fundamentally changed.

In analysing these points it is possible to draw conclusions about the extent to which traditional models still operate in current mental health services.

ARE THE LANGUAGE, CONCEPTS AND IDIOMS FROM THE FOUNDATIONS OF PSYCHIATRY STILL HEARD IN CURRENT MENTAL HEALTH SERVICES, AND IF SO, HOW?

The Greeks distilled mental health complexes into behavioural disturbances, mania and melancholia (Porter 2002). Bentall (2003) notes that Emil Kraepelin, the German psychiatrist (born 1856) is widely credited with being the central figure in the history of psychiatry. Bentall (2003) notes that Emil Kraepelin identified mental illnesses as being diseases of the brain, i.e. being physical in cause. He identified broad categories of mental illness, and although his position changed over time, he settled on psychosis, manic depressive illnesses (which he took to include all mood disorders) and paranoia (Bentall 2003).

It is striking that since the 1880s the ways in which atypical human behaviours are described has remained largely unchanged. Since those times there have been major advances in brain imaging that show the impact of external events (Bentall 2003); a greater understanding of the impact of trauma (Crawford, Nobles and Leary 2003); or child sexual abuse (Read *et al.* 2001; Spauwen *et al.* 2006); and knowledge about the increased risk of psychosis arising from the urban environment (Boydell and McKenzie 2008). In other words, the understanding of aetiology has developed remarkably, but conceptualisation of distress of the mind remains firmly that of an illness. This has serious consequences. Seeing a problem as an illness locates it under the aegis of the medical profession, and central to the response is psychopharmacology. Bentall (2009) and Mosher, Gosden and Beder (2004) highlight the exponential rise in the income of drug companies worldwide, the control they have over research into mental health problems, and their influence on the classification of mental illness (and the significant expansion in diagnostic categories). This means that, within the context of moves towards more social and psychological approaches in policy and practice, there is a powerful industry with vast financial resources funding research and influencing policies – and some would argue (e.g. Mosher *et al.* 2004) that this is a specific strategy to reinforce the idea of mental distress as a biological illness.

THE EXTENT TO WHICH THE POSITIVE CHANGES ARE EXPERIENCED BY THE MAJORITY OF SERVICE USERS

A good test of the extent to which service users are experiencing treatment and care that is beyond traditional psychiatry is to review the interventions that are received in the most clinical of settings (i.e. the inpatient environment). In the report into the use of the Mental Health Act 1983 (Amended), the Care Quality Commission (CQC 2011a) set out the percentage of patients who had participated in different activities during weekday office hours:

- Fifty-three per cent – talking groups

- Twenty-seven per cent – non-verbal therapy

- Fifty-two per cent – creative expression.

The report also included data on activities in the evenings and on weekends, and the percentages were significantly smaller (e.g. talking groups were seven per cent evenings, and five per cent on weekends).

It is possible to conclude that, although there is some significant uptake of psychological and social interventions, this is by no means the norm. The model of inpatient provision still appears to be a treatment-based regime as the default.

The CQC's national survey of community mental health services in 2011, which received responses from 17,000 service users (representing a 33% response rate) identified that 89 per cent had been on medication for their mental health problem. Eighty-seven per cent of people who had been prescribed medication in the last 12 months (i.e. a total of 14,949 respondents) said they were on medication for more than 12 months. Fifty-three per cent of respondents who saw a mental health worker (i.e. 16,710 respondents) said that their mental health worker had discussed talking therapy with them (39 per cent of those who saw a NHS mental health worker actually received therapy). A sub-cohort of 3656 service users who felt able to work were asked about the support they received, and 43 per cent said that they did not receive support in finding work, but would have liked this (CQC 2011b). These examples of findings represent an overall picture of a mental health service where medical interventions such as prescribing are apparently superordinate to psychological and social supports.

The payments by results (PbR) regime introduced into the National Health Service (NHS) has established a model of commissioning in which providers of services are financially rewarded for results achieved rather than for activity. In mental health services the framework for deciding tariffs uses 'care clusters' – categories into which service users are allocated, based on symptoms or associated need rather than diagnosis (Jobbins 2012). Despite the assertion that the categories are not based on diagnosis, the decision-making tree of 20 clusters uses language that draws on diagnostic categories. The Department of Heath clustering tool includes categories such as psychosis, affective disorder, dementia and depression. At the top of the tree (the so-called super-clusters) are psychotic, non-psychotic and organic (DoH 2012). Mental health services nationally are being structured around the care clusters to enable the PbR model to be operated – and rather than moving away from a traditional psychiatric model, care clustering entrenches the idea that people can be described as belonging to a category defined by symptoms. As Perkins states:

> personal strengths, goals, social circumstances, activities, values, beliefs, etc., are considered only in so far as they inform decisions about diagnosis, treatment, support and prognosis. (Perkins 2012, p.15)

THE EXTENT TO WHICH THE POWER BALANCES BETWEEN PROFESSIONALS AND SERVICE USERS HAVE FUNDAMENTALLY CHANGED

Policymakers and services have increasingly, over time, articulated a wish to see people who use services have a greater say in their treatment and care. The extent to which this is being achieved is measured in the CQC's national survey of community mental health patients. The findings of the 2011 survey show that 56 per cent of respondents stated that their views were definitely taken into account in deciding which medicine to take. A further 31 per cent said 'to some extent' (CQC 2011b). Interpreting this can be problematic because the way in which respondents make sense of 'taken into account' might not be clear. They may, for example, have interpreted this to mean that their wishes prevailed. As for the response 'to some extent', it may not be unusual for respondents in any health sector to rate their involvement in the prescribing process in this way. This highlights an issue worth considering. The model of relationship still remains that of the expert doctor and the patient.

The same survey asked about whether service users' views were taken into account in deciding the content of their care plan. Fifty-four per cent said definitely (CQC 2011b). That figure is telling, in that the concept of involvement in the care plan still maintains a model of service users being involved in something which is in the ownership of the service (Perkins 2012). Even with the conservative model of involvement, only 54 per cent of the 10,399 responses to that particular question indicated that service users felt their views were definitely taken into account.

There may be an incremental shift along a continuum from lesser to greater involvement in treatment and care, but the normal construct is still one of expert services and grateful patients. As Perkins (2012, p.17) states: '…professionals define the patient's reality in terms that their profession has invented…' The goal should be to move away from professionals authoring the stories of people's lives, to the person and professionals working alongside each other (Bracken and Thomas 2005).

EQUALITIES AND THE PREVALENCE OF THE TRADITIONAL MODEL OF PSYCHIATRY

Chapters 4 to 12 highlight inequalities affecting people from groups with protected characteristics. Mental health services routinely lead to poorer outcomes for these groups, and there are raised levels of service uptake for many. Current models used within the mental health system contribute to the higher rates of detention, and higher rates of diagnosis of psychotic disorders among certain groups of black people (CQC 2011c). There is a strong association between childhood sexual abuse and high levels of use of mental health services (Phillips and Jackson 2012). Suicide and self-harm is greater for people who are lesbian, gay and bisexual (see Chapter 9). People in urban areas with lower socioeconomic status are over-represented in mental health services (Boydell and McKenzie 2008). Exposure to repeated discrimination (e.g. for reasons to do with sex, race, sexuality, age) is associated with developing serious mental health problems (Myin-Germeys and van Os 2008).

Research that considers social factors often refers, for example, to susceptibility to developing mental health problems as a result of biogenetic factors. This stress vulnerability approach locates an initial problem within the individual (Myin-Germeys and van Os 2008). It is a means of answering the question as to why not all people who are exposed to the same social factors and early life influences develop a mental health problem similarly. This kind of approach is rooted in what Rapley, Moncrieff and Dillon (2011, p.8) describe as 'the contemporary mythology of interiorized, individualized mental pathology'.

The main problem with the interiorised, medicalised approach to mental health is the decoupling of experiences from resultant behaviours. Psychiatry's way of conceptualising mental distress and constructing a treatment system that disproportionately captures 'vulnerable groups' (Mgutshini 2012) is worthy of interrogation. There is now an extensive body of literature that critiques the utility of viewing madness as an illness (e.g. Bentall 2003; Bracken and Thomas 2005; Foucault 2009; Rapley *et al.* 2011).

The groups covered by the Equality Act 2010 and identified as having protected characteristics are defined in this way precisely because The Equalities Review (2007) considered an extensive body of research that highlighted the inequalities they faced. These inequalities are often manifested as discrimination, stigma, unfair treatment and, in worst case scenarios, traumatic events or series of events. Reviews of service user narratives identify 'insights of disempowering and depersonalizing experiences which often leave affected individuals feeling upset, devalued and helpless within a medically dominated system' (Mgutshini 2012, p.72) – this despite a mental health system that believes itself to be progressive and engaging in approaches that recognise whole people rather than just symptoms.

In reality people who have faced trauma or other negative life and social experiences are treated within a mental health system which mental health system which pathologises them. Workers in mental health services are reported as being stigmatising (Office of the Deputy Prime Minister (ODPM) 2004), and being a user of mental health services is stigmatising in wider society. Johnstone (2011) writes about the category error of asking the question as to whether certain traumas cause psychosis. For example, she suggests a more helpful approach to questioning, such as 'Can traumatic events traumatize people?' (2011, p.109). According to various critiques and reviews of service user experiences, traditional models of psychiatry do not see the experiences in people's lives as being central. In the search for symptoms and reinforcers of diagnosis, the person's narrative is lost, and this is particularly detrimental to people from groups with protected characteristics, because their life is often one imbued with the kinds of social circumstances and experiences that are associated with high levels of service use or poorer outcomes.

CASE STUDY 13.1: THE SEARCH FOR SYMPTOMS TAKES PRIORITY OVER THE SEARCH FOR MEANING

Becky was picked up by the police in her local supermarket, shopping naked. She was assessed in the police station by a doctor and a further assessment under the Mental Health Act 1983 (Amended) was arranged, to see whether she needed to be detained in a psychiatric hospital. During the first assessment the doctor noticed scars from superficial lacerations to Becky's wrists. Her GP had no record of self-harm, but during the assessment the doctors and approved mental health professional asked about how the wounds had occurred. Becky stated that they were scratches from her friend's cat.

Becky had her first admission to psychiatric hospital for assessment. She was given a diagnosis of psychotic breakdown, partly because of the inner voices that she was disturbed by, noted as delusions by the clinical team. During Becky's admission professionals on the ward tried to talk about her life and the scarring. One nurse noted in the records that she suspected possible childhood sexual abuse; however, intrusive voices that Becky was hearing made conversations difficult and the priority was to stabilise her illness.

When Becky was discharged she was keen to move away from her local area because she was embarrassed about having gone shopping naked. She resigned from her job on the front desk at her local council, as she knew visitors would recognise her and she was already under investigation for a poor attendance record. The community mental health team offered support with obtaining accommodation through the council, assistance with securing state benefits, and referral to a job club to explore options for part-time work.

Becky had two more breakdowns within four months of her first discharge and she received care under the crisis team. The team believed that the upheaval in Becky's life (work, accommodation) was triggering further breakdowns and making her illness problematic and entrenched. Her diagnosis was changed to schizophrenia. As more details of Becky's life emerged during her treatment and care it became apparent that she had been the victim of sustained sexual abuse between the ages of 9 and 16 – perpetrated by her father, uncle and their drinking partners. Professionals in the community mental health team believed that this was critical in understanding what had caused Becky's schizophrenia, and they referred her for therapy.

Becky made good use of the therapy, working out how she would cope with the increasing isolation she was feeling as her social networks were falling away. She spoke about her experiences of sexual abuse and the impact this had on her life, including possibly being a cause (at least in part) of her developing schizophrenia.

Questions

- Do you think that Becky's experience of sustained sexual abuse could have left her unscarred emotionally and psychologically?
- Do you think that hearing voices or seeing things that others cannot see or hear is an automatic sign of a mental illness?
- Suggest ten possible ways in which Becky's diagnosis of schizophrenia may negatively affect her life.
- Did Becky's life story play a prominent enough part in her care and treatment?
- What are the top three responsibilities of mental health services as seen through the prism of Becky's case? List up to 15 roles and tasks that the mental health services fulfilled in relation to Becky.
- What other roles and tasks might they have fulfilled?

Various studies show high rates of childhood sexual abuse in the population of women who are admitted to psychiatric hospital at around 50 per cent (see Chapter 5). One study showed that once discharged, women reported sexual abuse at rates as high as 85 per cent (Read *et al.* 2004). A system that has at its heart cure, care and containment (Perkins 2012) is designed with inbuilt inequalities. This is because groups with a protected characteristic are likely to use services in higher numbers because of what has happened to them, not because of who they are. Experiences of psychiatric services where their traumas and experiences are seen as secondary (Bracken and Thomas 2005) inevitably have a disempowering effect on people who already face disempowerment. Due to the stigma surrounding the utilisation of psychiatric services, it is not seen as desirable to use them. Western medicalised diagnostic labelling increases stigma (Fernando 2005). People from protected groups have to contend with the interaction between the discrimination that they face because of their identities, and the stigma that their use of mental health services entails.

There is insufficient space in this chapter to go through the details of alternatives. There are some approaches that have been subjected to rigorous research methodologies. In one study of the open dialogue model only 33 per cent of a cohort with psychosis had used neuroleptic medication and at two-year follow-up, 81 per cent had no residual symptoms (Seikkula, Alakare and Aaltonen 2011). There are also extensive volumes of personal narratives, such as *Living with Voices* (Romme *et al.* 2009), and compendiums such as the useful *Alternatives Beyond Psychiatry* (Stastny and Lehmann 2007), covering services and approaches that side-step traditional psychiatry and benefit the individual in critical areas of functioning for people who might otherwise have been drawn deep into the psychiatric system.

CONCLUSION

This chapter has presented arguments to demonstrate that modern mental health services are still significantly influenced by traditional psychiatry. This is despite the articulation of policymakers and services that they wish to see new models and approaches that keep service users central and which work to the principles of recovery (with the focus on people's strengths and capacities).

Certain groups protected under the Equality Act 2010 are more likely to use mental health services, and this may bring an additional layer of discrimination and inequality to their lives. Further, the inequalities, traumas and negative experiences that play a causal role in their mental health problems often receive only secondary attention in a service environment where the search for symptoms and surveillance for signs of relapse take precedence.

REFERENCES

Bentall, R. (2003) *Madness Explained: Psychosis and Human Nature.* London: Penguin Books.

Bentall, R. (2009) *Doctoring the Mind: Why Psychiatric Treatments Fail.* London: Allen Lane Publishing.

Boydell, J. and McKenzie, K. (2008) 'Society, Place and Space.' In C. Morgan, K. McKenzie and P. Fearon (Eds) *Society and Psychosis.* Cambridge: Cambridge University Press.

Bracken, P. and Thomas, P. (2005) *Postpsychiatry: Mental Health in a Postmodern World: International Perspectives in Philosophy and Psychiatry.* Oxford: Oxford University Press.

CQC (Care Quality Commission) (2011a) *Monitoring the Mental Health Act 1983 in 2010/111.* London: CQC.

CQC (2011b) Community Mental Health Survey 2011. Accessed at www.cqc.org. uk/public/reports-surveys-and-reviews/surveys/community-mental-health-survey-2011 on 31 May 2012.

CQC (2011c) *Count Me In 2010: Results of the 2010 National Census of Inpatients and Patients on Supervised Community Treatment in Mental Health and Learning Disability Services in England and Wales.* London: CQC.

Crawford, J., Nobles, W. and Leary, J. (2003) 'Repatriations and Healthcare for African Americans: Repairing the Damage from the Legacy of Slavery.' In R. Windrush (Ed.) *Should America Pay: Slavery and the Raging Debate on Repatriations.* New York: HarperCollins Publishing Inc.

DoH (Department of Health) (2012) Mental Health Clustering Booklet 2012-13. Manual. London: DoH. Accessed at www.dh.gov.uk/prod_consum_dh/groups/dh_digitalassets/@dh/@en/documents/digitalasset/dh_132656.pdf on 6 June 2012.

Equalities Review, The (2007) *Fairness and Freedom: The Final Report of the Equalities Review.* London: The Equalities Review.

Fernando, S. (2005) 'Is stigma universal?' *OpenMind 135*, 25. London: Mind.

Foucault, M. (2009) *History of Madness.* (First published in English in 2006.) Abingdon: Routledge.

Jobbins, D. (2012) 'Commissioning New Mental Health Services.' In P. Phillips, T. Sandford and C. Johnston (Eds) *Working in Mental Health: Policy and Practice in a Changing Environment.* Abingdon: Routledge

Johnstone, L. (2011) 'Can Traumatic Events Traumatize People? Trauma, Madness and "Psychosis".' In M. Rapley, J. Moncreiff and J. Dillon (Eds) *De-medicalizing Misery: Psychiatry, Psychology and the Human Condition.* Basingstoke: Palgrave.

McCulloch, A. and Lawton-Smith, S. (2012) 'UK Mental Health Policy Development: A Framework for Meaningful Change.' In P. Phillips, T. Sandford and C. Johnston (Eds) *Working in Mental Health: Policy and Practice in a Changing Environment.* Abingdon: Routledge

Mgutshini, T. (2012) 'Mental Health.' In M. Greenfields, R. Dalrymple and A. Fanning *Working with Adults at Risk from Harm.* Maidenhead: McGraw-Hill.

Mosher, L., Gosden, R. and Beder, S. (2004) 'Drug Companies and Schizophrenia.' In J. Read, L. Mosher and R. Bentall (Eds) *Models of Madness: Psychological, Social and Biological Approaches to Schizophrenia.* Hove: Brunner-Routledge.

Myin-Germeys, I. and van Os, J. (2008) 'Adult Adversity: Do early environment and genotype create lasting vulnerabilities for adult social adversity in psychosis?' In C. Morgan, K. McKenzie and P. Fearon (Eds) *Society and Psychosis*. Cambridge: Cambridge University Press.

ODPM (Office of the Deputy Prime Minister) (2004) *Mental Health and Social Exclusion: Social Exclusion Unit Report*. London: ODPM.

Perkins, R. (2012) 'UK Mental Health Policy Development: A Counter-argument.' In P. Phillips, T. Sandford and C. Johnston (Eds) *Working in Mental Health: Policy and Practice in a Changing Environment*. Abingdon: Routledge.

Phillips, L. and Jackson, A. (2012) 'Gender-specific Mental Health Care: The Case for Women-centred Care.' In P. Phillips, T. Sandford and C. Johnston (Eds) *Working in Mental Health: Policy and Practice in a Changing Environment*. Abingdon: Routledge.

Porter, R. (2002) *Madness: A Brief History*. Oxford: Oxford University Press.

Rapley, M., Moncreiff, J. and Dillon, J. (Eds) (2011) *De-medicalizing Misery: Psychiatry, Psychology and the Human Condition*. Basingstoke: Palgrave.

Read, J., Mosher, L.R. and Bentall, R.P. (Eds) (2004) *Models of Madness: Psychological, Social and Biological Approaches to Schizophrenia*. Hove: Brunner-Routledge.

Read, J., Perry, B., Moskowitz, A. and Connolly, J. (2001) 'The contribution of early traumatic events to schizophrenia in some patients: a traumagenic neurodevelopmental model.' *Psychiatry 64*, 319–345.

Repper, J. and Perkins, R. (2012) 'Recovery.' In P. Phillips, T. Sandford and C. Johnston (Eds) *Working in mental Health: Policy and Practice in a Changing Environment*. Abingdon: Routledge

Romme, M., Esher, S., Dillon, J., Corstens, D. and Morris, M. (2009) *Living with Voices: 50 Stories of Recovery*. Birmingham: PCCS Books.

Seikkula, J., Alakare, B. and Aaltonen, J. (2011) 'The comprehensive open-dialogue approach in Western Lapland: II. Long-term stability of acute psychosis outcomes in advanced community care.' *Psychosis: Psychological, Social and Integrative Approaches 3*, 3, October, 192–204.

Spauwen, J., Krabbendam, L., Leib, R., Wittchen, H.U. and van Os, J. (2006) 'Impact of psychological drama on the development of psychotic symptoms: relationship with psychotic proneness.' *British Journal of Psychiatry 188*, 527–523.

Stastny, P. and Lehmann, P. (2007) *Alternatives Beyond Psychiatry*. Berlin: Peter Lehmann Publishing.

Tang, S. (2012) 'The Care Pathway Approach: A Contemporary, Inclusive and Outcome-focused Rationale for Service Provision.' in P. Phillips, T. Sandford and C. Johnston (Eds) *Working in Mental Health: Policy and Practice in a Changing Environment*. Abingdon: Routledge

Chapter 14

CONFLICTS WITHIN
THE EQUALITIES AGENDA

Hári Sewell

INTRODUCTION

The Equality Act 2010 includes a public sector duty to promote good relations between those who share protected characteristics and those who do not. A person may have a protected characteristic and still be prejudiced and discriminatory to someone else who is covered by a different protected characteristic. The single equalities approach promoted by the Equality Act does not automatically unite people by virtue of having a common experience of inequality and prejudice. This chapter explores some of the potential conflicts within the equality agenda and offers ideas for tackling the challenges that arise.

FORMS AND FOUNDATIONS OF CONFLICT
Competing for resources

The bringing together of work on all protected characteristics is likely to involve the unifying of approaches and resources such as equalities posts, teams and stakeholder engagement forums. Back office functions that once helped to analyse and present service utilisation data by ethnicity, and perhaps sex and age, are now producing data on eight or nine protected characteristics. The legacy of major programmes such as *Delivering Race Equality in Mental Health Care* (Department of Health (DoH) 2005) may mean that race achieves greater prominence than other protected characteristics. The view that race deserves greater priority is reinforced by statements made in the press by high-profile commentators. For example, following the launch of the national mental health strategy *No Health without Mental Health* (HM Government 2011), *The Guardian* newspaper online version carried the headline of a blog 'Put race quality in mental health back on the agenda' (*The Guardian* 2011). The striking thing about this was that the national mental health strategy included a section on equalities, including race. Race had, however, lost its pre-eminent position of having a discrete strategy (DoH 2005), and this provoked concern. *The Guardian* blog was representative of many comments made at the time, bearing testimony to the view that not all inequalities are equally significant. It might just as well have been the case, however, that a race equality strategy would have provoked concern from interest groups covering other protected characteristics, given that the strategy was launched in a context where it was known that the Equality Act 2010 would come into force within a matter of weeks.

The rationale for resource allocation across protected characteristics needs to be clear. There is no formula that can be applied to make such a decision. It can only be achieved through data analysis and the balancing of corporate views with those of stakeholders and community groups.

Insufficient attention to group formation

The bringing together of all equalities issues into a single governance arrangement (such as an equality and diversity sub-committee or group) raises the possibility that people with different styles of working will need to operate in partnership, with scant attention having been paid to their unique histories. Apart from working styles, there may be a clash of belief systems (see the following section). Committees or stakeholder engagement forums that move from a single identity focus to an equality-wide focus may suddenly bring people with diverse interests together to work in partnership. Those responsible for coordinating such forums need to ensure that time is allocated to developing group cohesion. This might be through offering opportunities for participants to interact outside of business, to get to know each other personally. There is a wealth of literature on running groups effectively (e.g. Preston-Shoot 2007). Such knowledge needs to be applied to the development of new groups covering the equalities agenda.

Clash of belief systems

A single equalities approach that unifies work with traditional faith communities alongside engagement with the lesbian, gay and bisexual interest groups may lead to conflicts surfacing. Carr (2010) and Macaulay (2010) highlight this tension in trying to reconcile homosexuality with having a faith. There are other potential conflicts, such as someone from a traditional patriarchal culture working with a woman as a colleague or chairperson for a group. The possibilities for prejudice from another group are myriad. The role of services is to speak about these conflicts openly and to acknowledge the emotions that are generated. As Lindsay and Orton (2011, p.4) state, 'emotion will be around, but usually not as an acknowledged and valued part of the decision-making process'.

It is worth noting that clashes in belief systems may affect employees in mental health services, irrespective of the fact that they are required to comply with equalities policies. These may cause internal dissonance, or may be played out in disagreements with service users or colleagues.

BOX 14.1: EXAMPLES OF CLASHES OF BELIEF SYSTEMS

- A Christian social worker is asked to accompany a service user to a lesbian, gay and bisexual (LGB) centre to make an introduction. The social worker feels that he is entering an immoral place and tries to avoid the task.

- A training session on faith and spirituality is held in a mosque to try and engage local imams. A Christian social worker objects to attending.

- An older Pakistani man helping a female Muslim community development worker to run an engagement event continually instructed her in tasks. Though internally she objected as a liberated woman, she felt powerless to challenge him because she was aware of his belief about her role in that context. She anticipated that a challenge would have been seen as impertinent.

- An African staff nurse on a ward observed two female patients kissing and said that they would bring down the wrath of God. One of these patients retorted with a racist slur. The ward manager tried to resolve the situation, but stated his bewilderment as to how two people who knew what it feels like to be discriminated against could be so blatantly discriminatory.

Local history of adversarial relationships

Before bringing together workstreams into a single working group, it will be beneficial to investigate whether there are histories of adversarial relationships amongst the members. Local areas often have a number of people who have been involved in engagement and lobbying activities. Many of these people are able to chart changes from Community Health Councils to Public and Patient Involvement Forums, to Local Involvement

Networks and the current model of healthcare consumer rights protection, Healthwatch England (see Chapter 21). A long period of working in a local area enables the development of many positive and collaborative relationships, but it can also give rise to serious conflicts, and where potential conflicts arise because of belief systems, these can be wounding.

THE ROLE OF MENTAL HEALTH SERVICES IN HELPING TO RESOLVE CONFLICTS

In reality, mental health services cannot be held responsible for resolving some conflicts that are rooted in religious traditions. For example, if someone lives according to the will of God (according to their understanding of the scriptures), training or discussion will not persuade them otherwise. The best that can be hoped for is that people will find a way to maintain a professional role, notwithstanding their personal views. This does not mean, however, that mental health services are passively involved in such conflicts. Good management practice can go some way towards helping to minimise the chances of differences becoming disagreements and dissent.

Impact assessments

The Equality Act 2010 places a requirement on public authorities to have due regard to the need to eliminate unlawful discrimination, harassment and victimisation (see Chapter 1). In having due regard, public authorities will need to make some form of assessment of the impact that their policies, functions and decisions have on the protected characteristics. The Equality and Human Rights Commission website provides regularly updated information on undertaking assessments. The key point to note here is that relative need and priority can be determined when the impact on different protected characteristics is considered. This can contribute to providing a rationale for why investment of time and resources is being made.

Joint Strategic Needs Assessments

The requirement for health and local authorities to undertake Joint Strategic Need Assessments (JSNAs) arose from the Local Government and Public Involvement in Health Act 2007 (Crown 2007a). The purpose is to create a 'big picture' assessment of need to a local population. The guidance on JSNAs goes on to state: 'JSNA is a tool to identify the health and well-being needs and inequalities of a local population to inform more effective and targeted service provision' (Crown 2007). With a clear, well informed analysis of local need, it is possible to provide a rationale for decisions about relative investment. The more recent toolkit *Joint Strategic Needs Assessment: A Springboard for Action* defines a needs assessment as 'a systematic method for reviewing the issues facing a population, leading to agreed priorities and resource allocation that will improve health and well-being and reduce inequalities' (Local Government Improvement and Development (LGID) 2011, p.46).

Establishing an informed set of priorities might not quell disappointment experienced by particular groups but it might help minimise feelings of unfairness.

Community engagement in priority setting

The engagement of communities in priority setting is a key way in which expectations about resource allocation can be managed. The ten steps presented in the guidance on JSNAs (adapted from *National Standards for Community Engagement* produced by Communities Scotland 2005) can be usefully followed by any organisation delivering mental health services, and not solely the health commissioning bodies and local authorities to whom the guidance was addressed. Step 8 in the guidance suggests that information should be fed back to those with whom a consultation has taken place (Crown 2007). The whole process of engagement can serve to ensure that priority setting is understood and appreciated, if not completely agreed with (see Chapter 21).

Community development

Services can play a proactive role in educating and developing the understanding of communities. The respected *National Occupational Standards for Community Development* includes a core area on taking action with community groups to deal with conflict (Lifelong Learning UK 2009). Rather than avoiding conflict or acquiescing in the legacy of long traditions, services need to find ways to respectfully engage in dialogue about tolerance and equality, making it clear that the attempt is not to change fundamental beliefs, but to ensure that behaviours are compliant with the law.

Developing the workforce

A typical solution to developing the workforce is to offer training. The provision of knowledge may be achieved through training or e-learning modules, but honest reflection about beliefs and values will require other approaches (see Chapter 19). One of the main obstacles in working through beliefs on the part of staff which lead to conflict is intolerance for honest discussion and debate. As Bennett, Kalathil and Keating (2007) state, training often teaches staff just to say the right things and adopt behaviours that conform to expectation. There is merit is clarifying behaviours that are acceptable, at least as a starting point. More meaningful development of the workforce on equalities requires managers to be prepared to include reflection and honest discussion as part of supervision.

Ensuring emotional intelligence of the equalities lead

The field of equalities if fertile with opportunities for emotional pyrotechnics. Issues of unfairness, prejudice, injustice, feeling accused, and discrimination are the substance of hurt and anger. Many equalities leads will be covered by one or more protected characteristics and often choose to work in the field of equalities because of their passion for the work. Organisations need to capitalise on the benefits of this passion, and also to help develop an ability to recognise, understand and respond to emotions in themselves and others. Goleman (1995) calls this 'emotional intelligence'.

Medium-term planning

Not every priority can be addressed each year, but a planning timetable of three to five years allows for effort and resources to be targeted towards different protected characteristics over time. Expectations can be managed with interest groups who feel that there is insufficient focus on objectives for their protected characteristic. It will be important, however, that plans are adhered to and that commitments made are delivered upon.

CONCLUSION

Conflicts arise in the equalities agenda for a number of reasons. Disadvantaged groups may be unified by virtue of the fact that they face inequality, but as groups and individuals, there are still opportunities for conflict. Disagreements about resource allocation, clashes of belief systems, and local histories of difficult relations are some reasons why work on equalities may be fraught with conflict. Mental health services have a role to play in understanding and managing these conflicts with realistic expectations that deep-rooted feelings might not be immediately malleable to change, but behaviours might be containable.

REFERENCES

Bennett, J., Kalathil, J. and Keating, F. (2007) *Race Equality Training in Mental Health Services in England: Does One Size Fit All?* London: Sainsbury Centre for Mental Health.

Carr, S. (2010) 'LGBT Identities, Religion and Spirituality.' In P. Gilbert (Ed.) *Spirituality and Mental Health.* Brighton: Pavilion.

Communities Scotland (2005) *National Standards for Community Engagement.* Edinburgh: Scottish Executive.

Crown (2007) *Guidance on Joint Strategic Needs Assessments.* London: Department of Health.

Crown (2007a) *Local Government and Public Involvement in Health Act.* London: The Stationery Office.

DoH (Department of Health) (2005) *Delivering Race Equality in Mental Health Care: An Action Plan for Reform Inside and Outside Services and the Government's Response to the Death of David Bennett.* London: DoH.

Goleman, D. (1995) *Emotional Intelligence: Why It Can Matter More Than IQ.* London: Bloomsbury Publishing.

Guardian, The (2011) 'Put race equality in mental health back on the agenda.' Accessed at www.guardian.co.uk/society/joepublic/2011/mar/01/race-equality-mental-health#start-of-comments on 9 April 2012.

HM Government (2011) *No Health without Mental Health: A Cross-government Mental Health Outcomes Strategy for People of All Ages.* London: Department of Health.

LGID (Local Government Improvement and Development) (2011) *Joint Strategic Needs Assessment: A Springboard for Action.* London: LGID.

Lifelong Learning UK (2009) National Occupational Standards for Community Development. London: Lifelong Learning UK. Accessed at www.fcdl.org.uk/publications/ on 3 September 2012.

Lindsay, T. and Orton, S. (2011) *Groupwork Practice in Social Work. (First published in 2008.)* Exeter: Learning Matters Ltd.

Macaulay, R.J. (2010) '"Just as I am without one plea": a journey to reconcile sexuality and spirituality.' *Ethnicity and Inequalities in Health and Social Care 3,* 3, 6–13.

Preston-Shoot, M. (2007) *Effective Groupwork.* (First published 1987.) Basingstoke: Palgrave Macmillan.

Chapter 15

THE IMPACT OF COST CUTTING ON EQUALITIES

Hári Sewell

INTRODUCTION

Politicians and leaders of local services routinely state that cost-cutting measures will be reviewed and care will be taken to prevent any form of disproportionate impact on people from groups protected under the Equality Act 2010. This chapter questions whether sometimes well-intentioned analysis about the impact of changes on equality is accurate and sufficiently robust. Further, this chapter presents some concrete illustrations of how service changes that are expected to be universally challenging end up by contributing to a disproportionately negative impact on people from black and minority ethnic (BME) backgrounds, which could be avoided.

OBVIOUS ERRORS
Robbing Peter to pay Paul

A big risk in times of financial restraint is the reduction of budgets in areas that are more removed from the front line and those which are sometimes considered to be luxuries. The national evaluation of community development workers undertaken by De Montfort University (National Mental Health Development Unit (NMHDU) 2011) illustrated that an early response to the public sector cuts initiated by the Coalition Government in 2010 was a 50 per cent reduction in the numbers of mental health BME community development workers (CDWs) commissioned by health services nationally. Rationales for cutting these posts included the fact that the national strategy that led to the creation of the posts had ended (i.e. *Delivering Race Equality in Mental Health Care*, Department of Health (DoH) 2005); NHS trusts (commissioners or providers), faced with the need for budget reductions, needed to look first at non-clinical posts; and finally, the outcomes derived from these posts were less easy to identify (NMHDU 2011). There are, however, conflicting arguments. For example, the effectiveness of relatively low-grade CDWs was often measured against success in achieving macro organisational objectives. The success or failure to deliver those objectives cannot legitimately be seen as the sole responsibility of these workers. Organisations operate as systems, and it is rarely the actions of lone, low-level staff that are responsible for organisational failures (Torrington, Taylor and Hall 2007).

A legitimate criterion in deciding on service cuts is the extent to which a service or activity is considered to be core. There is no standard definition of 'core'. Statutory functions and contractual obligations are usually appropriately prioritised. Despite a belief that it is obvious which services are core or critical, it remains a matter of judgement as to which services are protected. Any support function is vulnerable, and those which are enabling of staff to do what they should be doing anyway are at greatest risk. Delivering fair and equitable services is the responsibility of all employees, so roles that support equality in organisations are typically more vulnerable.

Cutting posts of services that support equality is often a short-term fix with negative long-term consequences. People with protected characteristics under the Equality Act 2010 often face a complex set of problems in their lives (hence the protections of the Act), and as a consequence their demand on mental health services is greater. For example, Black African and Black Caribbean groups use services in significantly higher numbers than might be expected, based on numbers in the population (Care Quality Commission (CQC) 2011a). An analysis of the cost of inequality published in 2006 highlighted that the spend in these groups was about three times the spend on the white population (Sainsbury Centre for Mental Health 2006).

There are other examples of resources that have the potential to deliver savings and efficiencies. The provision of specific services for women who have been abused is likely to deliver improved service user outcomes, and therefore efficiencies and savings, given the fact that nearly 50 per cent of women in inpatient services have experienced childhood sexual abuse (Read 1997). There is evidence that there is a dose–response relationship between abuse and hearing voices (Bentall 2003). Mental health services bear the cost of repeat admissions and ongoing prescribing for women who have been traumatised. Service models that get to the root causes of women's troubles are ultimately more efficient; as the National Audit

Office has indicated, one in five psychiatric hospital admissions could be avoided (National Audit Office (NAO) 2007).

Where there are doubts about whether posts or specialist resources are delivering the efficiencies expected, it is better to review the way in which they are functioning and to work as a system to improve effectiveness. Deleting posts and closing services that seek to reduce inequalities can have the effect of never moving beyond the bedding-in stage. Future initiatives may lead to the creation of a team or role that has to start again, and which in turn may be cut for reasons similar to the case for predecessor roles – thus creating an ever increasing body of evidence on what supposedly does *not* work, and very little on what does.

The argument is not that posts, services or initiatives with a principal focus on equality should be protected from budget cuts, or that they should be maintained when there is a lack of evidence of impact and effectiveness. The point is that initiatives that have the potential to improve efficiency and provide a quality of service that is equitable across all groups should not be seen as easy targets.

Most of the negative impact on equality as a result of budget cuts does not come through the reduction or loss of specific posts or services. Budget cuts to health and social care mainstream services are likely to have an adverse impact on equality. There have been a number of commentaries on the current round of cuts resulting from the economic recession since 2008. *The Guardian* newspaper ran a special report in May 2011 in which six commentators highlighted the impact of the budget cuts in a number of sectors on women (*The Guardian* 2011). The point made throughout the six articles was that cuts which may not be targeted at women have a disproportionate impact on women and cumulatively worsen the disadvantage faced by women. (The articles covered legal affairs, Westminster culture, jobs, child benefit, education and social care.)

Public sector organisations or those fulfilling public functions are required under the Equality Act 2010 to undertake assessments of impact on equality (see Chapter 1) when they are making changes or budget reductions. When these are actually done, the robustness depends on the skill of the assessors and the willingness of the organisation to identify unequal impacts. If an organisation identified that a proposed service cut was going to have an unequal impact, it would need to have a legally compliant justification for why it was continuing regardless, or else would need to make amendments to avoid being in breach of the law. (One justification might be that, while an individual service change will have a negative impact on equality, as part of a bigger suite of changes the overall effect will be the reduction of inequality.)

BOX 15.1: ASSESSMENT OF IMPACT ON EQUALITY – AN EXAMPLE

Tryshire Mental Health Foundation Trust had proposals to close 30 per cent of their inpatient beds, and deemed that as black populations used beds in proportionately higher numbers, there would be a negative impact on equality in relation to these groups.

Tryshire Trust were, however, re-investing some of their savings derived from the bed closures into high-intensive home support. They created specific roles within the new team to work with the BME community, and the new office base was located in the area most populated by the black community. The consultation on the assessment of impact on equality generated positive comments from the BME community, who felt that the overall changes would bring more positive outcomes.

Organisations have a vested interest in identifying as few negative impacts on equality as possible. The public sector budget reductions signalled in the Government's Comprehensive Spending Review in October 2010 were significant (Crown 2010). Leadership teams, faced with national cuts of up to 21 per cent over three years (in councils), will have confidentially weighed different options for savings, knowing that each quarter without saving money merely worsens the challenge. The cuts required of individual organisations will vary, but even National Health Service (NHS) organisations (which were protected in the 2010 Comprehensive Spending Review) will probably be reluctant to abandon their plans, having arrived at proposals, which can then be subjected to an assessment of impact on equality.

There are myriad ways in which budget cuts can have a negative impact on protected groups in mental health. The following do not present an exhaustive exploration of impacts. Rather, they explore a few examples to illustrate the technique and approach that is needed to truly identify the impacts of cuts on equality.

REDUCTION OF SERVICES THAT ARE USED IN DISPROPORTIONATELY HIGH NUMBERS

Notwithstanding the high levels of dissatisfaction reported by black groups about inpatient services (Mental Health Act Commission 2006), they, and other protected groups who use inpatient services in disproportionately high numbers, will be afforded some form of safety and intervention. It is unlikely where hospital services are cut that community-based alternatives will be as available in equitable volumes. One consequence is that the number of community treatment orders is likely to increase beyond their current patterns, already reported as being of concern by the sector regulator (CQC 2011b). Further, the removal of support or containment without alternatives may leave some people vulnerable to exploitation, and even increase the possibility that they may become a greater risk to others, with negative long-term implications. It is not so much the loss of the specific inpatient services that is disproportionately negative for some protected groups, but rather the disproportionate increase in the numbers who fall through gaps in services.

REDUCTION OR LOSS OF SERVICES THAT WERE PARTICULARLY ACCESSIBLE OR TARGETED TO PEOPLE FROM PROTECTED GROUPS

Some mainstream services have a generic brief but attract disproportionately large numbers from some protected groups. In some cases the numbers may not be disproportionately higher, but a mainstream service may be considered to be a safe place for service users because of a culture that has developed, probably because of a staff member or team that worked there. See the example below.

BOX 15.2: CHANGE OF CULTURE WITH NEGATIVE IMPACT ON EQUALITY – AN EXAMPLE

Ladywood House resource centre was reconfigured from a traditional day centre into a skills and education centre for mental health service users. The manager of the day centre was a lesbian and her deputy was a gay man. Another member of staff was also a lesbian. Whilst other members of the team were not particularly open about their sexuality, the service was seen as safe by gay, lesbian and bisexual service users. The culture was responsive to people's needs regardless of their sexuality, and the material available and language used (e.g. about relationships) positively acknowledged the possibility of people having a sexual orientation other than heterosexuality.

In the transition to the new education and learning service model the manager secured a role in a community mental health team (which was a positive move for her) and the deputy left the organisation. The culture of the new centre, along with the service model, meant that people who were gay, lesbian or bisexual no longer had a safe place to go. This aspect of the service was not taken into account in the Assessment of Impact on Equality (see Chapter 1) because it was not part of the specification of the service. It was a benefit that had emerged, rather than one which had been designed. The reality, however, was that for people who were gay, lesbian and bisexual, this was a significantly negative impact on equality.

REDUCTION OR LOSS OF SERVICES THAT WERE GEOGRAPHICALLY ACCESSIBLE TO PEOPLE FROM PROTECTED GROUPS

As services are reconfigured and consolidated on a smaller number of sites, it is possible that the location of new services could create barriers in terms of access for particular protected groups. A service that operates at a site located at the top of a hill with no direct bus route is likely to constitute a physical barrier for service users who are disabled with regard to mobility. There may be less obvious negative impacts on equalities that might not be identified when the consequences of service changes are being considered as part of an Assessment of Impact on Equalities.

BOX 15.3: NEGATIVE IMPACT OF RELOCATING SERVICES – AN EXAMPLE

The Belvedere Hospital was being closed in a service reconfiguration, which was being consulted upon and being described as a positive move to newer facilities. The newer Templeton Hospital site did boast newer facilities for inpatients, but the walk to the site was past an adjacent park where a gruesome and well publicised rape had taken place. A large proportion of women who attended outpatient appointments found the walk intimidating on dark winter evenings. Given the fact that around 50 per cent of women who have been inpatients will have experienced some form of sexual violence (Read, Mosher and Bentall 2003), sexual safety needed to be paramount. The NHS trust responded to challenges about this plan by saying that patients could discuss with their consultant psychiatrist if they felt unsafe, and appointments would be planned in daylight where possible. The response did not fully address the fact that this meant that (a) the onus would be on women to reveal their fear, (b) getting a daylight appointment would only be guaranteed where possible and (c) women were in effect having their choice reduced by condensing the hours when they might have an appointment time.

The three examples set out above illustrate that the impacts of service cuts may not be sufficiently explicit to be easily picked up in Assessments of Impact on Equality. Adverse impacts will be missed where there is a disincentive to identify obstacles to speedy implementation of change or where the level of knowledge and expertise of the assessor is not extensive. This chapter now turns to identifying the costs and consequence of overlooking the negative impact of cuts on equality. An appreciation of the consequences may encourage a more detailed and expert analysis of changes to prevent costly problems emerging further downstream.

CONSEQUENCES

Consequences are considered at the level of individuals, organisations and society.

Consequences of cuts on people from protected groups

Certain groups were defined as having protected characteristics in the Equality Act 2010 (see Chapter 1) because there was a convincing body of evidence indicating that these groups faced obstacles in many aspects of their lives, which led to an unequal society (The Equalities Review 2007). Where mental health services make cuts and fail to identify the ways in which they perpetuate or worsen inequality, this will have a compounding impact on people from the protected groups. These ill-effects are played out in many individual stories of misery and poorer outcomes. The loss of support services and a social network will be challenging for all people who rely on mental health services, and for people from protected groups there is another layer of complexity. Older people, for example, may face a more profound sense of isolation as a result of the loss of a service, because Western societies have become reliant upon a technologically driven expert model of care and treatment and are therefore not geared up towards providing support networks beyond family and friends (Lubben and Damron-Rodriguez 2003). Gay, lesbian or bisexual people with mental health problems may find navigating new relationships more problematic because they are confronted with a world that is orientated around heterosexuality, and typically is homophobic (Carr 2010). The loss of services and support will drive up isolation and depression, and although this may not come to the attention of services, it will erode the quality of many lives, in the kinds of personal stories that go unseen behind headline comments, that there are no avoidable negative impacts on equality, when those in charge of service reconfigurations defend their decision.

Consequences of cuts on organisational culture

The relentless pursuit of savings has the insidious effect of supplanting almost all other priorities. Front-line services, which are typically described by ruling political parties as being protected, are eventually considered by NHS trusts as inevitable fair game as a source of financial savings (The King's Fund 2011). As organisations focus on significant budget reductions, the tolerance for previously unthinkable decisions increases (Sewell 2012). Against this backdrop considerations about equality are caught on a see-saw of aspirations: at one end there is the aspiration for speedy achievement of service reductions to meet harsh financial targets, and at the other end the wish to provide personalised services. As leaders in organisations communicate their focus on savings, they also potentially communicate to the workforce (whether explicitly or implicitly) that equalities is a luxury that cannot be afforded. Phrases such as 'everyone has to take a hit' fail to recognise that the cutting of posts or services that help to address inequality serves to perpetuate further inequality.

Organisational culture is affected when front-line staff and their managers see services that are valued by service users being cut. At this clinical/practitioner level staff face the reality of not being able to deliver personalised services to protected groups. A consequence of this is the emergence of a culture that accepts that service users must fit into the existing models of services. The idea of *service user-led services* becomes anachronistic rhetoric, whilst personalisation is increasingly considered to be nothing but an unattainable sentiment (*Community Care* 2011). Individual budgets may be delivered according to social care targets, but the culture of services may still be to seek savings through standardising practices, thus ironing out unique responses that front-line workers intend to be their way of meeting individual needs.

When staff work in an intense and sustained austerity climate the consequences are negative. As a study of 1160 employees undertaken after the 2010 Comprehensive Spending Review states: 'negative emotional experiences are a well-known reaction to radical and continuous change' (Keifer *et al.* 2011, p.2). The increasing threat (or experience) of overload, loss of role or loss of employment shifts the focus from service users. The consequent impact on equalities can be seen in the reduction of creativity and focus on achieving the absolute essentials of the job.

Consequences of cuts on society

The unmet needs of individuals and groups cost society dearly (Marmot 2010). People from protected groups who no longer engage with services, or who do not benefit from the interventions, treatment and care offered by services, are likely to cost society. This cost is financial, but there are also negative impacts in terms of lack of community cohesion (National Social Inclusion Programme 2009). Specifically, this means that people from protected groups become either more isolated, with increasingly complex problems, or they come to the attention of others in ways that create anxiety, fear or discontent. Society may experience greater visibility of social problems (e.g. more women misusing substances to suppress distress resulting from abuse) or greater fear (e.g. exaggerated media reports of aggression or violence by men who have not had their mental health needs met). Problems with meeting the needs of protected groups at individual and organisational levels will inevitably have negative consequences for society. Despite challenges to the findings of *The Spirit Level* (Wilkinson and Pickett 2011), the book presents convincing analysis of research that shows that more unequal societies suffer more social problems.

MITIGATING THE RISKS THAT CUTS WILL DISPROPORTIONATELY AFFECT PROTECTED GROUPS

This chapter has so far offered evidence that cuts will not be uniform in their impact. If left unmitigated the consequences will be more negative for people from protected groups. The Equalities Act 2010 provides a mechanism for mitigating the impact of any service change or policy development. The Equality and Human Rights Commission (EHRC) issued guidance on implementing the Act in January 2011, called *Equality Analysis and the Equality Duty: A Guide for Public Authorities*. Assessments of Impact on Equality are described as a protective approach to identify potential inequalities, rather than a mechanistic adherence to centrally predetermined processes. The guidance was updated in the context of the public sector cuts agenda. *Equality Analysis and the Equality Duty* reiterates the requirement under law to:

> have 'due regard' to the need to eliminate unlawful discrimination, harassment and victimisation as well as to advance equality of opportunity and foster good relations between people who share a protected characteristic and those who do not. (EHRC 2011a, p.1)

The document does, however, state that while the legislation does not prevent public bodies from implementing cuts that have a differential impact on different groups, the decisions must be fair and transparent. Where organisations show 'due regard' in a transparent, legally compliant way, and they identify that adverse impacts will disproportionately affect protected groups, public bodies must consider whether to make adjustments to plans, stop and rethink, or take steps to ameliorate these consequences.

There can be no preset way of ameliorating negative consequences on protected groups. Each local proposal will potentially have an impact according to the demographics, needs and patterns of service use in the area. It is essential that organisations are focused not only on being legally compliant but also on preventing longer-term negative consequences on communities, as already set out in this chapter. A robust analysis of impact on equality will already have provided information that clarified immediate and longer-term impacts. The model in Table 15.1 illustrates that amelioration of inequality on protected groups can only realistically be achieved by drawing on different aspects of an organisation. An organisation's approach to analysing its business, and the resultant discourse is informed by the theories and paradigms used. (Stacey 2007). The model in Table 15.1 suggests impact on equality should be analysed using the following aspects of an organisation: it's morals, operation, strategy, financial objectives and its social responsibility.

CONCLUSION

The cuts agenda is a reality of public services, and will be for some time, regardless of whether this is stated explicitly or is part of a mantra of efficiency savings and improved productivity. Given the reality of the decisions that leaders are faced with, it is important that organisations are equipped with capabilities to prevent the widening of inequalities. These capabilities cannot come through prescribing actions or providing examples that may not be transferable to the unique realities with which organisations are faced. The amelioration of negative potential impacts on equalities requires organisations to take seriously the challenge to fulfil their legal and moral duties, and for the passion of their rhetoric to be matched by the seriousness with which they undertake the task of assessing impacts on equalities.

Table 15.1: The perspectives employed by organisations to ameliorate inequalities when making cuts

Perspective	Moral	Operational	Strategic	Financial	Social Responsibility
Requires:	Clarity about organisation's ethics and values and the commitment to equality.	Expertise in analysing how inequalities are manifest in mental health for protected groups.	Knowledge of public health and the impact of inequalities on population health needs.	Understanding of how the failure to meet diverse needs causes inefficiencies.	Commitment of organisations to show leadership and contribute to social and societal gains.
Looks for:	Indications that choices of cuts are in conflict with organisation's values.	Creation of services gaps and barriers to access for protected groups.	Long-term adverse implications on the goals of the organisation.	Likelihood that effort will not achieve improved outcomes.	Evidence that organisation is insular and in self-preservation mode.
Ameliorates inequalities by:	Keeping the organisation's values central to decision making.	Anticipating in concrete ways the possible negative impacts on inequalities.	Designing plans that enable the organisation to meet its goals consistently over time.	Identifying invest-to-save opportunities through planning long-term.	Contributing to a social system that recognises that fairness and equality bring societal gains.

REFERENCES

Bentall, R. (2003) *Madness Explained: Psychosis and Human Nature.* London: Penguin Books.

Carr, S. (2010) 'LGBT Identities, Religion and Spirituality.' In P. Gilbert (Ed.) *Spirituality and Mental Health*. Brighton: Pavilion.

Community Care (2011) 'The state of personalisaton.' Accessed at www.communitycare. co.uk/static-pages/articles/the-state-of-personalisation/ on 8 December 2011.

CQC (Care Quality Commission) (2011a) *Count Me In 2010: Results of the 2010 National Census of Inpatients and Patients on Supervised Community Treatment in Mental Health and Learning Disability Services in England and Wales.* London: CQC.

CQC (2011b) *Monitoring the Mental Health Act 1983 in 2010/111.* London: CQC.

Crown (2010) *Comprehensive Spending Review 2010*. London: HM Treasury.

DoH (Department of Health) (2005) *Delivering Race Equality in Mental Health Care: An Action Plan for Reform Inside and Outside Services and the Government's Response to the Death of David Bennett*. London: DoH.

EHRC (Equality and Human Rights Commission) (2011a) Equality Analysis and the Equality Duty: A Guide for Public Authorities. Accessed at www.equalityhumanrights.com/uploaded_files/EqualityAct/PSED/equality_analysis_guidance.pdf on 6 June 2012.

EHRC (2011b) Making Fair Financial Decisions. London: EHRC. Accessed at www.equalityhumanrights.com/uploaded_files/EqualityAct/PSED/making_fair_financial_decisions.pdf on 3 September 2012.

Equalities Review, The (2007) *Fairness and Freedom: The Final Report of the Equalities Review*. London: The Equalities Review.

Guardian, The (2011) 'How the Coalition's blind spot on equality is letting women down.' *Special Report*, pp.6–7.

Keifer, T., Conway, N., Harley, J. and Briner, R. (2011) *Employee Responses to the Cuts: A Survey about the Experiences of Change in the Public Services*. London: International Centre for Governance and Public Management and Birkbeck College, University of London. August.

King's Fund, The (2011) *How is the NHS Performing? Quarterly Monitoring Report. April*. London: The King's Fund.

Lubben, J. and Damron-Rodriguez, J. (2003) 'An international approach to community health care for older adults.' *Family and Community Health 26*, 4, 338–349.

Marmot, M. (2010) *Fair Society, Healthy Lives*. London: The Marmot Review.

Mental Health Act Commission (2006) *Count Me in: The National Mental Health and Ethnicity Census: 2005 Service User Survey*. London: Mental Health Act Commission.

NAO (National Audit Office) (2007) *Helping People through Mental Health Crises: The Role of Crisis Resolution and Home Treatment Teams*. London: NAO.

National Social Inclusion Programme (2009) *Vision and Progress: Social Inclusion and Mental Health*. London: National Social Inclusion Programme.

NMHDU (National Mental Health Development Unit) (2011) *National Evaluation of the Community Development Workers*. London: NMHDU.

Read, J. (1997) 'Child abuse and psychosis: a literature review and implications for professional practice.' *Professional Psychology: Research and Practice 28*, 5, 448–456.

Read, J., Mosher, L.R. and Bentall, R.P. (Eds) (2004) *Models of Madness: Psychological, Social and Biological Approaches to Schizophrenia*. Hove: Brunner-Routledge.

Sainsbury Centre for Mental Health (2006) *The Cost of Race Inequality. Policy Paper No 6*. London: Sainsbury Centre for Mental Health.

Sewell, H. (2012) 'Race, Ethnicity and Mental Health Care.' In P. Phillips, T. Sandford and C. Johnston (Eds) *Working in Mental Health: Policy and Practice in a Changing Environment*. Abingdon: Routledge.

Stacey, R. (2007) *Strategic Management and Organizational Dynamics: The Challenge of Complexity*. Harlow: Pearson Education Ltd.

Torrington, D., Taylor, S. and Hall, L. (2007) *Human Resources Management*. Harlow: Financial Times/Prentice Hall.

Wilkinson, R. and Pickett, K. (2011) *The Spirit Level: Why Equality is Better for Everyone*. London: Penguin Books.

Chapter 16

GOOD ENOUGH PLANS AND STRATEGIES

Getting the Balance Right for Effective Planning and Decision Making – from Expediency to Pragmatism

Melba Wilson

INTRODUCTION

The National Health Service (NHS) has long experience of operational and strategic planning as part of ongoing change and improvement. This is based on developing an evidence base. One example (and one that is intended to incorporate the patient's perspective) is the NHS Institute's experience-based design (EBD) programme, which brings patients and staff together to re-design services (see www.institute.nhs.uk).

Discussion in black communities[1] has concerned why the existing evidence base regarding the mental health of black and minority ethnic (BME) communities has not been more effectively integrated into health and social care planning and implementation. Black Mental Health UK – an organisation that works (a) for a reduction of inequalities in the treatment and care of people from African Caribbean communities who use mental health services; and (b) to inform those communities about how

---

1   The focus in this chapter is on black and minority ethnic (BME) communities. Many of the points made can equally apply to other constituent communities (women, older people, children, people with disabilities), and also in relation to areas of religion and sexual orientation. The focus on race here is not intended to suggest hierarchy. Rather, it is a useful frame of reference for highlighting key points based on the literature and evidence. For a fuller set of references please refer to the work of the Mental Health Equalities Programme with the National Mental Health Development Unit (www.nmhdu.org.uuk/our-work/mhep/). In particular, the document *Mental Health Equalities Programme Sustainability and Legacy Plan* has a wide range of references and resources relating to all protected characteristic groups.

to influence the strategic development, policy design and implementation of services – states that:

> Inequality in mental health services between Black people and the majority White population has been the subject of ongoing debate and study for decades. It is well documented that people from BME communities and African Caribbeans in particular fare worse under the British mental health system. (www.blackmentalhealth.org.uk/index. php/home/about-us)

Service users and carers voice frustration at the lack of progress in improving services, given what is already known from available evidence (Kalathil *et al.* 2008). Others (see, for example, Fernando 2002; Fernando, Ndegwa and Wilson 1998) focus on the impact of bias and the hegemony of Western views of mental illness, and have pointed out that apparent contradictions in research findings and inquiry reports impact negatively upon clinical practice (Fernando 2002; Fernando, Ndegwa and Wilson 1998).

Sewell (2009) argues that the 'relatively low prioritisation of taking ethnicity, race and culture (ERC) into account arises from a lack of clarity about why it is essential.' He continues:

> Research has failed to enable consensus to be achieved about the role that ethnicity, race, culture, racial identity and ethnic identity play in patterns of mental health service utilisation. There is strong evidence that each of these factors have an impact on the relationship between services and BME service users and that these lead to poorer outcomes… The absence of a detailed understanding of precisely why there are differences according to ERC leads to an absence of a response, or a partial one. (Sewell 2009, p.29)

A major point of discussion concerns the fact that, notwithstanding existing widespread evidence (for example) in relation to the over-representation of black Caribbean people in mental health services (Care Quality Commission (CQC) 2011); 'Delivering Race Equality' programme (National Mental Health Development Unit (NMHDU) 2010), misinterpreting or ignoring the evidence can still lead to erroneous conclusions, and therefore inadequate service delivery responses (Kalathil *et al.* 2011).

Specifically in relation to Caribbean communities and the over-representation of black men in mental health services, the literature points to causal factors such as the impact of stigma and discrimination (Office of the Deputy Prime Minister (ODPM) 2004; Sainsbury Centre for Mental

Health 2002) and/or to inequality as a result of social determinants such as isolation, joblessness, poor education and migration (Bhugra *et al.* 2011; Kirkbride and Jones 2010; Morgan 2011).

Inaction, critics argue, can lead to:

- delays in investment and implementation

- activity which lacks purpose (i.e. no clear linkage with strategic or operational plans)

- light touch performance management

- poor service responses, experiences and outcomes for people from BME communities.

Service reconfiguration, consultation and organisational change are complex and lengthy processes. To minimise risk, organisations may adopt planning approaches which rely on *expediency* – i.e. delivering a means to an end. Decisions may be taken from a default position ('Let's go with what we know or have done in the past'). In mental health terms, these are not necessarily the kind of effective or evidence-based approaches that produce desired results from an end user's point of view. In the context of BME communities, this position can, at best, be unsatisfactory; and at worst, be seen as demonstrating a refusal to accept the need for change.

This chapter explores on what basis it can be determined whether planning and evidence gathering/integration, as part of service redesign, is 'good enough' – that is, 'good enough' to usefully inform outcomes for people of all ages and backgrounds who use mental health services, as well as satisfying the need for organisational accountabilities in adapting to change.

In relation to equality and equity, as in other areas, it is important to have proactive and sensitive leadership and decision making. This can take the form of mutually productive collaboration as part of a process of identifying whether and when work within given structures, processes and mechanisms *effectively* utilises the evidence base and yields sufficient mutual benefit – in other words, when there is a shift to be made from *expedient* approaches to *pragmatic solutions* – i.e. solutions based on cause and effect and practical lessons for change.

Specific areas highlighted here are:

- *structural responses* – e.g. in relation to the current architecture resulting from NHS reform

- *clinical responses* – e.g. how clinicians can assimilate different models into practice, such as a social anthropological approach exemplified by the explanatory model of working with clients

- *procedural responses* – the practical tools that enable change to be measured effectively (equality impact assessment, mental well-being impact assessment).

STRUCTURAL RESPONSES

The Coalition Government's plans for NHS reform signal a move away from centrally driven service targets and towards outcomes that matter most to people at a local level (Richardson and Cotton 2011). As such, they offer a clear opportunity to develop plans and promote progress on equity and access in the new health and social care architecture, where the emphasis is on outcomes and engagement.

Clinical commissioning groups (CCGs) will commission most services on behalf of patients, including:

- planned hospital care

- rehabilitative care

- urgent and emergency care (including out of hours)

- most community health services

- mental health and learning disability services.

Once established, the CCGs will be statutory public bodies, with powers and responsibilities set out in legislation. By October 2011, there were 266 'pathfinder' CCGs in operation across England (see www.nhsconfed. org/priorities/NHS-reforms/The-new-commissioning-landscape/ Pages/Commissioning-reform.aspx).

The Department of Health has stated that within the new structures:

The joint local leadership of CCGs and local authorities through the health and well-being board will be at the heart of this new health and social care system [and that] one of the key benefits of establishing health and well-being boards will be to increase the influence of local people in shaping services by involving democratically elected councillors and through local HealthWatch, so that services can better meet local need, improve the experience of service users, and improve the outcomes for individuals and communities. (DoH 2011c, p.16)

These changes represent an early and timely opportunity for CCGs to help to ensure equity in meeting the needs of their populations. They should also, it is hoped, enable communities to build on work already undertaken in predecessor structures to inform how services are commissioned and developed.

The Department of Health describes the health and well-being strategy as a 'unique opportunity for the health and well-being board members to explore together the local issues that they have not managed to tackle on their own' (DoH 2011c, p.20). It identifies three key themes:

- a focus on outcomes

- promoting integration

- engaging the public.

A key issue is data – its collection and use. With regard to opportunities under the NHS reform mechanisms, the NHS Confederation (Richardson and Cotton 2011) identified a range of actions for improving outcomes, including the need to develop and maintain integrated databases to permit more accurate assessment of *equality and access data* as well as information relating to transfers between services for children, adults and older adults (Richardson and Cotton 2011, p.13).

Likewise, the review of the 'Delivering Race Equality' programme (Wilson 2010), the five-year action plan to promote improvements in mental health outcomes for people from BME communities, identified the need for existing learning to be sustained and used in policy development and implementation. Included within this was the need for 'better use of data to inform commissioning and provision intentions in health and social care' (p.46).

The Operating Framework for the NHS in England 2011–12 identified that 'patient experience must be a key arbiter of all NHS services'; and that 'PCTs and providers should continue to ensure that appropriate systems are in place to capture the views and experiences of patients, service users and carers.' Data sources cited include:

- local and nationally coordinated patient surveys

- real-time feedback collected at the point of care (e.g. SMS texting, Patient Experience Trackers, kiosks)

- complaints data

- patient-reported outcome measures (PROMS).

(DoH 2010, p.25)

The Operating Framework for the NHS in England 2012–13 reinforces that 'the experience of patients, service users and their carers should drive everything the NHS has to do...' (DoH 2011a, p.8). New guidance for the NHS Operating Framework 2012/13 (DoH 2011b) will require clinical commissioning groups and primary care trusts (PCTs) to demonstrate systemic steps to ensure the retention of engagement with patients and the public on planned developments; and importantly, to demonstrate whether plans 'give due regard to the public sector equality duty (PSED), including whether equality objectives are integral' (DoH 2011b, p.19).

CLINICAL RESPONSES

At an individual level (i.e. the interface between clinicians and service users and carers or consumers) it is becoming increasingly clear that the interaction should be one based on developing and maintaining an equal partnership. A significant body of work (for example, Bhui and Bhugra 2003; Kleinman, Eisenberg and Good 1978) argues for the importance of translating cultural norms into a clinical language for practical application. Kleinman (2008, p.22) argues that 'this will...mean that students and practitioners acquire those interpretive skills of critical self-reflection that enable them to understand and respond to all those barriers that cause doctors to fail at the art of healing.' In a cross-cultural sense, there is much to recommend taking this explanatory approach to aid understanding of how to improve services.

A new tool, 'Making Good Decisions in Collaboration' (MAGIC), developed by The Health Foundation (2012a), aims to promote shared decision making between patients and clinicians. It is based on work with healthcare professionals in foundation trusts in England and a health board in Wales. The tool is based on the premise that shared decision making 'requires a big culture shift, breaking away from the traditional relationships between 'passive patients' and expert health professionals' (The Health Foundation 2012a, p.3). Although developed in a physical health context, MAGIC contains clear learning for work with people with mental health problems from diverse cultures.

PROCEDURAL RESPONSES

A number of procedural responses aimed at testing for improvement and change are available. The 'Plan, Do, Study, Act' (PDSA) tool (NHS Institute for Innovation and Improvement 2008) is one model used for developing service design and delivery. The four stages of the PDSA cycle are:

- **P**lan – the change to be tested or implemented

- **D**o – carry out the test or change

- **S**tudy – data before and after the change and reflect on what was learned

- **A**ct – plan the next change cycle or full implementation.

The model for improvement incorporates three questions:

- What are we trying to accomplish? (The aims statement.)

- How will we know if the change is an improvement?

- What changes can we make that will result in improvement?

Other procedural options include:

1. Equality Impact Assessment (EqIA) (NHS Employers 2009) – a tool for examining the main functions and policies of an organisation to see whether they have the potential to affect people differently. The purpose is to identify and address existing or potential inequalities resulting from policy and practice development. EqIAs should cover all the strands of diversity and will help trusts get a better understanding of their functions and the way decisions are made, by:

   - considering the current situation

   - deciding the aims and intended outcomes of a function or policy

   - considering what evidence there is to support the decision and identifying any gaps

   - ensuring it is an informed decision.

CASE STUDY 16.1: BRADFORD TEACHING HOSPITALS NHS FOUNDATION TRUST

Each department within the trust has undertaken initial EqIAs of all policies and functions. Full EqIAs have been carried out on those policies and functions that have the highest impact on equality groups. For further information see: www.bradfordhospitals.nhs.uk/about-us/e/impact-assessment.

---

2. Mental well-being impact assessment (MWIA). MWIA is a process that uses a combination of methods, procedures and tools to assess the potential for a policy, service programme or project to impact on the well-being of a population. MWIA makes evidence-based recommendations to strengthen the positive impacts and mitigate the negative impacts, and encourages a process to develop indicators to measure impacts (Cooke and Stansfield 2009).

CASE STUDY 16.2: SOUTH LONDON AND MAUDSLEY NHS FOUNDATION TRUST

MWIA on mental health service (Lewisham Rehabilitation Service). This tested the MWIA toolkit and demonstrated how indicators developed using MWIA can be collected over a period of time to demonstrate impact on mental well-being. The work identified three areas necessary for continuing to promote mental well-being:

- increasing people's decision-making skills
- promoting self-esteem by reducing stigma and discrimination
- increasing support networks.

The work resulted in the development of indicators based on the stakeholders' priorities, which were developed with the care coordinators who would be required to collect the data. For further information see: www.nmhdu.org.uk/our-work/promoting-wellbeing-and-public-mental-health.

CONCLUSION

A wealth of evidence exists to inform improvement of services to communities of diversity. Health and social care is undergoing rapid and continuing change, and this is a key opportunity for patient-centred planning, design and implementation. Commissioners and providers will need to demonstrate how they are incorporating the views and input of people who use services.

A new report by The Health Foundation (2012b) sets out the critical next steps for the NHS Commissioning Board, to make 'No decision about me, without me' a reality (p.1). These steps are:

1. The board must engage in the development of a strong narrative for shared decision making;

2.   The board must inspire others to play their part;

3.   The board must invest in the development of robust and meaningful measures of patients' involvement in their own care; and

4.   The board must pro-actively encourage the changes in service provision necessary to meet different expectations.

(The Health Foundation 2012b, p.4)

A pragmatic approach to influence day-to-day decision making and action planning will require the use of ideas, initiatives and a range of tools and techniques. These can deliver good patient-centred, evidence-based data and information that can address individual as well as organisational requirements.

REFERENCES

Bhugra, D., Gupta, S., Bhui, K., Craig, T., Dogra, N., Ingleby, J., Kirkbride, J., Moussaoui, D., Nazroo, J., Qureshi, A., Stompe, T. and Tribe, R. (2011) 'WPA guidance on mental health and mental healthcare in migrants.' *World Psychiatry 10*, 2–10.

Bhui, K. and Bhugra, D. (2003) 'Explanatory models in psychiatry.' *British Journal of Psychiatry 183*, 170.

Cooke, A. and Stansfield, J. (2009) Improving Mental Well-being Through Impact Assessment. Accessed at www.nmhdu.org.uk/silo/files/improving-mental-wellbeing-through-impact-assessment.pdf.

CQC (Care Quality Commission) (2011) *Count Me In 2010: Results of the 2010 National Census of Inpatients and Patients on Supervised Community Treatment in Mental Health and Learning Disability Services in England and Wales.* London: CQC.

DoH (Department of Health) (2010) The Operating Framework for the NHS in England 2011/12. Accessed at www.dh.gov.uk/en/Publicationsandstatistics/Publications/PublicationsPolicyAndGuidance/DH_122738.

DoH (2011a) The Operating Framework for the NHS in England 2012/13. Accessed at www.dh.gov.uk/prod_consum_dh/groups/dh_digitalassets/documents/digital asset/dh_131428. pdf.

DoH (2011b) The Integrated Approach to Planning and Assurance between DH and the NHS for 2012/13. Accessed at www.dh.gov.uk/en/prod_consum_dh/groups/dh_digitalassets/documents/digitalasset/dh_131976.pdf.

DoH (2011c) Joint Strategic Needs Assessment and Joint Health and Wellbeing Strategies Explained: Commissioning for Populations. Accessed at www.dh.gov.uk/en/Publicationsandstatistics/Publications/PublicationsPolicyAndGuidance/DH_131702.

Fernando, S. (2002) *Mental Health, Race and Culture.* Second edition. Basingstoke: Palgrave.

Fernando, S., Ndegwa, D. and Wilson, M. (1998) *Forensic Psychiatry, Race and Culture.* London: Routledge.

Health Foundation, The (2012a) Snapshot: MAGIC: Making Good Decisions in Collaboration. Accessed at www.health.org.uk/publications/snapshot-magic/.

Health Foundation, The (2012b) Summit Report: Leading the Way to Shared Decision Making. Accessed at www.health.org.uk/publications/leading-the-way-to-shared-decision-making/.

Kalathil, J., Collier, B., Bhakta, R., Daniel, O., Joseph, D. and Trivedi, P. (2011) *Recovery and Resilience: African, African-Caribbean and South Asian Women's Narratives of Recovering from Mental Distress.* London: Mental Health Foundation. Accessed at www.mentalhealth.org.uk.

Kalathil, J. et al. (2008) *Dancing to Our Own Tunes: Reassessing Black and Minority Ethnic Mental Health Service User Involvement.* London: National Survivor User Network.

Kirkbride, J. and Jones, P. (2010) 'The prevention of schizophrenia – what can we learn from eco-epidemiology?' *Schizophrenia Bulletin.*

Kleinman, A. (2008) 'The art of medicine, catastrophe and caregiving: the failure of medicine as an art.' *The Lancet 371*, 5 January, p.22.

Kleinman, A., Eisenberg, L. and Good, B. (1978) 'Culture, illness and care: clinical lessons from anthropologic and cross-cultural research.' *Annals of Internal Medicine 88*, 2, 1 February, 251–258.

Morgan, C. (2011) 'Social Disadvantage, Ethnicity and Psychosis.' *Conference presentation, Institute of Psychiatry*, 13 June.

NHS Employers (2009) www.nhsemployers.org/EmploymentPolicyAndPractice/Equality AndDiversity/Equality-Impact-assessments/Pages/EqualityImpactAssessment.Intro. aspx.

NHS Institute for Innovation and Improvement (2008) www.institute.nhs.uk/quality-and-value/experienced-based-design/the-ebd-approach-(experiences-based-design). html.

ODPM (Office of the Deputy Prime Minister) (2004) *Mental Health and Social Exclusion, social Exclusion Unit Report.* London: ODPM.

Richardson, A. and Cotton, R. (2011) No Health without Mental Health: Developing an Outcomes Based Approach. NHS Confederation Mental Health Network. Accessed at www.nhsconfed.org/mhn.

Sainsbury Centre for Mental Health (2002) *Breaking the Circles of Fear: A Review of the Relationship between Mental Health Services and African and Caribbean Communities.* London: Sainsbury Centre for Mental Health.

Sewell, H. (2009) *Working with Ethnicity, Race and Culture in Mental Health: A Handbook for Practitioners.* London: Jessica Kingsley Publishers.

Wilson, M. (2010) Delivering Race Equality in Mental Health Care: Race Equality Action Plan: A Five-year Review. London: National Mental Health Development Unit/Department of Health. Accessed at www.nmhdu.org.uuk/our-work/mhep/.

PART
IV

CHANGE AND EQUALITIES

Chapter 17

APPLYING MANAGEMENT RIGOURS

Hári Sewell

INTRODUCTION

This chapter sets out the case for ensuring that the usual management rigours are applied to leading and implementing the equalities agenda.

WHY THIS NEEDS ATTENTION

The link between the protected characteristics and identity has often meant that there is a disproportionately high number of staff from protected groups leading the agenda that matches their own identity, at least at the front line or junior grade management levels. For example, a report into black and minority ethnic (BME) community development worker (CDW) posts established as part of the 'Delivering Race Equality' initiative (Department of Health (DoH) 2005) highlighted that 69 per cent of post holders were from a BME background (Walker and Craig 2009). This is striking, given the fact that the Department of Health Implementation Guide posed the following question and response:

Do CDWs need to be recruited from BME communities?

No. But what they must do is to work with, on behalf of and closely with the BME community. There may, however, be compelling reasons why it is felt necessary for a worker to be employed from a particular ethnic background, but this is likely to be the exception and would need to be compliant with the Race Relations Act. (DoH 2004a, p.14)

The profile of those working on equalities for women, men, lesbian, gay and bisexual and faith reflect a similar pattern. It might be considered a matter of intuition that this should be the case, and there are good grounds for appointing someone with personal experience and an identity that enables greater ease in communicating and co-working with the target community they serve. A consequence, however, is that the staffing profile reinforces that view that tackling equality is largely the responsibility of members of the group in question (Dominelli 2008). Further, it communicates (perhaps unwittingly) that the matching of identity is of equal or greater importance than possessing the core knowledge and skills to deliver the role effectively. The equalities agenda may become a special interest subject as opposed to a key managerial requirement. Regulatory bodies place requirements on organisations to deliver outcomes, but in a research study into the views of those in leadership positions many participants highlighted that they felt that the equalities agenda suffered because the expectations set for it (e.g. by means of targets) were lower than they were for other areas of mental health and social care (Sewell and Waterhouse 2012). The Equality Delivery System (EDS) for the National Health Service (NHS) was launched as a non-mandatory framework for commissioners and providers of health services in partnerships with other partner agencies (Crown 2011). The EDS is consistent with the Coalition Government's priority to reduce the burden of targets, and is the first major single equalities toolkit in the NHS. However, there is no statutory compulsion attached to it, and so the best managerial skills in NHS organisations are dedicated to other agendas which, if breached, would jeopardise senior jobs and organisational viability.

Compliance with the Equality Act 2010 will require an assessment of impact on strategy, policies or service change on equality. Although there is no longer a standardised model for Equality Impact Assessments (EqIAs), the Equality and Human Rights Commission (EHRC) highlights the need to make some assessment of impact as a requirement under the Equality Act 2010. The Commission provides regularly updated guidance on undertaking Assessments of Impact on Equality on its website. EqIAs were considered to follow a specific methodology and published individually. The distinction made with the new terminology introduced by the EHRC was the shift from a need to follow a particular methodology (i.e. process driven) to demonstrating that the impact on equality had been assessed.

A good test of the commitment to implementing equalities in an organisation is how effectively the usual management rigours are applied. The benefit of applying management rigours is discussed below under the following subjects:

- strategic management

- commissioning

- financial management

- human resources (HR) management

- change management and project management.

STRATEGIC MANAGEMENT

The EDS for the NHS highlights the role of planning commissioning as a critical. Outcome 1 is listed as: 'Services are commissioned, designed and procured to meet the health needs of local communities, promote well-being, and reduce health inequalities' (Crown 2011, p.28).

There are a number of activities that are elements of the strategy process. Scragg (2010) identifies strategic issues as:

> those that fundamentally affect the policies of the organisation, for example in terms of its mission and values, the services it provides, the people who use the service and the financial health and the effectiveness of its management. (Scragg 2010, p.21)

It is clear that an organisation will need to have a detailed understanding of the issues in relation to each of the nine protected characteristics: how they relate to staffing; issues in research about needs; quantitative and qualitative data about service utilisation; and engagement of stakeholders, including service users, community and voluntary sector services. Additionally, the impact of current service utilisation, analysed according to the nine protected characteristics, needs to be understood, and in particular the opportunities for greater efficiency. It should immediately be apparent that this level of analysis, informed by a good knowledge of all nine protected characteristics is not something that can be done effectively without specific knowledge and education in the issues around equalities and mental health. Also apparent is a degree of inevitability that poor strategic analysis and development of solutions will lead to weak performance in managing equalities.

BOX 17.1: A KEY QUESTION FOR SENIOR MANAGERS

A key question for senior managers should be: 'How do we assure ourselves that we have the expertise to incorporate compliance with the Equality Act 2010 into our strategic planning, and do we have the commitment to make strategic decisions about service configurations and organisational and staff development to ensure that needs are effectively met and equitable improvements in service user outcomes are achieved?'

Equalities need to be incorporated into all strategy and planning. There also, however, needs to be a discrete function of strategic planning for equalities. In this way the equalities agenda can begin to achieve some parity with other functions within an organisation.

COMMISSIONING

Leaders in provider mental health organisations reported their views that equalities is largely absent from the commissioning agenda (Sewell and Waterhouse 2012). Two aspects of commissioning are important: population needs assessment, and the development of commissioning strategies and procurement. The NHS and Social Care Act 2012 established a new public health system in England and Wales, and this includes the transfer of public health duties to local authorities. This is intended to enable the assessment of population needs to be informed by an integrated analysis of needs. The inequalities that arise in populations may be considered on the basic of class, geography, lifestyle and other social determinants (Marmot 2010). The Equality Act 2010 requires that inequalities are analysed in relation to the protected groups. The same epidemiological analysis needs to be applied to the protected groups, and the understanding of population mental health needs to take account of differences.

CASE STUDY 17.1: EQUALITIES IN POPULATION NEEDS ASSESSMENT

The suicide prevention strategy being developed in a mainly rural local authority area identified high-risk groups, including young men, farmers, doctors and people with mental health problems who had an admission to a psychiatric hospital. The first draft of the strategy did not present data on the risks associated with being lesbian, gay or bisexual (LGB). When challenged, the public health department stated that they had no data available because sexuality was not always known (for example, not all gay, lesbian or bisexual people who commit suicide have disclosed their sexuality). Without a strong local lobby group the department struggled to formulate a response to the high-risk group. Eventually, through working with a national charity that lobbies for and supports the improvement of society and services for LGB people, the public health department was able to include some relevant objectives in their suicide prevention strategy. These included working with partners to prioritise the gathering of data on sexuality in general practice, as a first step towards developing a better response and targeting of suicide prevention activities.

> An additional outcome from this episode was that the public health department produced a series of fact sheets that provided local data and information in relation to the groups with protected characteristics, to aid future population needs assessment.

The illustration in Case Study 17.2 demonstrates how reducing inequalities through commissioning processes requires the usual standards of data gathering and analysis to be applied across the entire equalities agenda. The understanding of needs will help to inform local commissioning strategies.

The procurement stage of commissioning creates opportunities for reducing biases in the process itself. This is, however, not the focus in this chapter, but rather the content of specifications for services to meet commissioning priorities. Service specifications describe the functions to be fulfilled by a provider. The process of developing service specifications needs to be well informed by a knowledge of what is required to reduce inequalities. For example, a specification for a therapy service (e.g. under the policy 'Improving Access to Psychological Services', known as IAPT) might need to include specific requirements to monitor provision to ensure accessibility to men. This would be important, given the data that shows that men accounted for 35 per cent of uptake for psychological therapies for anxiety and depression (Royal College of Psychiatrists (RCPsych.) 2011). Though the report anticipates some over-representation of women, given the higher prevalence of anxiety and depression among women, there is still lower than expected take-up by men. Further, a study into men's health suggests that depression is underdiagnosed in men (Men's Health Forum 2010). Equality for *all* protected characteristics needs to be considered in relation to *all* relevant service specifications.

FINANCIAL MANAGEMENT

Chapter 18 sets out the financial case for tackling inequalities. It is obvious that budgets should be identified for work on equalities, and that this should be based on commissioning strategies or work plans. It is also important, however, that return on investment should be effectively considered. It is not discriminatory to seek evidence of outcomes from targeted initiatives to improve equality. Caution needs to be exercised to prevent interrogation of value for money and effectiveness from being used as an excuse to cut funding by being more stringent for equalities initiatives than for other aspects of the organisation.

HUMAN RESOURCES MANAGEMENT

Human resources management covers a range of functions, including workforce planning, resourcing people, i.e. employment and retention of staff, workforce and organisational development, performance management and employee relations (Armstrong 2009). Organisational development and workforce development are covered in Chapters 19 and 20.

Of particular interest in this chapter is the recruitment and retention of staff, and performance management. Two perspectives are considered. One relates to the HR management of the workforce generally, and the other to staff in posts specifically focused on the equality agenda.

The process of identifying the knowledge and skills needed in a service and developing job descriptions in the NHS was largely shaped by the development of the Agenda for Change Knowledge and Skills Framework (KSF), originally published in 2004 (DoH 2004b). Agenda for Change provides national job profiles to serve as a basis for local job descriptions and person specifications. Job descriptions routinely include some reference to working with diversity or equal opportunities. Other organisations will have their own systems for agreeing the content of job descriptions. The whole process of defining roles and filling posts with the ideal candidate is influenced significantly by the knowledge, skills and attitudes of those involved in the process. A large proportion of HR functions are fulfilled by line managers, and where there are gaps in knowledge, skills and attitudes, this will affect the process.

> A further factor affecting the role of line managers is their ability to do the HR functions assigned to them. People-centred activities such a defining roles, interviewing, reviewing, providing feedback, coaching and identifying learning and development needs all require specific skills. Some managers have them: many don't. (Armstrong 2009, p.97)

Managers, incomplete comprehension of equalities undermines their ability to carry out these HR functions to best effect. For example, a manager may develop an interview question such as, 'Tell us how equal opportunities applies to this post?' This is not necessarily as specific and helpful as it might be, and the abilities of the manager will affect the assessment of the responses given by candidates.

BOX 17.2: EXAMPLE OF POSITIVE INTERVIEW QUESTIONS

Positive interview questions for a mental health practitioner role could be:

> Tell us how inequalities become manifest in the lives of people with various protected characteristics who use our services. Tell us ways in which you can help to reduce inequalities in your practice. Provide examples from your past practice of where you have taken specific steps to reduce inequalities.

Another dimension to consider is the appointment of staff or consultants whose role it is to fulfil specific functions to address inequality. The design of job descriptions and the selection of staff needs to recognise that there is a body of knowledge that is required, not purely from personal experience but based on some form of study. A woman who is passionate about injustice to women may bring energy and commitment to a role, but if the role is to promote gender equality and she does not know about findings from research into men's mental health, the appointment might not be appropriate without some specific development work. Even considering just women's mental health, there is a wealth of research and knowledge without which a worker will be less well equipped to deliver a role to the same standards of technical competence that might be expected of another role. Further, there will be universal skills that will be required, such as recording, report writing, presenting and project management, which should be in the possesion of post holders where such functions are required. Organisations can sometimes, erroneously, be persuaded by a narrow intuitive knowledge. There is also an assumption on occasions that when working in one area of equalities that knowledge and skills can be transferred to another or that attitudes are right. In fact, there are conflicts which might mean, for example, that a BME worker with strong roots in a faith community is hostile to homosexuality. (See Chapter 14 on conflicts within the equalities agenda.)

The performance management of staff is a core function of line managers (Scragg 2001). For the workforce generally, performance management of staff will require prior organisational specification of standards and minimum expectations. For equalities, the types of standards that lend themselves to performance management are to do with data capture rather than quality of practice. Most practice is not observed by line managers. (Case notes reviews are a proxy and these don't happen routinely.) The indicators of the strength of practice tend to be overall service outcomes (e.g. repeat admissions, admissions in emergency, length of stay). The analysis of routine data to identify inequality is variable, with age, gender and ethnicity more routinely captured. The ability of organisations to understand the messages from equality data is limited. For example, although sex has always been captured in service-use data, the meanings of variations for men and for women are often not recognised and responded to (Men's Health Forum 2010; Phillips and Jackson 2012). This points to the need for more expertise within organisations, in relation to inequalities for the different protected characteristics.

Staff working in specialist services that target groups with protected characteristics often bring a level of engagement and empathy not experienced in other parts of the mental health system. A service for LGB people, run largely by LGB staff, may offer a unique service appreciated by the service users. There may, however, be aspects of performance that require attention. Line managers need to have the clarity of leadership to manage performance so as to ensure that service users receive the best possible service, without fear of being unfairly criticised for being discriminatory. There is a sense of powerlessness that can sometimes dog line managers, and rather than achieving the goal of a quieter life, avoidance causes resentment on the part of colleagues. Consequences are that service users get an inferior service, and the group with protected characteristics attracts negative comments. Avoidance of tackling poor practice merely entrenches discrimination. Content knowledge and affinity with service users are only part of the contribution to be made by specialist staff. The excellent and massive contributions made by the majority should not be overshadowed by line managers' avoidance of tackling the weak performance of a few.

CHANGE MANAGEMENT AND PROJECT MANAGEMENT

The delivery of specific equalities initiatives needs a level of change management and project management equal to that for other initiatives and projects in an organisation. This means that governance and managerial oversight need to be in place. The excellent *Managing Change in Health and Social Care Services* (Scragg 2010) draws on traditional texts and modern theories to present key aspects of managing change. Managers and leaders in organisations need to be alert as to whether equalities initiatives are given the same focus.

The human aspects of managing change in relation to equalities need to be understood and managed. Traditional texts highlight various reasons why people may resist change. Change in relation to equalities brings into focus some particular emotional dimensions. Some staff may believe that certain aspects of the equalities agenda are being handled incorrectly. For example, some staff seriously objected to the collection of data on sexuality as part of the annual 'Count Me In' census of mental health inpatients, coordinated by the Care Quality Commission. It is common for senior academics to suggest that the appropriate response to ethnicity within mental health services is simply to provide a personalised service to everyone. It is important that those with responsibility for managing change have the emotional intelligence (see Goleman 1995) to be mindful of the emotional component of change around equalities, and invoke strategies to manage these.

CONCLUSION

Equalities initiatives need to be managed with the same rigour as any other aspect of organisational delivery. This might be considered obvious, but there are a number of factors that interfere with the ability of organisations to manage equalities effectively; these might include, for example, deference to the knowledge and commitment of staff who share an identity with the target group with which they work, or lack of specificity on the part of organisational leaders about acceptable standards.

REFERENCES

Armstrong, M. (2009) *Armstrong's Handbook of Human Resources Management Practice.* London: Jessica Kingsley Publishers.

Crown (2011) The Equality Delivery System for the NHS (Amended January 2012). London: Department of Health. Accessed at www.eastmidlands.nhs.uk/about-us/inclusion/eds/ on 5 March 2012.

DoH (Department of Health) (2004a) *Mental Health Policy Implementation Guide: Community Development Workers for Black and Minority Ethnic Communities: Interim Guidance.* London: DoH.

DoH (2004b) *The NHS Knowledge and Skills Framework (NHS KSF) and the Development Review. Policy.* London: DoH.

DoH (2005) *Delivering Race Equality in Mental Health Care: An Action Plan for Reform Inside and Outside Services and the Government's Response to the Death of David Bennett.* London: DoH.

Dominelli, L. (2008) *Anti-racist Social Work.* Third edition. Basingstoke: Palgrave. (Original work published in 1997.)

Goleman, D. (1995) *Emotional Intelligence: Why It Can Matter More Than IQ.* London: Bloomsbury Publishing.

Marmot, M. (2010) *Fair Society, Healthy Lives.* London: The Marmot Review.

Men's Health Forum (2010) *Untold Problem: A Review of the Essential Issues in the Mental Health of Men and Boys.* London: Men's Health Forum.

Phillips, L. and Jackson, A. (2012) 'Gender-specific Mental Health Care: The Case for Women-centred Care.' In P. Phillips, T. Sandford and C. Johnston (Eds) *Working in Mental Health: Policy and Practice in a Changing Environment.* Abingdon: Routledge.

RCPsych. (Royal College of Psychiatrists) (2011) *National Audit of Psychological Therapies for Anxiety and Depression. National Report 2011.*

Scragg, T. (2001) *Managing at the Frontline: A Handbook for Managers in Social Care Agencies.* Brighton: Pavilion.

Scragg, T. (2010) *Managing Change in Health and Social Care Services.* Brighton: Pavilion.

Sewell, H. and Waterhouse, S. (2012) *Making Progress on Race Equality in Mental Health.* London: NHS Confederation.

Walker, R. and Craig, E. (2009) Community Development Workers for BME Mental Health: Embedding Sustainable Change. Accessed at www.nmhdu.org.uk/our-work/mhep/delivering-race-equality/dre-archive/dre-archive-community-development-workers/ on 5 May 2012.

Chapter 18

TACKLING INEQUALITY IN SERVICE DELIVERY

Melba Wilson and Hári Sewell

INTRODUCTION

Taking a cost-effective approach to equality requires a good understanding of the costs and consequences of *in*equality. This is even more necessary in a climate of economic austerity, stringent cutbacks and propensity for short-term cost-cutting exercises. This chapter makes the case for taking the long view, for developing approaches in service delivery that avoid waste of effort and resources and ultimately achieve greater value for money in terms of improved service user outcomes and experiences.

Timely and effective responses to people with mental health problems give excellent value for money (Centre for Mental Health 2010a, 2010b). In its policy paper on the economic and social costs of mental health problems in 2009/10, the Centre for Mental Health noted:

> Providing good quality parenting support to people with young children, extending access to psychological therapy, early identification of distress at work, diverting offenders with mental health difficulties from custody and assisting people with severe mental health problems into paid work all make a massive difference to people's lives and create both immediate and long term savings to public finances and to the wider economy. (Centre for Mental Health 2010a)

Key areas of focus in the financial case for tackling inequality in service delivery include taking account of:

- the costs of repeated admission and detention
- inadequate care pathways
- lack of early intervention.

These, in turn, have a knock-on effect which leads to poor experiences and outcomes, and therefore rising costs to maintain an ineffective status quo.

These areas of wasted resources are precisely the ones that are most closely associated with people in the groups with protected characteristics (as set out in Part II of this book). For example, Caribbean people have high detention rates; older people experience poor care pathways due to age discrimination; and women in inpatient wards have high rates of childhood sexual abuse, which may not be addressed in the clinical interventions. These are illustrative, but do indicate the priority areas for improving efficiency in service delivery for vulnerable groups, who are often people covered by protected characteristics.

DRIVERS FOR CHANGE

The cost of mental ill-health in England in 2011 was £105.2 billion a year. The figure includes the costs of health and social care, lost output in the economy, and the human costs of reduced quality of life (Centre for Mental Health 2010b). The financial case for addressing inequality rests not just in the costs to mental health services, but also in this wider context. More equal societies are more productive (Marmot 2010).

The imperative to make savings can have the impact of creating a greater focus on equalities (Sewell and Waterhouse 2012). Over a period of growth between 1997 and 2010, the National Health Service (NHS) needs now to make £15–£20 billion in efficiency savings by 2013–14. Ways have to be found to release money from the whole system to reinvest in quality improvements. The focus will be on redesigning services to improve quality and productivity, encouraging innovation, and preventative interventions (National Mental Health Development Unit (NMHDU) 2010). A detailed economic case for service redesign was constructed by the former Sainsbury Centre for Mental Health in relation to black people (their categorisation) (Sainsbury Centre for Mental Health 2006). The report, based on 2004–05 data, estimated that between £97.6m and £109.5m could be saved if the average spend per black service user was the same as for a white service user. Such detailed studies have not been undertaken in relation to all individual protected characteristics, but the lesson can be extrapolated to other groups.

In considering the financial case for addressing inequality, there are two sides of the coin to be considered. On one side there are cases for increasing efficiency, as set out in various publications (e.g. Centre for Mental Health 2010a; Naylor and Bell 2010), and within these the need to consider the implications for groups with protected characteristics. On the other side is the need to understand the nature of the inequalities as experienced by people in relation to their protected characteristics, and how increased efficiency can be achieved by better meeting their needs.

Inefficiencies in mental health services for people covered by protected characteristics usually result from:

- disproportionately high numbers accessing services in a crisis

- preventable use of high-cost specialist mental health services

- lower impact levels resulting from interventions, leading to poorer outcomes (such as longer lengths of stay and repeat admissions)

- use of services in disproportionately high numbers due to socioeconomic factors

- provision of services which do not address the underlying problems.

Identifying inefficiencies in mental health services for people with protected characteristics: An example

Affington Mental Health NHS Foundation Trust used a RAG rating system (red, amber, green, to denote priority) to identify the extent to which the criteria set out above applied to groups with the protected characteristics. This provided a snapshot of the hotspots for improving efficiency and contributed to thinking about an overarching cost improvement programme (see Table 17.1). Sex, for example, which covers men and women, was rated red for 'underlying problems not addressed' because for women there was some evidence that issues rating to childhood sexual abuse were sometimes not addressed, and the self-destructive behaviours exhibited by some men were not routinely addressed.

Table 18.1: Hotspot equality areas for improving efficiency

	Admission in Crisis	High use of specialist services	Poor service outcomes	Use of services in high numbers	Underlying problems not addressed
Age	R	A	R	G	A
Disability	A	A	R	A	G
Gender reassignment	G	G	R	G	G
Marriage and Civil Partnership	G	G	R	G	G
Pregnancy and maternity	G	G	R	G	A
Race	R	R	R	R	R
Religion or belief	G	G	R	G	A
Sex	A	A	R	A	R
Sexual orientation	G	G	R	A	R

Key:

R = red (requirement for urgent attention)

A = amber (attention required)

G = green (currently no critical issues identified)

Undertake the same exercise in your organisation or service to see where the hotspots might be for improving efficiency. Draw on service use data and qualitative information about experience.

DEVELOPING A COST-EFFECTIVE APPROACH IN SOUTHWEST LONDON

Taking a specific example of improving efficiency in relation to the groups covered by protected characteristics, this section examines work in London which is aimed at developing a cost-effective approach to mental health and social care, and highlights work underway in Southwest London, aimed at addressing issues of long-term conditions and out-of-hospital care, including mental health. These provide useful examples of how taking account of people's diverse needs and planning for the long term can lead to greater efficiencies.

The King's Fund report (Naylor *et al.* 2012) identifies a number of key messages in relation to cost, inequality and quality of care, including the following:

- Many people with long-term physical health conditions also have mental health problems, and these can lead to significantly poorer health outcomes and reduced quality of life.

- People with long-term conditions and co-morbid mental health problems disproportionately live in deprived areas and have access to fewer resources of all kinds. The interaction between co-morbidities and deprivation makes a significant contribution to generating and maintaining inequalities.

- Collaborative care arrangements between primary care and mental health specialists can improve outcomes with no, or limited, additional net costs; and clinical commissioning groups should prioritise integrating mental and physical health care more closely as part of their strategies to improve quality and productivity in health care.

Work to create models of mental health care for London set out the case for change for mental health services in London (London Health Programmes 2011). It reinforced the message of the National Mental Health Strategy, *No Health without Mental Health* (HM Government 2011), of improving outcomes for people with mental health problems through high-quality services accessible to all. The case for change acknowledged that:

London's mental health services face particular challenges…including higher than average numbers of people with complex needs, refugees and asylum seekers, and people with a dual diagnosis of mental illness and drug or alcohol problems. (London Health Programmes 2011, p.7)

The models of care which resulted from this work focused on two key aspects:

- the care received by people experiencing a crisis

- the care received by people with long-term mental health conditions.

Recommendations for improvement included:

- refocusing existing services

- shared care arrangements as integral

- a navigator role to facilitate access to services

- working in partnership.

The London Health Programmes acknowledge that implementation for both models will necessarily reflect local strategies, service configurations and levels of investment; and that plans will need to include 'the profile of investment and benefit realisation that reflects the starting point for each health economy and the pace of change considered affordable'.

A local case for change

Ongoing work in Southwest London is building on the ideas set out in the *Case for Change* (London Health Programmes 2011). The draft report of a clinical working group in Southwest London set out the challenges at a local level, in helping to establish and make real a case for change (Better Services, Better Value for South West London 2011). The report identified four themes:

- rising demand for healthcare: more people, needing more care in the future

- needing to do more with less: the reality of financial pressures

- achieving the highest possible standards of care and meeting patients' expectations

- responding to changes in staffing arrangements and shortages of skilled health professionals.

The work identified that an inherent principle in the case for change is that it 'may not be feasible to keep on doing what we've always done to meet the health needs of local residents' (Better Services, Better Value for South West London 2011, p.4). The draft report also identified and made recommendations for better coordinated and managed services. This was a key message from stakeholders who were consulted. So it can be seen that the aim is to work practically, work efficiently and, most important of all, work with the people who use the services.

EXPLORING COST-EFFECTIVE APPROACHES

When thinking about how best to meet needs within a context of financial constraints, a number of approaches are worth exploring, including the following.

- Personalisation – as a means of helping to ensure that people are in control of the support they need to live in the ways they wish to live (NMHDU 2010). Skills for Care (2012) has identified person-centred practice to achieve positive outcomes as a core standard for social care managers, and states in its refresh of standards that 'individuals must be given opportunities to express their needs, desires, preferences and wishes to be afforded a service that is personal to them' (Skills for Care 2010).

- Use of talking therapies – the improving access to psychological therapies programme offers extended scope to children and young people, those with physical health long-term conditions and mental health issues, those with medically unexplained symptoms, and those with severe mental illness. Outcomes are focused on:

  ◦ improved access to evidence-based psychological treatments

  ◦ improved mental health and well-being

  ◦ more people with lived experience of these situations involved in leading the changes

  ◦ more people able to resume or start normal working lives (Mullins 2011).

- Involving the voluntary sector – The King's Fund describes the voluntary and community sector (VCS) as 'an excellent example of why localism in health care can be so effective' (Nayler *et al.* 2012). It identifies that 'overall, the NHS spends £3.4 billion annually in the voluntary and community sector, [and that it]... has a strong track record of working with communities and supporting individuals to manage their health better' (Weaks 2012).

A joint King's Fund/National Council for Voluntary Organisations paper (Curry *et al.* 2011) makes a number of recommendations for improving the role of the VCS within the health and social care reforms. These point to the need for better engagement within the new structures; development of better funding mechanisms; and better strategic development by the sector.

CONCLUSION

This chapter has highlighted the fact that mental health services will inevitably be inefficient if the provision of services fails to achieve equitable improvements in outcomes for people from the groups with protected characteristics. Responding to the financial case for tackling inequality is about taking action to create changes in service delivery. This action should start with the aims of commissioning for good outcomes, and developing and maintaining services which reflect the diverse needs of the whole community; and it should be underpinned by the views and input of people who use the services. It necessarily involves taking account of the financial and political imperatives which govern health and social care frameworks. Efficient and targeted service delivery is *effective* service delivery.

It is not a quick fix. Meeting the needs of diverse groups will often require personalised approaches and changes to services. Realigning services to better meet needs will sometimes require some redistribution of resources. It can, however, generate lasting and long-term change such that costs and benefits are more closely correlated with needs.

REFERENCES

Better Services, Better Value for South West London (2011) Draft Clinical Report of Long-term Conditions and Out of Hospital Care (Including Mental Health). Clinical Working Group. Accessed at www.southwestlondon.nhs.uk/haveyoursay/bsbv/Pages/default.aspx.

Centre for Mental health (2010a) *The Economic and Social Costs of Mental Health Problems in 2009/10.* London: Centre for Mental Health.

Centre for Mental Health (2010b) *The Economic and Social Costs of Mental Health Problems in 2009/10, Updated Analysis. October.* London: Centre for Mental Health.

Curry, N. et al. (2011) *The Voluntary and Community Sector in Health: Implications of the Proposed NHS Reforms.* London: The King's Fund/National Council for Voluntary Organisations.

HM Government (2011) *No Health without Mental Health: A Cross-government Mental Health Outcomes Strategy for People of All Ages.* London: Department of Health.

London Health Programmes (2011) *Mental Health Services: Case for Change for London.* London: London Health Programmes.

Marmot, M. (2010) *Fair Society, Healthy Lives.* London: The Marmot Review.

Mullins, K. (2011) 'The Aspirations of the IAPT Programme.' Presentation to SMI Stakeholder Event, 23 November. Accessed at www.iapt.nhs.uk/smi-/ on 1 May 2012.

Naylor, C. and Bell, A. (2010) *Mental Health and the Productivity Challenge: Improving Quality and Value for Money.* London: The King's Fund.

Naylor, C., Parsonage, M., McDaid, D., Knapp, M., Fossey, M. and Galea, A. (2012) *Long-term Conditions and Mental Health: The Cost of Co-morbidities.* London: The King's Fund.

NMHDU (National Mental Health Development Unit) (2010) *Paths to Personalisation in Mental Health: A Whole System, Whole Life Framework.* London: NMHDU.

Sainsbury Centre for Mental Health (2006) *The Cost of Race Inequality. Policy Paper No. 6.* London: Sainsbury Centre for Mental Health.

Sewell, H. and Waterhouse, S. (2012) Making Progress on Race Equality in Mental Health. London: NHS Confederation. Accessed at www.nhsconfed.org/Publications/ on 3 September 2012.

Skills for Care (2012) Manager Induction Standards – Refreshed 2012 web edition. Accessed at www.skillsforcare.org.uk on 1 May 2012.

Weaks, L. (2012) Do Local Voluntary Organisations Hold the LKey to Improving Health Outcomes? Accessed at www.kingsfund.org.uk/blog/vcs_health_outcomes.html on 1 May 2012.

Chapter 19

ORGANISATIONAL DEVELOPMENT APPROACHES

Hári Sewell and Cheryl Brodie

INTRODUCTION

Compliance with legislation, policy and objectives to promote equality needs to be subject to the same management and leadership rigours as for any other area of responsibility in an organisation.

This is perhaps obvious, but many problems that arise in the delivery of this agenda do so because the usual rigours have not been applied.

A typical error in organisations, irrespective of the subject or specialism in question, is to focus on one aspect of an organisation, seeking the proverbial 'magic bullet' to solve problems. The reality is that most organisational problems are not down to a single aspect. This chapter focuses on organisational development (OD), because implementing the Equality Act is similar to implementing any change and requires understanding the whole system. It is only by taking an organisational development approach that there will be consistent improvements in equality over time.

WHAT IS ORGANISATIONAL DEVELOPMENT (OD)?

There is much confusion about what OD is and why it is useful. That is in large part due to OD's gradual emergence as a field with distinct knowledge, values and skills beginning in the 1980s. The founders of OD include Warren Bennis (1969), Edgar Schein (1969) and Richard Beckhard (1969), who were innovative in bringing together disciplines such as psychology, sociology, systems theory and management literature to achieve change within organisations.

There is a plethora of definitions of OD; however, this one avoids the jargon: 'OD is a field of knowledge and practices that guides an organisation to change to become more effective in a sustainable and healthy way.'

The goal is organisational effectiveness and improvement, and the focus is on looking at the whole system and how the parts (sections, departments teams and individuals) impact on each other.

Mistakenly, OD is sometimes seen as an approach to achieving change by focusing only on one aspect of an organisation – for example, rewriting the strategy or changing the structure. Although there is much evidence to the contrary, it is often hoped that all can be improved with an exciting strategic plan, or by rearranging the coloured boxes on a new structure chart.

However, as far back as the 1980s, there were models that began to consider the human dimensions of change: put simply, what makes people behave and do things differently. One of these is the 'McKinsey 7S' framework, which offers a sound approach to combining all of the essential factors that sustain good organisations (Waterman, Peters and Philips 1980). The model identifies seven aspects of an organisation that need to be given attention if change is to be effective and sustained. The seven aspects all begin with s: *strategy, systems, structure, skills, style, staff* and *shared values* (which last embraces all the other six).

Although the McKinsey 7S model is very useful, it is important to remember that this is just a particular construct. The key point to note is that the McKinsey model recognises the multiplicity of factors involved in bringing about change, and the way they interact and impact on each other. A simple example would be an organisation wanting to collect more information from staff. Obviously, the organisation would need to ensure that staff changed their behaviour to comply with this request; however, instructing people is rarely enough to get full compliance. Other aspects need to be considered – for example, the time involved, why the information is needed, how it will be stored and accessed.

Since the development of the McKinsey 7S model there has been a rise in rich data obtained in organisations about how to deliver and manage change – for example, through the work of Kanter (1983) and Kotter (1996; Kotter and Cohen 2002). OD has therefore been taken more seriously as a knowledge, skills and values set that helps organisations to become more effective.

The consistent lesson from all studies in OD is that no one individual is responsible for 'developing the organisation'. It is a collective responsibility, with the greatest burden of responsibility on those who are charged with leadership. It is the leaders who need to combine collecting and interrogating hard data, and changing the behaviour of staff.

HOW AN OD APPROACH SUPPORTS
THE EQUALITIES AGENDA

At the outset of this chapter it was noted that the equalities agenda needs to be subject to the same management rigours as for any other development within an organisation. This means that, when thinking about implementing any strand of the Equalities Act, the impact on the whole organisation needs to be considered. However, there is a further dimension and complication that needs thinking through: the impact of emotion. One of the striking features about working with difference is that it often generates uncomfortable and difficult emotions (see, for example, Macaulay 2010). Tackling unfairness, inequality or discrimination can often trigger challenging feelings, and sometimes these feelings are subconscious and not understood. For someone who experiences unfairness or inequality, this can generate anger and outrage. For those who are seen as perpetrating inequality, as part of a social class, society or system, they can feel accused and guilty, even when they know that they personally have done nothing wrong.

The intensity of unease may vary from one protected characteristic to another but, as explored in Chapter 14, there are sometimes conflicts between equalities agendas, leading to emotions ranging from acute embarrassment to anger (for example, where devout faiths try to accommodate homosexuality).

As stated above, OD needs to take account of how humans behave. However, when implementing the equalities agenda, understanding of the emotional aspect of change becomes paramount (Kanter 1983). Understanding the root causes of why change or development is slow or non-existent is still very important; however, a major aspect of this is understanding the emotion surrounding the way people and relationships function.

To help understand emotion, the concept of 'emotional intelligence' was coined by Daniel Goleman (1995), and it is becoming increasingly common in discourse around change in the National Health Service (NHS) and social care. Put simply, it is about understanding why, at crucial moments, the heart overrides the head when choosing how to act, and why passion overrides reason. Emotionally intelligent people understand this, and even though they have prejudices, as we all do, they can act as if they have none. Incorporating emotional intelligence into managerial practice will go some way towards indentifying and responding to some of the barriers to implementing initiatives to reduce inequality.

CASE STUDY 19.1: UNDERSTANDING THE EMOTIONAL ASPECT OF CHANGE

Carl was associate director in a mental health foundation trust. He was responsible for ensuring that the sexuality of inpatients was collected with other biographical data. Over the course of 18 months Carl reported the dissatisfaction of management after each quarterly report that showed very little progress towards the target of 85 per cent data compliance. Ward managers were told that they were failing to fulfil their management obligation, and harsh memos and warnings were issued.

On a managers' seminar the subject of data collection about sexuality emerged as a topic of conversation during a discussion about something else. Angry feelings emerged from the managers. Some felt that the executive had deliberately chosen a challenging matter in order to exercise their authority. Others felt that the requirement was fundamentally wrong because it was intruding into people's private lives. Others were supportive of the initiative in principle, but felt that the lack of appropriate training or briefing for staff and managers was bound to undermine it. Further, because of the ignorance and prejudice around homosexuality that emerged in the organisation, gay, lesbian and bisexual staff were feeling alienated from the organisation. Other staff felt that their concerns about the process around data collection were erroneously taken as signs of prejudice.

Brandy, the assistant director for OD, was present at the managers' seminar and assessed that increased pressure and sanctions were not achieving the intended aims of the executive. She discussed with Carl how best to bring the workforce on board. They arranged for some well-informed briefings and discussion groups at which attendance was voluntary. During the briefings the reasons were explained why the data was needed, and participants discussed sensitive ways of collecting it. The findings were used to inform a decision by the executive to support some managers' workshops, where they too were able to explore their own thoughts and feelings and develop understanding about why and how the data would be used.

Within the following six months, data collection on the wards steadily increased from 7 per cent to 78 per cent. Though this was still some way off the target, there was evidence of a sea change in attitude and behaviour amongst the staff teams.

The example in Case Study 19.1 illustrates how the instructions and sanctions of management can be ineffective if the emotional aspects of change are not taken into account and responded to. Returning to the McKinsey 7S model (Waterman *et al.* 1980) it is apparent that Carl was also ignorant about how to manage the emotional aspect of change. Initially Carl assumed that the staff were uncooperative and difficult. Carl had naively thought that he could tell his subordinates what to do and that this would be a 'reasonable management request' (a term used in employment law).

In contrast, the staff were outraged. Didn't Carl realise what their workload was? Did he really think he could just keep asking them for extra work? Had he no idea what would happen if they asked such sensitive questions? Did he ever think about what their role was? Referring back to the 7S model: Carl had not considered the shared values, the skills nor the systems (the procedures, processes and routines) that characterise the way important work is to be done.

The OD approach provides a framework for analysing the causes of problems and barriers in implementing change (Kotter 1996). It trains the managerial eye to view the entire organisational landscape. It would be naive of managers to ignore the complexity of implementing change in the equalities agenda, given the legacy of inequalities documented in Part II of this book. This is particularly the case if managers and leaders of organisations wish to see sustained, meaningful change, rather than just achieving the satisfaction of ticking a box to say that a target or objective has been met, whether locally determined or not.

RISK ASSOCIATED WITH A PARTIAL APPROACH TO IMPLEMENTING EQUALITIES

The workforce in mental health services is the most valuable and costly resource (Audit Commission 2006). The risks associated with poor workforce management in relation to equalities and diversity are captured in Chapter 20. Failure to capitalise upon all talents and deal with problems in relationships among workers, or even resentment amongst staff who experience their organisation as paying undue regard to equality in workforce management, are all concerns that are dealt with in Chapter 20.

The organisational risks associated with partial implementation of the Equalities Act 2010 and attendant guidance are myriad. Risks in the NHS are typically grouped in categories such as governance, financial, legal, reputational, workforce and clinical. There is interplay between all of these risks. A bad legal ruling against an organisation will have a potentially adverse impact on reputation, and it is likely to have a negative financial impact, not just because of the costs of fighting a case, but because of consequential lost revenue if detrimental commissioning decisions are made.

In practical terms, failure to lead the implementation of equalities and ensure that clear objects are managed effectively might lead to:

- disempowered staff who identify a need but are unable to meet it

- superficial achievement of targets with little change of substance (e.g. number of people trained with little impact on practice)

- gap between rhetoric of leaders and reality of front-line staff, creating resentment in front-line managers and staff

- money wasted on failed initiatives, such as development programmes for black and minority ethnic (BME) staff which fail to achieve goals because the organisation is ambivalent

- reputational damage resulting from incidents, if staff make claims against the organisation on the basis of any protected characteristic

- poor relationships with stakeholders

- legal costs at employment tribunals.

CASE STUDY 19.2: FAILURE TO LEAD THE IMPLEMENTATION OF EQUALITIES

Karen, a community psychiatric nurse, has received positive feedback in her annual appraisal for several years. Her practice has been held in high regard, and successive team managers have paired new nurses with her to ensure that they have exposure to the best practice. Karen has a visual impairment.

In the last year the trust has moved to electronic recording on domiciliary visits. All staff were issued with electronic tablets that are linked to the electronic patient record system to enable real-time recording. Karen has found it difficult to use her tablet on the road, despite the functions designed to improve accessibility for people with visual impairments. This related to the layout of the forms on the software used by the trust. Despite the fact that managers have said that Karen could still record on paper and use a desktop computer later, she has felt that the organisation had been discriminatory. For example, when staff were told that they could leave early on New Year's Eve, Karen was told that perhaps she should stay behind because no doubt she had recording to do. In staff meetings the assistant director publicly said that everyone was able to 'see' the benefit of using the tablets, and then added 'well almost everyone' with a raise of eyebrows and a stare in

Karen's direction. Such comments became more frequent, and Karen's manager began asking repeatedly if she still felt that she was in the right job.

Eventually Karen resigned and took out a claim for discrimination on the grounds of disability. The trust lost the case and paid compensation. As a result commissioners said that they wanted reassurance that the workforce was appropriately trained. In a defensive act the trust executive commissioned a raft of equality training and engaged an external expert to review the single equalities scheme to identify gaps. The total cost, including staff release time, was estimated at over £200,000. Both the episode and the trust's response had a negative impact on its credibility amongst staff and local stakeholders. The local media ran a negative campaign.

A POSITIVE MODEL – THE EQUALITIES ORGANISATIONAL DEVELOPMENT TOOLKIT

In 2010 the National Mental Health Development Unit (NMHDU) commissioned a piece of work to explore how the development of equalities could move away from a focus on training to focusing on reviewing the organisation as a whole. A toolkit published by NMHDU in 2011.

In the process of developing the Organisational Development Toolkit, NMHDU piloted the work with St Andrew's Healthcare. The learning from the pilot is described within the toolkit itself, and it makes explicit the fact that development of the organisation required not just acknowledgement of the feelings that were expressed (or suppressed), but appropriate responses as well.

Description of the toolkit

The toolkit is named 'Equalities is a Management Issue', confirming the premise, as stated earlier in this chapter, that reducing inequalities needs to be subjected to the same disciplines and governance as are required for other strategies.

The toolkit illustrates responsibilities at different levels within an organisation and makes suggestions about how to move from aspirations around tacking inequality to their practical application. The idea was to support organisations to reflect on what good might look like for them, as opposed to imposing a fixed model of 'the right way to do things'.

The toolkit stresses that implementing equalities involves everyone in the organisation doing something differently.

The ideas are divided into four levels within the organisation:

- board or executive – this takes an OD approach

- service manager or lead professional – a manager or leader covering a range of services

- team manager, e.g. a community mental health team manager, ward manager, or manager of a particular service

- individual – anyone, at any level, whether they manage or not.

Why the toolkit is considered to be a positive model

For reducing inequality in health services to be a reality, we must focus on outcomes. The toolkit took this approach by suggesting a variety of ideas to demonstrate not only sound process, but really effective results.

The starting point was an analysis of data to identify where there is inequality. Sources of data include:

- patient experience

- patient stories and feedback

- GP feedback

- patient survey

- staff survey

- complaints PEAT (Patients Environment Action Team) scores

- nursing care indicators.

The analysis was then used to set objectives in service plans, that should be translated into individual objectives at appraisal. Examples are set out below.

- Reduce sexual assaults on female patients.

- Increase the numbers of older people who have access to new services, e.g. crisis intervention.

- Reduce the disproportionate rates of compulsory detention of BME service users in inpatient units.

- Ensure balanced range of effective therapies – such as peer support services and psychotherapeutic and counselling treatments, as well as pharmacological interventions that are appropriate and effective across genders, social class and disabilities.

This approach is a departure from the more common inequality awareness-raising workshops, and suggests the focus should be on measurable improvements. To achieve these hard targets will require a great deal of soft skills and emotional intelligence.

How the toolkit can be used for maximum impact

The way the toolkit can be used is demonstrated by the case study at St Andrew's (NMHDU 2011).

St Andrew's is the UK's largest not-for-profit mental healthcare charity. They provide an extensive variety of care pathways, through medium to low secure and pre-discharge services, and also offer a variety of more specialist treatments, including treatments for autistic spectrum disorder and Huntington's disease. In supporting the NMHDU's project to test their draft Equalities Organisational Development Project (EqODP) toolkit, St Andrew's took the following preliminary steps:

- secured commitment from the senior management board

- identified a director lead

- identified an internal project lead who met with the EqODP leads from the NMHDU to explore the project options.

The starting point was curiosity about the reasons why BME staff had a disproportionate number of disciplinaries. However, preliminary meetings with the EqODP leads broadened the areas that St Andrew's wished to explore. They were defined as:

- the extent to which a disproportionately high proportion of their BME nursing staff worked at night

- the perceptions and realities of the contributions made by night staff to service user care, and the value placed on them

- the relationship between potentially negative perceptions and experiences of night staff, and the high proportion of BME staff within this section of the workforce.

The project gathered data from organisational workforce reports and from well facilitated focus groups, exploring the issue from the perspectives of:

- night shift nursing staff

- day shift nursing staff

- ward managers

- senior staff.

This approach therefore considered an organisational challenge from a variety of perspectives, going well beyond a one-dimensional approach that would focus solely on one issue (for example, skills).

The OD approach considered many of the 'McKinsey 7S' factors, exploring how strategy, systems, structure, style, skills, staff and shared values all impacted on each other.

The project identified that daytime staff and managers held the view that night-time nurses were, as a group, less competent than their daytime counterparts. Night-time staff felt undervalued and overlooked, and were in fact undermanaged. There was not, however, an explicit association between the number of BME staff and negative perceptions.

The potential solutions that were developed suggested that teams be managed as a whole, and that a light be shone on much of the good practice that happened at night but was rarely seen. It was suggested that training be given at night, and that managers should on occasion do part of their duties at night. The project raised the consideration as to whether the St Andrew's charity might use a rotational approach that had been successful elsewhere.

EXERCISE 19.1: SIMPLE EQUALITIES ORGANISATIONAL DEVELOPMENT SELF-ASSESSMENT

Use the following chart reproduced from the Equalities Organisational Development toolkit as a simple self-assessment tool, to prompt initial ideas about the starting point for implementing the Equalities Act 2010 within your own organisation.

Table 19.1: Self-assessment tool

Ideas	We are already doing this	We would like to do this	Priority and timescale
1. Have equalities as a standing agenda item, including assessments of the impact of policies and functions on protected groups, and review achievements annually.			
2. Review representation of protected groups in services and set targets and SMART objectives to bring about change.			
3. Evaluate the impacts of one of your policies in depth and extrapolate the learning across other areas of business or protected groups.			
4. Collect, analyse and publish workforce data relating to recruitment, selection, access to training, career progression, grievances and disciplinaries. Draft a strategy to prioritise and address these issues, with clear milestones.			
5. Pick one or two issues from the equality and diversity agenda and embed into working practices as an exemplar project for managing organisational change.			
6. Organise a 'reducing inequalities' staff conference. Celebrate successes; create interest and involvement by generating ideas from staff.			
7. Develop an award scheme for staff who have taken action which has reduced inequality or had an impact overcoming challenges faced by specific target groups.			
8. Include commitments to equality and diversity in core values, mission statement and strategic plans.			
9. Have champions – encourage board members/exec directors to lead on specific equalities areas or have one member of the board as the lead on this area.			
10. Use self-assessment tools to help understand where you are and where you want to be.			
Your ideas…			

Source: NMHDU; Crown copyright 2011

FROM ASPIRATION TO ACTUALISATION – KEY ESSENTIALS

Moving from intention to action is a very hard path, summed up in the proverb 'The road to hell is paved with good intentions.' Capturing the essence of the Equality Act 2010 and embedding it in the culture will be a change, and change, as we have all experienced, is mostly difficult. That is why it is often recommended to work with OD specialists who can bring process skills and expertise to implementing something new. The first step is for people to understand why the Equality Act was needed, and to have a chance to think about what needs to change, as well as how to make it happen. The goal is greater ownership and understanding the meaning of what people are asked to do differently.

There are a number of key writers on making change happen – for example, John Kotter's highly regarded books *Leading Change* (1996) and the follow-up *The Heart of Change* (Kotter and Cohen 2002) describe a popular and helpful model for understanding and managing change. Each stage acknowledges a key principle identified by Kotter, relating to people's response and approach to change, a process in which people see, feel, and then change. The starting point is persuading leadership that something needs to be done and having aims and objectives around the equalities agenda.

CONCLUSION

One only has to look at how health organisations and others struggle to implement health and safety legislation to realise that implementing legislation is hard. Implementing the Equality Act 2010 is more challenging because of the strong emotion it evokes. However, the changes required by this legislation need to be treated with the same leadership vision and management discipline as any others. To do this an OD approach is necessary, bringing together all the aspects of an organisation and not pretending that a short information workshop is going to make any difference at all.

REFERENCES

Audit Commission (2006) *Managing Finances in Mental Health. A Review to Support Improvement and Best Practice. National Report.* London: Audit Commission.

Beckhard, R. (1969) *Organisation Development: Strategies and Models.* Reading, MA: Addison-Wesley.

Bennis, W.G. (1969) *Organisation Development: Its Nature, Origins and Prospects.* Reading, MA: Addison-Wesley.

Goleman, D. (1995) *Emotional Intelligence: Why it Can Matter More Than IQ.* London: Bloomsbury.

Kanter, R.M. (1983) *The Change Masters.* New York: Simon & Schuster.

Kotter, J. (1996) *Leading Change.* Boston, MA: Harvard Business School Press.

Kotter, J. and Cohen, D. (2002) *The Heart of Change: Real-Life Stories of How People Change their Organisations.* Boston, MA: Harvard Business Press.

Macaulay, J.R. (2010) '"Just as I am without one plea": a journey to reconcile sexuality and spirituality.' *Ethnicity and Inequalities in Health and Social Care 3*, 3, 6–13.

NMHDU (National Mental Health Development Unit) (2011) *Equalities Organisational Development Toolkit.* London: NMHDU.

Schein, E.H. (1969) *Process Consultations: Its Role in Organisation Development.* Reading, MA: Addison-Wesley.

Waterman, R.H., Peters T.J. and Phillips, J.R. (1980) 'Structure is not organisation.' *Business Horizons 23*, 3 June, 14–26.

Chapter 20

SKILLING
THE WORKFORCE

Hári Sewell and Cheryl Brodie

INTRODUCTION

Workforce development is about developing the people in an organisation to improve the way services and activities are delivered. It is likely to be driven by some of the following elements: analysis of and response to the policy environment, organisational objectives and individual and team needs (Scragg 2001).

Workforce development is sometimes seen in isolation as purely improving the capabilities, knowledge and skills of staff. This chapter on skilling the workforce takes the approach that workforce development is part of the development of the overall capacities of an organisation and system (i.e. a system of partners essential for delivery of comprehensive care and treatment). Chapter 17 on applying management rigours to the equalities agenda, and Chapter 19 on organisational development, set a broader context for understanding how skilling the workforce contributes to wider organisational capacities.

In this chapter, skilling the workforce incorporates more than just the development of skills in the purest sense, and includes the knowledge, skills and attitude required to provide good mental health care to all people, mindful of the particular needs of people with protected characteristics.

This chapter is deliberately not entitled 'training', because since the 1990s there has been a move away from the idea that organisations train staff members who are passive recipients of knowledge and skills. The emphasis is now on learning as a self-directed and work-based process that leads to improved performance. This might be provided by coaching or mentoring opportunities, for instance (Chartered Institute of Development (CIPD) 2012).

DRIVERS FOR DEVELOPING THE WORKFORCE

It would be naive to suppose that the catalyst for staff development is always rooted in a desire to see better performance by individuals and/ or the organisation. As well as altruistic intentions, other drivers for workforce development include political manoeuvring and reputational management of an organisation. For example, an inquiry into the death of a service user who committed suicide on an inpatient ward may have identified that the deceased was a victim of homophobic abuse from fellow patients, with complicity on the part of staff. In such a case a training programme around sexual orientation may be invoked even in a climate where cuts are being made to the learning and development budget. Such a decision may not be driven by a purely moral or ethical imperative – other reasons could include pre-empting an investigation from the regulator; pacifying a powerful lobby group; managing the corporate reputation internally and externally; responding to pressure from commissioners; or responding to legislation.

A key question to bear in mind is why a senior management team would want to spend a large sum of money on the workforce.

The ways in which staff knowledge, skills and attitudes are developed have changed over time, largely as a result of shifts in political agendas or new development in thinking within the human resources management discipline. It is important to understand these developments when considering the best ways of identifying the needs of staff and ensuring that their knowledge, skills and attitudes are enhanced accordingly. Different approaches are outlined below.

COMPETENCY-BASED APPROACHES

These seek to describe the knowledge and skills required to perform some stated functions at a particular level. For example, a senior clinician with supervisory responsibilities will be expected to have an understanding of inequalities and how they are manifest in the lives of service users and staff, and they may also be required to know the legislation underpinning this area. The competency-based approach sets out 'what good looks like' and requires only evidence that a particular individual has achieved the described level of competence, rather than evidence of activity such as training in that area. This approach is akin to an outcomes-based approach where the main interest is the end result, rather than the mechanism for achieving it (Fletcher 1991).

INPUTS-FOCUSED AND ACHIEVING TARGETS

Under the 1997–2010 Labour Government there was a preponderance of targets in the public sector set with the intention of raising standards and creating uniformly high service quality across the country. An unintended consequence of this was that the inputs were sometimes identified as targets because they were easier to measure (i.e. the number of people trained in a subject is easier to measure than the number of people able to fulfil particular functions to an agreed acceptable standard). A second unintended consequence was the focus of organisations on ticking a box demonstrating that they had met a particular target by any means necessary. This could include categorising a rushed briefing session on a topic in a team meeting as 'training'.

As Chapter 19 points out, a large component of developing competence in equalities is dealing with the emotional content. Inequality brings up issues around unfairness, which leads to debates and strong emotions about what constitutes unfairness and the relative roles of perpetrators and victims. The legacy of the tendency toward short, focused inputs (training or briefing sessions) continues, fuelled by the shrinking of resources for learning and development arising from public sector budget reductions. This poses risks that equalities training loses out owing to the lack of time or expert delivery to unearth and explore the emotional content alongside the hard knowledge and skills being taught.

ADULTS AS ACTIVE LEARNERS

A positive advance in the world of learning and development is the increased emphasis on staff being active in their own learning. This marks a shift from centrally delivered training courses requiring off-site attendance (with all the associated travel and opportunity costs) to learning where individuals are encouraged and supported to access the development best suited to meet their unique development needs.

Another advantage of the emphasis on adults as active learners is that individuals assume responsibility for identifying the gaps in their knowledge and skills and ensuring that the appropriate learning takes place. Experts in learning and development become consultants to help and guide, replacing the doctor–patient model where the trainer makes the diagnosis and suggests the cure (Schein 1990). Instead, they can suggest a range of methods that the learner can follow to acquire the knowledge, attitude or skill required, and learners can choose a methodology that suits their learning style (Kolb and Fry 1975).

SHIFT FROM TRAINING
TO PERSONAL DEVELOPMENT

The shift from training to personal development denotes the increased utilisation of other interventions to improve knowledge and skills, such as mentoring, shadowing, job rotation, action learning sets, coaching, supervision, and group reflective practice. All these methods encourage reflective practice and provide opportunities for thinking about client work and unconscious processes (Obholzer and Roberts 1994). This is particularly valuable when learning about equalities because it is through talking and challenge that individuals can see where their prejudice lies. The group supervision model is particularly useful if well facilitated. It is retrospective and experience-orientated, and it is designed to promote and develop the group's overall competence by facilitating the group process, as well as extending and improving levels of professional knowledge. It also encourages openness and uses the experience of group members in uncovering the process that is going on within the group (e.g. competition and rivalry, or fight or flight) (Bion 1961).

It is relatively easy to tick a box confirming that staff know they must treat people equally regardless of race or sex, but a completely different level of learning is required to hold a group reflective practice session discussing why black men stay on mental health wards longer than white men with the same level of health needs. In the second option there is the possibility to talk about the emotions involved in treating someone who somehow seems different, and to share feelings about issues that arise (Schon 1983). Awareness of feelings opens up the possibility of choice. Instead of denial there is room for interest and thinking of strategies and solutions which can improve an individual's skills and the outcome for clients. This is not an easy learning method, but it is more effective in finding improved ways of working (Obholzer and Roberts 1994).

In health and social care, where many roles are based on judgement, interventions other than off-site training hold the potential to bring about more sustained improvements in individuals. These other approaches reflect a shift to a more person-centred approach to developing individual members of the workforce.

Despite the shift in approach by specialists in human resources or personnel, many publications suggesting improvements in the mental health workforce in relation to equalities cite staff training where there is a standard, usually didactic approach as being desirable (Commission for Social Care Inspection (CSCI) 2008).

APPROACHES TO KNOWLEDGE AND SKILL DEVELOPMENT ON EQUALITIES

Focus on individual protected characteristics

One of the biggest challenges in workforce development in relation to equalities is determining whether a single equalities programme is to be pursued, or whether there are sufficient resources to provide development on individual protected characteristic (and whether such an approach is in fact desirable).

Generalised equalities approach

It is clear from research (Sewell and Waterhouse 2012) that the adoption of a single equalities approach, if not implemented accurately, can lead to a weakening grasp of the matters of significance in relation to each of the protected characteristics. The tension remains, then: the Equality Act 2010 and subsequent policies and frameworks such as the Equality Delivery System in the NHS (Crown 2011) push services towards a single equalities approach, but there are different interpretations as to what is required. Some of these approaches are more detrimental than others. For example, one interpretation of adopting a single equalities approach is to think about equalities in a general sense. Typically this would mean focusing on issues such as dignity and person-centred approaches, in the belief that no specialist knowledge is required – just openness and a preparedness to allow individual wishes and needs to be responded to in care planning; this approach is often described as 'personalisation'.

There is a drawback of assuming that personalisation automatically addresses inequality for all the protected characteristics. In reality the best way to address inequality is to understand how inequalities are played out in people's lives.

CASE STUDY 20.1: PERSONALISATION: THE MAIN DRAWBACK

Elizabeth is a social worker who believes strongly in personalised approaches in the provision of health and social care services. Though her client, Candice (who had her first admission), does not have a personal budget for social care, Elizabeth tries to support her to control the direction of her care as much as possible. Elizabeth asks questions to prompt Candice to think about as many aspects of her life as possible. She asks about what Candice might like to do with her days: education, volunteering, employment, etc. Elizabeth asks about what kind of accommodation Candice would like, what area, any amenities she would like nearby, would she like it to be somewhere where, if she found a boyfriend, he would be able to stay over? Elizabeth asks Candice to just say what is important to her in rebuilding her life, and to try and incorporate these into her care plan.

Candice is a lesbian and found Elizabeth's assumption and references to her boyfriend to be disturbing. Candice felt privately that hostility from her parents about her sexuality precipitated her breakdown, and this was reflected in her own and her family's silence on this issue at the point of admission. Candice was seeking new accommodation precisely because she felt that the homophobia and hostility at home would be detrimental to her mental health. Candice found Elizabeth's assumptions about her sexuality to be hurtful and alienating. Despite Elizabeth's attempt to be inclusive and work towards personalised care, she had missed a most important aspect of equalities.

Personalised approach

The illustration in Case Study 20.1 demonstrates how a generalised approach can still create shortcomings when considering staff development needs. The illustration used a thoughtless assumption to make the point, but there are other issues that arise in assuming that personalisation covers equalities adequately. A lack of knowledge about the drivers for inequality means that certain inequalities might be lost. For example, a personalised approach may enable a woman to speak about how she would like to be treated on a ward, but if the staff are not aware of the fact that nearly 50 per cent of women on impatient wards are likely to have experienced childhood sexual abuse and other sexual violence (Read 1997), sufficient planning cannot be put in place to take account of this in staffing rotas and planning activities when male and female wards are adjacent.

For each protected characteristic there will be factors that need to be at the forefront of workers' minds. Such a factor could be the issue that some linguistic minorities will give the impression of understanding English more than they can; or that an older person acquiesces in a decision because it is generationally normal to be grateful for any care and support. The role of power and systems in silencing people from protected groups needs to be incorporated into knowledge that is drawn upon professionally. Workers need to know how trends of traditionally poor service outcomes indicate that specific actions need to be taken, otherwise these trends may well continue on the negative trajectory. Personalised approaches on their own will not stem this.

Human rights-based approach

The human rights-based approach to equalities is described in Senghera (2010). The articles of the European Convention of Human Rights were incorporated into domestic law under the Human Rights Act 1998 (Crown 1998) and there is an approach to addressing inequalities that ensures that individual human rights are given centrality in planning and delivering care. As in the personalisation approach, individual need is seen as the driver for fairness, but the risks are similar. These relate to a failure to recognise errors and negative trends that are likely to go unabated unless they are known about and tackled explicitly.

Fragmented focus on one or two protected characteristics

One approach to mitigating the risk of a generalised approach is to pursue development programmes that are based on individual protected characteristics. There is some merit in this. Some leading academics and voices of authority criticise the system of grouping together all equalities and not giving a special identity to race, for example (*The Guardian* 2012). If practitioners are exposed to development in one protected characteristic, it is probable that they will achieve more depth, more understanding of applicability to practice. There are two main risks, however. First, that certain protected characteristics will be covered (e.g. race) because of the political sensitivities and volume of data supporting an argument, whilst others (such as disability) may be relegated to a future programme that never materialises. Second, that such a model reinforces the view that individual identities can be seen in silos rather than in terms of a fluid movement between different aspects of self, as explained by the concept of intersectionality (see Chapters 2 and 3). A practitioner skilled in understanding race inequality in mental health may focus on this aspect and fail to address adequately the needs of an individual from the perspective of being a woman who experiences racism, sexism and discrimination due to pregnancy and maternity.

Single equalities

A single equalities approach to workforce development is likely to be delivered as interventions that cover all protected characteristics, either together or in modular sessions, with the whole programme eventually covering all protected characteristics with some discussion about the complexity of identity.

Best practice in the single equalities approach would strike a good balance between depth and breadth: depth in the subject area of each protected characteristic and the way in which inequalities are manifest, and breadth in comprehensive coverage of all protected characteristics.

KEY CONTENT FOR EQUALITIES DEVELOPMENT PROGRAMMES

This chapter is not intended to be prescriptive about the content of development programmes. Each area will need to take account of factors such as local priorities, community requests, outcomes from serious case reviews, and findings from local reviews of data on service utilisation. There are, however, some key aspects of content that should be considered as a minimum. These are set out below:

- legislative context

- definitions of terminology

- illustrations of how inequalities become manifest in mental health for each of the nine protected characteristics

- impact of histories of oppression and disadvantage

- power

- identity and personal experience

- evidence from service utilisation

- evidence from research

- positive practice.

As with the design of any development programme, the starting point has to be the delegates' existing experience, knowledge, attitude and skills. It is better that development is in stages, starting with the need for legislation and how to comply, followed by in-depth sessions with case studies based on the protected characteristics.

EVALUATION OF DEVELOPMENT PROGRAMMES

Although there is much training that is delivered, there is very little evaluation. Evaluating programmes is difficult, but much more effort should be made to ascertain the reaction of the learners, what change has taken place in behaviour, and the effects on outcomes (Kirkpatrick 1993).

As said earlier, anyone responsible for the development budget must be able to answer the question posed by senior management, 'Why spend budget on equalities?' In addition to the moral reasons, the answer should include a hard business case, working out how much bad practice may cost. (This could be the cost of someone staying longer in a hospital when they could be discharged, or the cost of a tribunal case for not complying with the law.)

INTERVENTIONS FOR IMPROVING KNOWLEDGE, SKILLS AND CAPABILITIES

It is a common problem that learning and development departments are reduced in lean times. This demonstrates senior managers' opinion that the cost of learning exceeds the benefits, and that if budgets are cut, activity will not be missed. Therefore, those holding the budget and resources must choose their development methods wisely. Effectiveness can only be demonstrated if thought is given at the outset to what is to be achieved – for example, a reduction in serious incidents, shorter stay on the wards, fewer hospital admissions, better patient satisfaction scores. E-learning is gaining popularity and is often cited as being cost-effective, flexible and convenient. This may well be true for testing knowledge, but not so good for improving practice in a department.

There are many methods to choose from. The common learning methodologies are defined below.

- *Shadowing:* Job shadowing is a career exploration activity that offers an opportunity to spend time with a professional currently working in a person's field of interest. It offers a chance to see what it is like working in a specific job and to have questions answered.

- *Mentoring:* Mentoring is a relationship between an experienced person and a less experienced person for the purpose of helping the one with less experience. The mentor provides advice and support, as well as wisdom.

- *Training:* Training usually refers to some kind of organised event such as a seminar or workshop that has a specific start and end date. It is often a group activity, but the word 'training' is also used to refer to specific instruction done one-on-one.

- *Coaching:* Coaching is the art of facilitating the performance, learning and development of another person. The coach uses a variety of techniques to enable the coachee to identify problems and generate their own solutions.

- *Team-based case studies and consultancy:* This is when a team comes together to review a case or serious incident. The starting assumption is that individuals want to do a good job, but systems and processes could be improved. The facts of the case or incident are established and a timeline and process map compiled by the group. The group identifies where improvements could be made without apportioning blame to any individuals. It is helpful to have a facilitator to guide the process.

- *Action learning sets:* An action learning set is a group of between four and seven people, who meet regularly to support one another in their learning in order to take purposeful action on work issues. A set member presents a problem and the participants then ask searching questions to enable the problem holder to identify a solution.

- *Supervision:* Supervision is a meeting between two people for the purpose of reflection, support and learning. It enables individual practitioners to develop their knowledge and competence and to consider accountability for their own practice. The meeting is usually with a more experienced professional, but peer supervision is also useful.

- *Group supervision:* This is where a group of staff reflect on their practice. It is often a self-selected group, rather than the whole team as above.

- *E-learning:* This is electronic learning that is delivered, enabled or mediated using technology for the explicit purpose of training in organisations. One form is training modules that can be completed at an individual's computer. Another method is web-based training which comprises technology that is used to deliver content to the end user without significant interaction with (or support from) training professionals, peers or managers. (For example, it can be a lecture delivered online.) There is also informal e-learning, where individuals browse the internet for knowledge they want.

- *Personal study:* This is where an individual chooses how they wish to learn.

- *Reflective journals:* This is where a group of people come together to discuss an interesting article.

THE ORGANISATIONAL CONTEXT – ENABLING OR BLOCKING

Chapter 19 emphasised the organisational development approach that places the knowledge and skills of the workforce within the context of other key elements of an organisation. A learning and development department or team will struggle to support the development of knowledge and skills unless certain aspects are in place:

- clarity about the real objectives being pursued and the model of equalities training acceptable to the organisation

- leadership from the board and senior management team

- clarity in organisational policies about acceptable standards of practice

- the culture of the organisation – unwritten understandings about what is acceptable

- organisational priorities in everyday working life

- resources freed for development.

THE DEVELOPMENT PLANNING CHECKLIST

This chapter is not prescriptive about what a development programme for equalities should look like, but certain aspects are worthy of consideration by the person or team responsible for ensuring that the development needs of the workforce are met. The checklist in Table 20.1 may serve as a useful resource for ensuring that essential elements have been considered in setting out a development programme for staff.

Table 20.1: Development planning checklist

Check	Tick	Notes
Is every protected characteristic covered somewhere in the period by the learning and development cycle (as set out in the organisational learning and development plan)?		
Is a full range of interventions being considered:		
• training		
• e-learning		
• consultation sessions		
• team learning		
• shadowing		
• mentoring		
Are development providers (internal or external) equipped and able to demonstrate:		
• expertise based on study and not solely on personal experience		
• knowledge of how protected characteristics interact		
Is the model of development clearly based on an *integrated* approach or *discrete* approach for each protected characteristic, and is this aligned to the organisational approach to equalities?		

CONCLUSION

Skilling the workforce requires corporate honesty about the precipitants of resource allocation to workforce development. The interventions suited to developing the staff in relation to equalities are those that engage the workforce as active learners, and those that include reflection and open dialogue. Making decisions about the approach to skilling the workforce in a single equalities approach is not a science. The benefit of achieving breadth across all protected characteristics should not come at the expense of depth, otherwise staff will know that there is inequality for different groups with protected characteristics, but will not necessarily know precise ways in which these are played out in mental health services. Staff need to be equipped to identify inequalities and discrimination, or the potential for these, and to be skilled at intervening effectively. Achieving this to a high standard across all protected characteristics is a challenge. Those planning staff development programmes need to be mindful of this and plan accordingly.

REFERENCES

Bion, W.R. (1961) *Experiences in Groups*. London: Tavistock Publications.
CIPD (Chartered Institute of Development) (2012) Coaching and Mentoring Factsheet. August. London: CIPD. Accessed at www.cipd.co.uk/hr-resources/factsheets/coaching-mentoring.aspx on 19 September 2012.
Crown (1998) *Human Rights Act*. London: Crown.
Crown (2011) The Equality Delivery System for the NHS. (Updated January 2012.) Accessed at www.eastmidlands.nhs.uk/about-us/inclusion/eds/ on 10 April 2012.
CSCI (Commission for Social Care Inspection) (2008) *Putting People First: Equality and Diversity Matters 1. Providing Appropriate Services for Lesbian, Gay and Bisexual and Transgender People*. London: CSCI.
Fletcher, S. (1991) *Designing Competence-Based Training*. London: Kogan Page.
Guardian, The (2012) 'Black and minority ethnic mental health participants "marginalised" under coalition.' 18 April, p.35.
Kirkpatrick D.L. (1993) *Evaluating Training Programs: The Four Levels*. San Francisco, CA: Berrett-Koehler.
Kolb. D.A. and Fry, R. (1975) 'Toward an Applied Theory of Experiential Learning.' In C. Cooper (Ed.) *Theories of Group Process*. London: John Wiley.
Obholzer, A. and Roberts, V. (1994) *The Unconscious at Work: Individual and Organizational Stress in the Human Services*. London: Routledge.
Read, J. (1997) 'Child abuse and psychosis: a literature review and implications for professional practice.' *Professional Psychology: Research and Practice 28*, 5, 448–456.
Schein, E.A. (1990) 'General philosophy of helping: process consultation.' *Sloan Management Review 31*, 3, Spring.
Schon, D. (1983) *The Reflective Practitioner: How Professionals Think in Action*. New York: Basic Books Inc.
Scragg, T. (2001) *Managing at the Front Line*. Brighton: Pavilion.
Senghera, R. (2010) 'Equality and Human Rights Approaches in the NHS: Making Spirituality in Mental Health Care Count.' In P. Gilbert (Ed.) *Spirituality and Mental Health*. Brighton: Pavilion.
Sewell, H. and Waterhouse, S. (2012) *Making Progress on Race Equality in Mental Health*. London: NHS Confederation. Accessed at www.nhsconfed.org/Publications/ on 3 September 2012.

Chapter 21

ENGAGING STAKEHOLDERS AND COMMUNITIES

Hári Sewell

INTRODUCTION

Engagement in health and social care covers a plethora of activities such as *consultation, partnership working, co-production* and *self-management* (El Ansari and Andersson 2011, p.46). When mental health trusts (along with other National Health Service (NHS) bodies) were required to meet core standards in seven domains, the 17th core standard was that 'the views of patients, their carers and others are sought and taken into account in designing, planning, delivering and improving health care services' (Crown 2004). The sector regulatory body used the core standards as the basis for assessing the fitness of organisations, and evidence of compliance with Standard 17 included demonstrating mechanisms such a reviews of complaints, surveys, exit interviews, as well as consultation forums and one-off events. Despite the evolution of regulatory mechanisms that provide clarity about effective practice in engagement, the legacy of managing such activities with imprecision remains. There is often a failure to consider and assess the impact of any engagement on service user outcomes.

Defining engagement is therefore a challenge. There does not appear to be consensus on a single model of engagement, and no standard volume on what constitutes good stakeholder engagement, nor the mechanisms for engaging individuals. 'Public and patient involvement (PPI) is increasingly important in UK health and social policy' (El Ansari and Andersson 2011, p.45), but this chapter eschews the term (and concept) 'PPI' on account of the limited scope for participation that is implicit in the words 'patient' and 'public'. There is a history of formalised involvement mechanisms in health dating back to Community Health Councils in 1974, and in 1992 the Local Voices initiative to promote patient involvement (Coleman *et al.*

2011). Public and Patient Involvement Forums were introduced under legislation (El Ansari and Adersson 2011), but were replaced by Local Involvement Networks (Stuart 2009), with greater emphasis on social care and community involvement. The Health and Social Care Act 2012 introduced HealthWatch England, which will support local HealthWatch organisations. These are intended to be consumer champions to ensure that service user and carer views are fed back to commissioners and providers (Coleman *et al.* 2011). This progression is relevant to mental health provision because of the lead role that health plays in the provision of mental health services. A broadening out of perspective is achieved when the role of Heath and Wellbeing Boards is considered. They have a clear role to develop a population needs assessment, based on engagement and input from local populations and taking into account a broad perspective of needs to inform commissioning from a public health perspective (Crown 2007; Local Government Improvement and Development 2011). Related earlier mechanisms of community engagement were the Local Area Committees established under the Local Government Act 2000. Specific to mental health were Local Implementation Teams (LITs), established to ensure the delivery of the *National Framework for Mental Health* (Department of Health (DoH) 1999). The LITs were designed to encompass local stakeholder views.

WHAT GOOD ENGAGEMENT LOOKS LIKE

The *Guidance on Joint Strategic Needs Assessments* (Crown 2007) included ten steps for effective community engagement adapted from *National Standards for Community Engagement*, produced by Communities Scotland (2005).

BOX 21.1: TEN STEPS FOR EFFECTIVE COMMUNITY ENGAGEMENT

- *Involve*: Identify and involve the people and organisations who have an interest in the issues which are being explored.

- *Support*: Identify and overcome any barriers to people's involvement (transport problems, timing, etc.).

- *Plan*: Gather evidence of necessary and available resources and use these to plan purpose, scope and timescale of engagement and actions.

- *Methods*: Agree to and use methods of engagement that are appropriate and fit for purpose.

- *Work together and with others*: Agree to and use clear procedures to enable participants to work with each other effectively and efficiently; work effectively with others who have an interest in the engagement process.

- *Share information*: Ensure that necessary information is communicated between participants.

- *Improve*: Actively develop skills, knowledge and confidence of all participants.

- *Feedback*: Feed back results to all those involved and affected.

- *Monitor and evaluate*: Work together to monitor and evaluate whether engagement has achieved its purpose.

- *Recognise*: People are different, and processes and services should take meaningful account of those differences.

(Crown 2007, p.15; Crown copyright 2007)

These steps are an excellent summary of community engagement, and can be applied beyond 'community' stakeholders such as voluntary sector providers, campaign groups and organisations, and other interest groups.

The final step, '*recognise*', is particularly relevant to the subject of this book. The established involvement and engagement frameworks in health and social care have been through many iterations because they have so often been criticised for being ineffective in achieving the intended goals. Even the new mechanisms under the Health and Social Care Act 2012 were publicly criticised for their likely ineffectiveness by eight major national charities in advance of their implementation (Coleman *et al.* 2011). A national, government-endorsed review of Joint Strategic Needs Assessments identified that 'in contrast to the wealth of information given by respondents on the technical needs assessment, accounts of how the public and people who use services were involved in assessing needs were far less detailed' (Ellins and Glasby 2011, p.37). Individuals, groups and organisations with identities or purposes aligned to one or more of the protected characteristics are more likely to be excluded from the mechanisms of engagement. (If established processes fail to engage the general population of those eligible to participate, so much the more likely are certain groups with protected characteristic to be overlooked.) The document *Good Practice in Community Engagement from an Equality Perspective* states: 'Despite progress in the development of community engagement, there can be a range of barriers to this, with evidence suggesting that equality groups remain under-represented' (Equality and Human Rights Commission (EHRC) 2009, p.iii).

BOX 21.2: SOME REASONS WHY SERVICES MAY BE LESS EFFECTIVE AT ENGAGING CERTAIN GROUPS

- Age: The profile of those engaged with organisations is likely to be older (retired), middle-class (with access to time and finances to participate). Many older people will, however, be excluded because:
  - Older people may have more challenges with physical access to traditional consultation meetings and engagement events.
  - Engagement through newer technologies may in effect exclude older people.
  - Energy levels may be a concern.
  - Boisterous events may be intimidating.
- Disability:
  - Physical access may present a barrier.
  - Hearing or seeing proceedings may present a barrier.
  - Potential physical or psychological discomfort may cause people to opt out.
  - Cost of engaging a carer may cause people to opt out.
- Gender reassignment:
  - As for other groups, fear of discrimination may cause people to opt out.
  - The possibility of being isolated may cause people to opt out.
  - Stigma may be a barrier.
- Marriage and civil partnership:
  - Caring responsibilities may be a barrier.
  - As for other groups, fear of discrimination may cause people to opt out.
  - Stigma may be a barrier.
- Pregnancy and maternity:
  - Physical access and comfort may be a concern.
  - Some women may have concerns about physical safety.

- Race:
  - Language may be a barrier in all mediums of engagement.
  - Concerns about discriminatory attitudes may lead to opting out.
  - Some people may have less access to spare time for economic and caring reasons.
  - Lack of trust.
- Religion or belief:
  - Secular proceedings may be a turn-off.
  - Concerns around a clash of values may lead to opting out.
- Sex:
  - Women may be put off by male-dominated engagement forums.
  - More caring responsibilities for women may be prohibitive.
  - Men may be under pressure with long hours at work.
- Sexual orientation:
  - Fear of discrimination may cause people to opt out.
  - The possibility of being isolated may cause people to opt out.
  - Stigma may be a barrier.

The challenges of ensuring equitable engagement are not primarily about inventing new mechanisms, but rather about identifying the barriers to equitable utilisation of mechanisms by all groups.

EXERCISE 21.1: MECHANISMS FOR ENGAGEMENT – IDENTIFYING WHAT BARRIERS THEY POSE FOR GROUPS WITH PROTECTED CHARACTERISTICS

In relation to each of the mechanisms for engagement set out below, consider the following questions:

- Are particular groups with protected characteristics more likely than others to face barriers in using these mechanisms?
- If so, which groups?
- What are these barriers?

- What can be done to address these barriers?
- Which barriers exist for other groups?
- Describe solutions to address these barriers.

Engagement mechanisms

(Reproduced from the Local Government Association (LGA) website; see LGA 2012.)

Design charrettes

A 'design charrette' is an intensive, participative workshop that brings people from different disciplines and backgrounds together to explore options for a particular area or site. This method is especially useful for getting people involved in shaping or changing planning, transport, landscape or other major projects affecting their communities.

Focus groups

Focus groups are guided discussions of a small group of citizens. They are normally one-off sessions, although several may be run simultaneously in different locations.

Online consultations

Online consultations seek people's opinions and expertise about important proposals or changes being made. They are especially useful when trying to make sure that the people who know most about the issue concerned have the chance to comment. By using the internet, an unlimited number of participants can be involved.

Online forums

Online forums are internet-based discussion areas where participants can post their views about topics and respond to other people's comments.

Opinion polls

A form of survey that measures the opinion of a selected sample of people and counts their 'votes'.

World café

A world café uses an informal 'café setting' for participants to explore an issue in small groups. Discussions on particular aspects are held in rounds of 20 to 30 minutes, after which participants move on to new groups and new discussions. The method is good at generating new ideas about the issue, sharing experience and exploring action in real-life situations. The event ends with a summary of all discussions that have taken place.

Participatory techniques

Participatory appraisal

Participatory appraisal (PA) is a 'family' of approaches that enable local people to identify their own priorities and make their own decisions about the future. The techniques were originally developed for use in rural areas and in developing countries, but because PA is very flexible and inclusive it is now used in many situations. It emphasises local knowledge and enables local people to do their own assessment, analysis, and planning, which makes it very effective in empowering communities.

Participatory budgeting

Participatory budgeting (PB) is one member of the participatory appraisal family. PB directly involves local people in making decisions about how to spend a defined public budget. Local people discuss and vote on spending priorities, and they also have a role in overseeing the process.

Participatory strategic planning

Participatory strategic planning (PSP) is another member of the PA family. It is a way of bringing a community together to help them jointly explain and agree with each other how they want their community or organisation to develop over the next few years.

Co-production

Co-production refers to a way of working whereby decision makers and citizens, or service providers and users, work together to create a decision or a service which works for them all. The approach is based on the principle that the people most affected by a service are in the best position to help design it.

User panels

User panels are regular meetings of service users about the quality of a service or other related topics. They help to identify concerns and priorities they and others may have and can lead to the early identification of problems or ideas for improvements.

A variation on this method is the citizens' panel, where large numbers of residents regularly complete questionnaires about the quality of local services.

Scrutiny methods

Citizens' jury

Citizens' juries consist of a small panel of non-specialists, modelled on the structure of a criminal jury. The group sets out to examine in detail something that local people have identified as being very important, and at the end they deliver a 'verdict'.

Consensus conference
A consensus conference is made up of a panel of citizens who question expert witnesses on a particular topic at a public conference. Their recommendations are then circulated widely.

Addressing barriers to groups with protected characteristics requires some preliminary consideration of diversity of need.

COMMITMENTS FOR EQUALITY IN ENGAGEMENT

Drawing on the knowledge about capacities, capabilities, experiences and anxieties of people from protected groups, five principles are now offered to help mental health commissioners and providers to benchmark their approaches to engagement:

1. Effort will be made to identify the different interest groups, stakeholders and partners in the local context, and an understanding of their needs will influence decisions.

2. The choice of mechanisms invoked will be influenced by the needs of different interest groups, stakeholders and partners in the local context.

3. Effort will be made to repair damaged trust by being open about limitations for what can be changed, and the level of influence that can be achieved over decisions and plans. Trust will be fostered by offering some 'quick wins', some of which respond specifically to the needs of protected groups.

4. The fact that there is a diversity of views and needs within any protected group will be catered for. There will be no expectation that a single view from an interest group either exists or will be forthcoming.

5. Grassroots engagement will be prioritised. It will be recognised that articulate voices that speak on behalf of groups sometimes identify significantly with commissioners and providers of services (perhaps as a result of class) and consequently develop unhelpfully close relationships. Effort will be made to compensate for this by engaging as many 'grassroots' people as possible, as frequently as possible.

CONCLUSION

Effectively engaging communities, and stakeholders generally, in a way that leads to demonstrable change, is a challenge. Engagement that fosters influence on the part of people and groups with protected characteristics is to be achieved by identifying at the planning stage who is to be engaged, and what barriers they are likely to face unless mitigating actions are taken.

REFERENCES

Coleman, A., Checkland, K., McDermott, I. and Harrison, S. (2011) 'Public and patient involvement in the restructured NHS.' *Journal of Integrated Care 19*, 4, 30–36.

Communities Scotland (2005) *National Standards for Community Engagement*. Edinburgh: Scottish Executive.

Crown (2004) Standards for Better Health. Guidance. London: Department of Health. Accessed at www.dh.gov.uk/en/Publicationsandstatistics/Publications/PublicationsPolicyAndGuidance/DH_4086057 on 5 June 2012.

Crown (2007) *Guidance on Joint Strategic Needs Assessments*. London: Department of Health.

DoH (Department of Health) (1999) *National Framework for Mental Health*. London: DoH.

EHRC (Equality and Human Rights Commission) (2009) *Good Practice in Community Engagement from an Equality Perspective*. London: EHRC.

El Ansari, W. and Andersson, E. (2011) 'Beyond value? Measuring the costs and benefits of public participation.' *Journal of Integrated Care 19*, 6, 45–57.

Ellins, J. and Glasby, J. (2011) 'Together we're better? Strategic needs assessment as a tool to improve joint working in England.' *Journal of Integrated Care 19*, 3, 34–41.

LGA (Local Government Association) (2012) www.local.gov.uk/web/guest/localism-act/-/journal_content/56/10171/3510950/ARTICLE-TEMPLATE.

Local Government Improvement and Development (2011) *Joint Strategic Needs Assessment: A Springboard for Action*. London: Local Government Improvement and Development.

Stuart, O. (2009) 'User participation in health care services.' *Ethnicity and Inequalities in Health and Social Care 2*, 4, 50–58.

Chapter 22

KNOWLEDGE MANAGEMENT, NEW TECHNOLOGIES AND EQUALITIES

Tony Jameson-Allen

INTRODUCTION

The use of new technologies can deliver some particular benefits and efficiencies in engaging people from groups protected by the Equality Act 2012. Technological solutions can help to overcome some of the potential barriers that may arise. This chapter aims to set out some practical thoughts and ideas for use in day-to-day service development, delivery and improvement. Organisations that actively encourage dialogue, listen and converse with their 'customers' are those most likely to deliver a service that is of a high quality, valued, successful and wanted! The effective use of modern technology – primarily web-based resources – can assist in removing many barriers faced by people – time constraints, mobility and physical access issues, audio and visual impairments, language barriers – and can help to reduce some cultural and belief system barriers. However, with all the technology available, which can be used to gather any amount of knowledge and data about services, failure to engage, actively listen and to have quality conversations with the people whom services are there to provide for renders such activity somewhat pointless. Today's technology and society's adoption of social media into mainstream life offers unparalleled opportunities of easy-to-access, speedy and cost-effective engagement with communities, groups and individuals. This chapter develops ideas raised in Chapter 21 on engaging stakeholders and communities, and also demonstrates applicability for other aspects of organisational knowledge management.

KNOWLEDGE MANAGEMENT

Knowledge management is concerned with the storage and the flow of knowledge: 'flows represent the ways in which knowledge is transferred from people to people or from people to a knowledge database' (Armstrong 2009, p.219).

The intention of this chapter is not to present an academic perspective on knowledge management, but rather to illustrate the ways in which embracing knowledge management and modern technology can enhance work on equalities.

THE CHANGED WORLD

People are no longer passive recipients of services, or indeed, of information. The worldwide web provides a plethora of instant resources offering advice, support and knowledge exchange. Any piece of information published or service provided can be compared, examined and checked out against similar examples from across a locality, region or country. Despite this, there remains a clear gap between the information-rich and the information-poor and there should not be any assumption that a reliance on technology will close this gap. However, effective use of it can ensure increased accessibility and opportunities for engagement from as wide a social circle as possible. Immediacy real time communication fuelled by modern technology and media.

There are inherent risks associated with the speed at which information now travels; inaccurate information travels fast. Organisations need to operate strategically in their planned engagement and communication of initiatives, and the agreed channels and use of social media should be identified in a robust strategy. Clear understanding of the workings of social media, in particular, is needed if an organisation is to adopt fully the use of the tools technology now affords us. Untimely release of unchecked materials or data can prove disastrous if published inappropriately. In this day and age of seemingly warp speed sharing, the idea that, once a document has been published on a website, deleting it from the site will remove it from the worldwide web is, at best, optimistic. It is necessary to be particularly vigilant with data and documents pertaining to service performance or plans for service change. How often do we hear of ministers or officials walking into buildings for meetings, carrying documents that are on view to the zoom lenses of the press? Copies are circulated on the web long before the news breaks on the more traditional media channels of radio or TV – by which time the focus becomes one of reputation management rather than communication!

Good forward planning is therefore essential when planning release of information that has been captured.

WHY TECHNOLOGY IN KNOWLEDGE MANAGEMENT IS NEEDED IN PROMOTING EQUALITIES

The written word, even in first languages, may not have the same currency as for mainstream audiences; use of internet-based media opens up options for using recorded media, additional visual cues to support messages, and an opportunity to link people and groups together to begin to develop common ground and shared understanding of the subject.

- Cultural understandings of terms and concepts may differ. A knowledge management-based approach supported by technology provides flexibility in disseminating the aims and opportunities afforded by an initiative/project/service.

- Many protected groups have a history of disengagement. People often feel that services do not have a good track record of communicating appropriately with them. There is a need to identify common ground, mutual goals, and an understanding of why groups should converse and engage.

- The costs incurred by traditional forms of face-to-face engagement and consultation are unsustainable in a lean economic climate. Costs for venue hire, equipment hire, catering, and payments for time and travel, are becoming increasingly restrictive. The traditional approach, whilst having many advantages in establishing rapport and shared understanding with communities, can limit engagement to those able and available to attend at a given time, on a given day.

- Using a combination of recorded broadcast (from professionally filmed material to webcasts recorded on a laptop or low-cost 'Flip'-type video cameras), the written word and supporting images, provides the opportunity to disseminate messages, and invitations to engage, in a variety of languages and formats – to best meet differing cultural and spiritual beliefs and audio and visual needs – and give communities the opportunity to access these at times best suited to the individuals concerned.

- Advertising and recruiting via traditional forms of media can now be easily supplemented by familiar 'social media' platforms such as Facebook, YouTube and Twitter – to name but three.

CASE STUDY 22.1: USING SOCIAL MEDIA FOR RAISING AWARENESS AND RECOGNITION OF ILLNESSES IN ACUTE GENERAL HOSPITALS

At the end of 2006 a project was launched with a toolkit aimed at raising awareness about a group of commonly encountered but often undiagnosed conditions in the acute general hospital arena. A modest budget was available to disseminate the messages and to develop supporting resources that would underpin the learning.

Delivery to such a wide target audience required clever and careful use of the resources available. Social media was the key to building and sharing these supporting resources. Coupled with attendance at key conferences to promote the toolkit, presentations and videos were produced to be shared and disseminated across the worldwide web.

YouTube, Facebook, Twitter and Vimeo all had a role to play. A slide pack had been produced to promote the toolkit. This was then automated and set to music. The impact of the combination of emotive music and strong images on people viewing the presentation was immediately clear to see. This was going to be a positive tool to use in the challenge of engaging hearts and minds.

The presentation was uploaded to YouTube, embedded in relevant websites, and later promoted via Facebook pages and through Twitter. Analytic data demonstrated excellent figures for the number of views and plays, with data of increasing subsequent visits to the project's pages.

The toolkit had been put together involving a wide range of people, including senior clinicians and people experiencing mental health and physical conditions. To underpin this, and with a small budget in mind (which would not facilitate development, printing and distribution of additional traditional material), video was used to capture stories and knowledge from people with personal experience of the conditions and from leading experts in the field. A single day of filming at a central location captured several hours of superb material, which was then turned into a series of 'podcasts'. These were then shared via the hospital's website, YouTube, Facebook, Twitter, etc., with the facility to add comments and ask questions about the content, facilitating wider access to a greater potential audience.

Orders for the toolkit continued to build, and feedback on the presentation and podcasts supported the decision to use social media as the chosen, cost-effective, method of spread and dissemination.

Collecting and collating large amounts of diverse information has probably never been easier. The use of online tools such as survey software, forms, databases and forums enables truly cost-efficient and cost-effective data collection. At the start of an initiative time and careful planning should be invested in identifying how best to present the requests for information, and what methods and formats will be most useful in engaging with the targeted demographic.

Knowledge, data and learning gained from initiatives using technology-based collection allows for highly portable resources to be shared, using a host of online vehicles including:

- podcasts

- YouTube

- Facebook

- Twitter

- fully interactive online conferencing and meeting facilities.

KNOWLEDGE MANAGEMENT AS A SOLUTION

Leading by example, a strong knowledge management approach starts at the top of any organisation, with investment in developing a healthy knowledge-sharing and management culture, and investment not only in the technology, hardware and software, but also in making sure that it is used to its maximum potential by staff and communities alike.

Some considerations when planning engagement and information capture/sharing

- *Data collection:* What information do we need? How best can we collect it? Why should 'customers' fill in your survey-quiz-comments form? What is their reward?

- *Capture:* How can we capture the information we need? Do we want to talk to people face-to-face? Over the phone? Will this allow people to voice their true thoughts and feelings and engage effectively? Or might they do that better in the privacy of their own environment, through writing or typing their thoughts?

- *Collecting evidence:* Of what your customers experience, and also of what is working and what is not.

- *Effective processing:* Think how to make the data captured useful – can it be presented in an attractive, easy-to-understand format? Can it be processed so that it can be made accessible in a variety of formats?

- *Efficient storage:* Ownership – whose knowledge is it anyway? Make it clear to all involved in planning the work, and also to all who engage and submit information to you, how it will be used, what will be published, where it will be published, and in what formats.

- *Dissemination:* If possible, ensure that participants in any initiative are given clear information on how, when, where and why they should engage, what the benefits will be, what kind of anticipated outcomes there are likely to be and, most important of all, where these can be viewed.

THE OPPORTUNITIES AND ADVANTAGES THAT EFFICIENT USE OF TECHNOLOGY OFFERS, SPECIFICALLY IN RELATION TO EQUALITIES

- *Audio or visual impairments:* Use of online media facilitates creative communication channels and ensures opportunity for people to use technology to maximise their abilities and opportunities to engage – for example, the use of screen readers on websites or documents; increasing font size; including images and easy-to-read materials to underline messages.

- *Physical access:* Offering online voting and surveys and commentary removes the barriers that face-to-face engagement can create – for those with home internet or local access through libraries or internet cafés, etc. There are no time constraints, no travel requirements, and there is less pressure to formulate instant responses in group settings.

- *Ethnicity and language:* In addition to screen readers, the ability to make documents and information accessible in alternative languages online eliminates the need for large print runs. Transcripts of podcasts or films can be produced, and/or films can include signing for the deaf.

- *Gender:* Utilising online facilities avoids potential cultural and gender issues which may have reduced or restricted potential engagement in traditional face-to-face group meetings. The lack of time constraints, and increased accessibility, also offer opportunity for those with parental or caring responsibilities to engage at a time that suits their needs.

- *Sexual orientation:* There are many well documented examples of people who have experienced discrimination from health and social care organisations because of their sexual orientation and assumptions made about their beliefs and personal choices. Online technology affords an opportunity to gather quantitative and qualitative data without influence. Anonymous submissions can be made without prejudice.

- *Age equality:* While the web is a new and emerging technology, its adoption into everyday society has continued at a breathtaking pace globally. The first port of call for NHS health care advice, information and assessment is increasingly the Web, with a huge amount of interactive resources to be found at www.nhs.uk. The fastest growing demographic of users registering on Facebook and YouTube for the past two years has been people aged over 50. On the internet, age is irrelevant.

FACEBOOK – A PLACE TO FIND PEOPLE AND OPINION

There are more than 750 million active users of Facebook, and 50 per cent of those log on in any given day. People spend collectively over 700 billion minutes per month on Facebook. There are over 900 million objects that people interact with (pages, groups, events and community pages), and an average user is connected to 80 community pages, groups and events. The average visitor to Facebook creates 90 pieces of new content each month. From a language perspective, there are more than 70 translations available on the site. In 2010 there was a 922 per cent increase in the number of users over the age of 55 (Facebook 2011).

CASE STUDY 22.2: BUILDING A WEBSITE

In February 2009 a new website to host and disseminate a government programme was to be built. A stakeholder group was available to advise and comment on the site build, through traditional channels of presentations at scheduled meetings (though the website was just one item on what was usually a busy agenda). Timescales were tight, but the ethos of sharing, inclusion and feedback was adhered to in ensuring the finished site was user-friendly and simple to access and navigate.

Twitter was used for the first time. An account was opened, initially to find out what Twitter was all about. The 'tweets' put out originally were orientated towards disseminating a few pieces of news related to mental health. Using hash tags '#' to label content, '#mentalhealth' resulted in the account gaining a number of people 'following' the updates. A number of these people would probably be classed as early adopters and already experienced users of Twitter, and used it to open conversations with other users, or for information gathering.

Initial tweets posted at the start of the web work were personal, describing some part of the working day (often late at night!) and giving a human element to what was being undertaken. In a short period of time regular comments and responses began to build up, and a noticeable group of people would often comment or respond. Rapport was building, as was the semblance of online conversations – not really what you might expect when limited to 140 characters per tweet.

As the site build began, screen shots and previews were posted via Twitter, with invites for anyone to comment or provide feedback on the look, feel and functionality of the site, and requests for ideas and suggestions. Many valid, helpful and interesting comments and suggestions came back via Twitter, on most occasions virtually instantly, which assisted greatly in developing and ultimately delivering a website which, judging by feedback from users and analytic data on the behaviour of site users, met and exceeded the original project plan.

New technology affords a simple, cost-efficient and portable suite of tools to support engagement, inclusion, feedback, sharing and learning among:

- staff
- service users and carers
- communities and interest groups
- stakeholders and interested parties.

CONCLUSION

The relatively new world of emerging technology, social media and online resources presents an opportunity for organisations to engage with their whole stakeholder base effectively and in an equitable manner, reaching out to potentially greater numbers of people who otherwise may not have the opportunity to engage, in a cost-effective and efficient way. Technology is being adopted, adapted and accepted into everyday life at an amazing rate. To ignore the opportunities technology offers because of organisational ignorance of its workings, or personal preferences and opinion, is to exclude a large proportion of a potential audience and customer base. Technology offers, in part, solutions to overcome many of the barriers faced by excluded or disengaged groups of people. Technology, and with it knowledge management, need to be understood, embraced and integral to any organisation's day-to-day operation and management.

REFERENCES

Armstrong, M. (2009) *Armstrong's Handbook of Human Resources Management Practice.* London: Jessica Kingsley Publishers.

CONCLUSION

Hári Sewell

The Equality Act 2010, in bringing together nine protected characteristics, creates a massive challenge. Front-line practitioners and managers are required to achieve a breadth of knowledge and understanding across nine areas of equality and maintain adequate depth in all. Organisations need to infuse all of their activities with an understanding of equalities, at the same time being fully equipped to run discrete programmes of work to address inequalities in mental health and to manage these with rigour on a par with other aspects of business.

In putting together this volume, it was my intention to cover the breadth of the mental health issues that can be seen to exisit in relation to the Equality Act 2010 encompassing all the protected characteristics and issues around implementation – and to do this some degree of depth as well. I hope this balance has been achieved. Trying to achieve it has involved a number of judgements: taking into account the reader's previous knowledge, the inevitable limit on length for individual chapters when attempting to provide an overview within a single volume, and allowing contributing authors to judge what to include from their areas of expertise. As a result, the contributions in this book reflect the tensions and judgements made by practitioners and managers in mental health, in relation to the amount of attention that can be given to equalities overall, and more specifically to each protected characteristic.

Some chapters act as useful summaries of information relating to the Equality Act 2010 and its protected characteristics; others serve to highlight the complexity of the challenges facing front-line practitioners and managers. However, I hope that you have found that there is learning across all of these chapters, and lessons that unify them. Key commonalities and themes that have run throughout are the following:

- People are complex, with multiple identities, and cannot be accurately seen through the lens of just one protected characteristic.

- Causal factors for inequalities are a mix between factors outside and inside of the mental health system. Similarly, solutions cannot be found by change addressed purely to the mental health sector. Public health and social care responses are also required.

- Mental health services have some inbuilt systemic inequalities, illustrated vividly in the chapters by Vincent (on age), and Carr (on sexuality) and Durairaj and Durairaj (on gender reassignment), and as evident in all the chapters in Part II.

- Addressing inequalities requires more than good intentions to treat people fairly – there are some specific ways in which inequalities emerge and these require knowledge of the subject matter. (Consider, for example, Durairaj and Durairaj's chapter on gender reassignment.)

- The ways in which the search for 'what is wrong' with people (i.e the search for symptoms) obscures the interest in what has happened to them, and the consequences for engagement and finding solutions (Chapters 4, 13 and 21).

Perhaps the most fundamental point evident within the book is the importance of strong leadership: staff on the front line are reliant on organisations to be good stewards of organisational resources, to ensure that inequalities are addressed.

Service users look to front-line staff to provide or facilitate services that meet their unique set of needs. Front-line staff look to their managers and leaders to provide the policies, resources and culture that allow inclusion and equality to thrive.

Without such leadership, patchy responses emerge, where the quality of response to diversity by front-line staff depends on their own personal inclination or chance knowledge about a particular aspect of equality. Robust leadership is not just about having the perfect plan. Partnership with people who have used, or may potentially use, services is essential, including the engagement of communities and stakeholders. It must be accompanied by an awareness that the complexity of identity relates not only to protected characteristics, but also to being a worker in mental health, and/or being service user. The responsibility is on mental health services to model positive approaches to employing people who are experiencing, or have experienced, mental health problems, and to tackle discrimination and stigma head-on.

Working towards equality in mental health is clearly not a sideline issue. It is not yesterday's agenda, nor is it the task of a minority within the mental health sector. I am grateful to the contributors to this book for putting forward such a powerful description of the developmental landscape for working towards improved equality in experience and outcomes for people who use mental health services. They have done so in sufficient depth to enable practitioners and managers to recognise that such knowledge should be used as a catalyst for action.

CONTRIBUTORS

Hári Sewell is Founder and Director of HS Consultancy and Honorary Senior Research Fellow at both the University of Central Lancashire and Buckinghamshire New University, UK. He has been published widely on race, ethnicity and equalities in mental health. Hári has worked in central government, local government and the NHS, including seven years as an Executive Director in a Mental Health NHS Foundation Trust. He was founder and first chair of the Social Care Strategic Network (Mental Health).

Jo Honigmann, MA, MSc, is a Partner in Just Equality, a human rights and equality consultancy focusing on areas that have an impact on disabled people and others affected by discrimination and social exclusion. A specialist in the fields of disability, discrimination and education, Jo has worked as a solicitor and more recently as a legal and policy consultant. Jo has been a member of the Law Society's Mental Health and Disability Committee since 2003, and was its chair from September 2008 to September 2010.

Melba Wilson has more than 20 years' experience in the public and voluntary sectors as a director, manager, activist and chronicler. Her focus is on health and mental health policy and practice in strategic planning, policy and analysis; corporate management; and partnership and leadership development and service improvement. Melba was formerly National Director of the Delivering Race Equality in Mental Healthcare programme, a five-year Department of Health action plan. A former journalist, Melba is currently an independent consultant, writer and researcher.

Eleanor Hope, a Community Organiser in New York, studied English Literature and Journalism before moving to London in 1989. While completing a degree in Cultural Studies, she produced a documentary on the student occupation in East London. Currently employed by the NHS as a Development Worker in Mental Health, she delivers 'race' equality training to staff and supports black and minority ethnic users to set up peer groups and become self-employed. She is also a freelance trainer delivering workshops in equalities, well-being and peer support.

Sue Waterhouse, RMN, RGN, Dip. in Nursing, MBA. Sue is a nurse by background. She has worked in mental health for in excess of 25 years. Her clinical experience has been in acute mental health, specialist secure services and women-only mental health services. For the last 15 years Sue has been campaigning for improved mental health services for women. She has researched and published in this area and has developed women-only services. Sue has worked regionally and nationally in gender equality and the wider equality agenda in mental health, and is currently working as a freelance consultant with HS Consultancy.

Barbara. A. Vincent, BSc, MSc, RMN, NT, was born and raised in the north of England. She has worked for over 30 years as a Mental Health Nurse in the NHS with older people with mental health problems. She started working with older people as a Nursing Assistant working in a care home and currently works as a Nurse Consultant in Dementia and Later Life Mental Health for Sussex Partnership NHS Trust.

Sarah Carr, PhD, is Senior Research Analyst at the Social Care Institute for Excellence (SCIE) leading on personalisation. She has also led work on service user and carer participation. Sarah is Honorary Fellow at the Faculty of Health, Staffordshire University, Visiting Fellow of the Centre for Government and Charity Management, Faculty of Business, London South Bank University and a Fellow of the Royal Society of Arts. She is a trustee of the Lesbian, Gay, Bisexual and Transgender (LGB&T) Consortium of Voluntary and Community Organisations and of the National Survivor and User Network (NSUN). Sarah is a long-term user of mental health services and has written on her experiences.

Marcel Vige, MSc, MSc, lectures in Psychology and Social Science for the Open University. Marcel has spent many years leading campaigns for the mental health charity Mind, focusing on minority ethnic communities and other marginalised groups. He also has a background in drug and alcohol advocacy provision and service development.

Scott Durairaj, PGC; in 2001, after ten years in the ambulance service as a Paramedic Duty Manager, Scott went on to work for the Commission for Racial Equality. Awarded a Postgraduate Certificate in Equality, Sociology and Global Politics with merit from the University of Central Lancashire, he contributed to the *Oxford Handbook of Mental Health Nursing* (2006). He is now studying for an MBA at the University of Sussex whilst leading on equality and human rights at Sussex Partnership NHS Foundation Trust.

Jourdan Durairaj, HND, having established himself in ethical design, has spent the past five years working in the field of health equality and human rights for both commissioners and providers. He has extensive experience founding health community engagement programmes and bringing authentic voices into service redesign. He successfully led a £250,000 funding bid for a rural black and minority ethnic patient advocacy service. He is interested in cultural bias within person-centred care.

Peter D. Gilbert, MA (Oxon), M Soc Work, MBA, is Emeritus Professor of Social Work and Spirituality at Staffordshire University, Associate Fellow at the University of Warwick and Visiting Research Fellow with the University of Sussex. A former director of social services in the UK, Peter has published books on spirituality and mental health, social work and leadership. He has been the national project lead for the National Institute's, and now National Forum's, spirituality and mental health programme since its inception in 2001. Peter is co-editor of *The International Journal of Leadership in Public Services*, and is currently working on a book on spirituality and end of life care.

Cheryl Brodie, Bed, MSc, FCIPD is a Learning and Organisational Development Consultant with management, business, market research, training and development experience gained in complex organisations, in both the private and public sector. Cheryl's interest is in getting to the heart of problems and delivering solutions whilst engaging stakeholders. Cheryl has worked as Assistant Director, Organisation Development in a Mental Health Trust for eight years and currently chairs a community social action forum to support projects that bring local change.

Tony Jameson-Allen, RMN, is an accredited Knowledge Management Consultant. Having worked across the public and private sectors in mental health and social care services for older people as a clinician, Tony moved into service improvement, knowledge sharing and user engagement, particularly in the field of dementia care. He is Director of Evolution Networking Ltd and continues to work with older people as a social entrepreneur, having founded a Community Interest Company focusing on sports-based reminiscence activities.

SUBJECT INDEX

AUTHOR INDEX